THE TAKING OF NEW YORK CITY

THE TAKING OF NEW YORK CITY

Crime on the Screen and in the Streets of the Big Apple in the 1970s

Andrew J. Rausch

Foreword by
Jami Bernard

APPLAUSE
THEATRE & CINEMA BOOKS

Bloomsbury Publishing Group, Inc.
4501 Forbes Blvd., Ste. 200
Lanham, MD, 20706
ApplauseBooks.com

Distributed by NATIONAL BOOK NETWORK

Copyright © 2025 by Andrew J. Rausch

All rights reserved. No part of this book may be reproduced in any form or by any electronic or mechanical means, including information storage and retrieval systems, without written permission from the publisher, except by a reviewer who may quote passages in a review.

Library of Congress Cataloging-in-Publication Data

Names: Rausch, Andrew J., author. | Bernard, Jami, writer of foreword.
Title: The taking of New York City: crime on the screen and in the streets of the Big Apple in the 1970s / Andrew Rausch; foreword by Jami Bernard.
Description: Essex, Connecticut: Applause, an imprint of Globe Pequot, the trade division of the Rowman & Littlefield Publishing Group, Inc., [2024] | Includes bibliographical references.
Identifiers: LCCN 2024013972 (print) | LCCN 2024013973 (ebook) | ISBN 9781493078714 (cloth) | ISBN 9781493078721 (ebook)
Subjects: LCSH: New York (N.Y.)–In motion pictures. | Crime in motion pictures. | Crime–New York (State)–New York–History–20th century. | New York (N.Y.)–Social conditions. | Nineteen seventies.
Classification: LCC PN1995.9.N49 R38 2024 (print) | LCC PN1995.9.N49 (ebook) | DDC 791.43/6587471043–dc23/eng/20240709
LC record available at https://lccn.loc.gov/2024013972
LC ebook record available at https://lccn.loc.gov/2024013973

∞™ The paper used in this publication meets the minimum requirements of American National Standard for Information Sciences—Permanence of Paper for Printed Library Materials, ANSI/NISO Z39.48-1992.

"New York is a mess, say these films. It's run by fools. Its citizens are at the mercy of its criminals who, as often as not, are protected by an unholy alliance of civil libertarians and crooked cops. The air is foul. The traffic impossible. Services are diminishing and the morale is such that ordering a cup of coffee in a diner can turn into a request for a fat lip."

—*New York Times* critic Vincent Canby (from his review for *The Taking of Pelham One Two Three*)

"When you leave New York, you are astonished at how clean the rest of the world is."

—Fran Lebowitz, *People* magazine, 1978

Contents

Foreword	ix
Introduction	1
1970: Black Film and White Anger	7
1971: The Blue Flu, *The French Connection*, and *Shaft*	17
1972: Grass Eaters and Meat Eaters, Charlie Chop-off, and *The Godfather*	49
1973: Cop Movies, Blaxploitation, and *Mean Streets*	79
1974: Murder Is Down, But NYC Has a *Death Wish*	113
1975: A *Dog Day Afternoon* in Fear City	145
1976: Travis Bickle Meets the Son of Sam	159
1977: The Night the Lights Went Out on Cherry Street	171
1978: Donnie Brasco and the Biggest Heist in US History	177
1979: *The Wanderers* and *The Warriors* Run the Streets	185
1980: The Last Batch of 1970s Crime Films	205
Selected Bibliography	231
Index	239
About the Author	257

Foreword

They say there is no such thing, yet I am that rare creature that supposedly does not exist—a native New Yorker, born and bred. How I see and experience my hometown may not be the way others do, but like all native New Yorkers, I have an unshakable belief that I am correct. (New Yorkers are not actually rude, but they are smug!) What others may view as noisy and crowded, I see as manifestations of exuberance and color. What others may think of as movies that underscore a nasty and toxic city, I see as triumphant depictions of my hometown's transcendental marvels.

One of my most treasured memories of homegrown moviegoing, which happened long before I became a film critic for New York City dailies—the *New York Post* and then the *Daily News*—was catching a double bill of Bruce Lee kung fu flicks in one of the genuinely seedy theaters along 42nd Street, the "old" Times Square, what I personally consider the *real* Times Square. I much prefer that to the current Disneyfied version, with its well-defined pedestrian lanes and high-def neon and bland fast-food eateries. The fake monks in their rented saffron robes stealing a cigarette in a doorway between shakedowns of softhearted tourists. The fake cartoon characters come to dingy life in threadbare plush outfits as they pretend to adore the kiddies who pose with them for overpriced photos. Where once were porno palaces are now costumed hucksters; I prefer genuine sleaze to the Halloween-party variety. To many New Yorkers, myself included, the bad old crime-ridden New York of the 1970s was at least genuine and made no apologies—infinitely preferable to the sanitized sleaze of today.

That old New York—gritty, crazy, quirky, a quicksand of crime and corruption—is the subject of Andrew Rausch's *The Taking of New York City: Crime on the Screen and in the Streets in 1970s Big Apple*. Rausch's book happily brings back the good old, bad old days. It allows us to return in memory—and if memory does not serve every single reader, then through the agency of cinema—to my beloved, crime-infested, dicey, porn-parlor-strewn New York of the 1970s.

I happened to come of age exactly in the era the author describes, starting it as a naive junior high schooler and finishing it in the swagger-filled, post-college years of first journalism jobs and late nights at Studio 54, all washed down by a cocktail of existential confusion. Because it was such an important time in my life, everything about 1970s New York City is etched in a special place, as if an unsanitary tattoo parlor tatted it there. The cacophony of that time, in that place, is manna from heaven: drugs, disco, dodgy characters, visceral subway graffiti with plump and vibrant lettering, and movies made on my own Mean Streets. *The Taking of New York City* offers up a smorgasbord of long-forgotten sensations and offers an antidote to much of the bland moviemaking that would follow in the next decade.

Rausch seems to know exactly how I feel, even though he grew up in—of all places that are anathema to this one—*Kansas!* Even so, Rausch's appreciation for the era's New York–based crime movies is rich and detailed. It had not occurred to me until I read this excellent book that even non-native New Yorkers could "get it" through the edgy brilliance of these movies, where form met function and delivered it all with a blast. Physically living in the very New York pictured or re-imagined in these spectacular cinematic roller coasters is not, after all, the only way to see, feel, and understand how vivid every day was back then.

It was probably Dustin Hoffman barking, *"I'm walkin' heah!"* to a pushy taxi driver in *Midnight Cowboy* (1969) that gave me the response that burbled up from me some years later when a guy tried to pick my pocket on an elevated No. 7 train platform.

I turned to the would-be criminal and barked, Ratso Rizzo style: *"Are you fuckin' KIDDING me?"* Did this lowlife not understand that I was the genuine article, a native New Yorker who might well bang on the hood of a Checker cab if one got in my way? Did he not know that I am a connoisseur of homegrown crime, not a potential victim of it? My New York-y ferocity made the bum back off.

The movies discussed in this book reflect my reality, and also advanced it when they first came out. In the chapter on *Klute* (1971) (my first-ever adult-rated movie, which I saw while underage by sneaking into the theater with my high school boyfriend and was blown away by the casual sexuality, not to mention Jane Fonda's haircut), Rausch quotes Donald Sutherland's remark about the city's "degradation, alienation, and the squalor." Exactly! You gotta problem with that? We embraced such sentiments as our coat of arms. To me, and as exemplified by many of these films, there was something noble about civic desperation.

These movies are about more than their locations, of course. As in *Mean Streets* (1973), they are often about how those locations figure into the lives of the characters, how those individuals succeed or fail at reconciling danger, excitement, and urban blight with matters of choice and character.

Still, the locations in these movies are all so intimately recognizable to New Yorkers. Needle Park—as in *Panic in . . .*—was a little scalene triangle near a major subway intersection where you could sit on a bench and enjoy a hot dog from Gray's Papaya and a spot of sunlight despite drug detritus crunching underfoot. Not far from Needle Park, in an alley mere steps away, Joe Turner (Robert Redford) in *Three Days of the Condor* (1975) meets his CIA controller (Cliff Robertson).

The subway—which, despite the word, includes elevated sections of overhead train tracks—is where cop Frank Serpico (Al Pacino) gives chase beneath the shifting light-and-dark strobe effect of the Broadway local that thunders above Ditmars Boulevard in Astoria, Queens. (I spent my younger years a few neighborhoods over.) There's Walter Matthau trying to prevent *The Taking of Pelham One Two Three* (1974) in that seminal subway hijack movie (that later gave Quentin Tarantino the names of his Reservoir Dogs), even if the Transit Authority demanded that the *Pelham* filmmakers remove all graffiti from the subway cars, which is kind of like insisting eggs be stripped of their shells.

My first apartment after college was in a seedy brownstone half a block from the path to the Central Park Reservoir, where I jogged partly for exercise but mostly hoping for a sighting of Jackie Onassis, who also used the crushed gravel path for her daily run, both of us passing every 1.58 miles the semi-spooky pump house where Laurence Olivier, armed with his dental drill, asked Dustin Hoffman, "Is it safe?"

So, was it safe, my beloved New York of the 1970s? Technically, it was not. Crime and distress everywhere you looked. And yet you have to admit that these movies mirror how utterly vibrant those times were. Menacing, sure. Down and dirty.

But also thrilling. You won't need a can of pepper spray to protect you while you go ahead and dig in!

Jami Bernard

Introduction

The United States was changing dramatically in 1969. That year is often pointed to as a demarcation line between two very different eras. If you were an older American in 1969, set in your ways, you'd have been shocked because, as Bob Dylan had pronounced five years earlier, the times were changing, and brother, they were changing *fast*. NASA put a man on the moon, and, just like that, science-fiction stories moved from the pulp magazines to the front page of the newspaper. A "hippie" music festival in Woodstock signaled a clear change in American pop music; Elvis and his gyrating hips were out, and long-haired rockers with electric guitars were in. American soldiers were still fighting an unwinnable war and laying down their lives overseas. Meanwhile, back home, more than a million anti-war protesters descended on Washington, D.C., demanding to be heard.

There were changes taking place in the Big Apple, too. Mickey Mantle, who had for two decades been the heart and soul of the Yankees, hung up his cleats and called it quits. Then there was the Stonewall rebellion, in which members of the gay community stood their ground and told the police and straight America that they'd had enough of their bullshit. The Marxist militants who called themselves the Weathermen had begun recruiting in NYC, and two hundred black and Puerto Rican students took over City College demanding the admission of more minorities. Twenty-one members of the Black Panthers were arrested and accused of coordinating attacks against the

NYPD and the Queens Board of Education. (All of them were later acquitted.)

That same year, director John Schlesinger made a movie in and about New York City called *Midnight Cowboy*. The film, about a couple of down-on-their-luck schlubs trying to survive on the mean streets of the city, was nominated for seven Academy Awards and won three (Best Picture, Best Director, and Best Adapted Screenplay). *Midnight Cowboy* was a great film, yes, but it was also the first *true* 1970s NYC movie. While it was filmed and released before the Seventies began, it was the first major film that gave America a glimpse of the cesspool New York City was rapidly becoming. This was America's introduction to a new Big Apple that was unlike the city they'd known before. The brightly dressed street gangs of *West Side Story* (1961) would soon give way to the barbarians in *The Warriors* (1979), and the bright, optimistic Manhattan Audrey Hepburn's call girl inhabited in *Breakfast at Tiffany's* (1961) would become the relentlessly bleak Manhattan where Jane Fonda's call girl in *Klute* (1971) would fight to stay alive. *Midnight Cowboy* played a huge role in changing America's perception of the city. The happy-go-lucky "Big Apple" tag would soon be replaced with the darker "Fear City" label due to the city's much-hyped crime problem.

But what caused the increase in crime in the 1970s? Where did it come from? There were numerous factors responsible, but the primary culprit was a city unemployment rate that routinely topped 10 percent and was significantly higher than anyplace else in the United States. Between 1969 and 1974, the city lost more than half a million manufacturing jobs. As a result, more than a million households found themselves dependent on welfare by 1975. The city then experienced a mass exodus, with nearly half a million people moving out. There were also massive cuts in law enforcement as a result of the city's financial woes. So, predictably, crime increased across the board, and "serious crimes," which included rape, felony assault, and murder, soared to record highs.

In *The Ungovernable City*, author Vincent J. Cannato paints a vivid picture of the time: "Stabbings, robberies, muggings, graffiti, arson, and rape began to strike a wider and wider portion of the population. Burglaries made people feel vulnerable, even in their once-safe homes and apartments. It wasn't just the reality of crime and sense of broadening disorder that hurt. It was the raw fear and perception of vulnerability that seeped into every interaction of daily life."

But, as we'll discuss in this volume, New York City wasn't quite the murderous hellhole the media purported it to be. Was it violent? Yep. Was it rundown to the point where it looked like bombed-out Beirut? Of course. Was it dangerous? You bet it was. But was it the most violent city in the world, or even the United States for that matter? No, it wasn't. But that was the image it got stuck with in the 1970s. And while that image did a lot to damage NYC's reputation and repel would-be tourists, it led to one unforeseen positive aspect—it brought revenue to a city in need of money from filmmakers seeking to exploit its very worst qualities.

The early 1970s were a time in which Hollywood seemingly handed over the reins to young upstarts who were inspired by the cinema of the French New Wave, Italian Neo-realists, and indie maverick John Cassavetes. These filmmakers, including the likes of Bob Rafelson, Martin Scorsese, Dennis Hopper, Terence Malick, Brian De Palma, Roman Polanski, Francis Ford Coppola, and others, sought to create art that was closer to reality than the artificial aesthetic Hollywood had been known for. Of course, two of those young Baby Boomer directors, George Lucas and Steven Spielberg, would eventually become known for big, flashy tent-pole productions that followed the traditional Hollywood aesthetic, leading to the late-Seventies blockbuster craze, but for a few years in the first half of the decade, happy stories and happier endings were replaced with downbeat storylines and ultra-bleak endings. Good guys stepped aside to make way for morally ambiguous anti-heroes. With all of this taking place, the crime genre was an obvious place to plumb for dark stories.

New York City, complete with its reputation as a violent hellhole teeming with rapists, muggers, and killers, along with its spray-painted everything and an appearance of post-apocalyptic urban decay, was the *perfect* place to make gritty, grimy, violent pictures about the underbelly of American society. In *Making Movies*, director Sidney Lumet recalls advice legendary Italian cinematographer Carlo Di Palma once gave him about lighting: "The secret lay in picking the right place to begin with and then doing as little as possible with it. Given the choice between two equally good exteriors or interiors, pick the one that's already the right color; the one that takes the least alteration by light. Paint if you have to, but try to find places that are closest to what you want to end up with." This same principle was applicable—when producers and directors wanting to give their crime films an air of authenticity chose to shoot in the Big Apple, a great deal of their work was already done.

The 1970s are often called the "Golden Age" of crime films because of the staggering amount of crime films, many of which were among the finest the genre has ever produced, made during that period. A great many of those pictures were shot in New York City. Although there were prominent American crime films made in that decade with stories that took place around the globe, *a lot* of them were centered in the "Rotten Apple." Many iconic gems—some of the most emblematic of the genre—were filmed there. These include *The French Connection* (1971), *Shaft* (1971), *The Godfather* (1972), *Mean Streets* (1973), *Serpico* (1973), *Death Wish* (1974), *The Godfather Part II* (1974), *The Taking of Pelham One Two Three* (1974), *Dog Day Afternoon* (1975), and *Taxi Driver* (1976), just to name a few.

While filmmakers came to the city to craft authentic crime pictures, there were occasions when the projects became more authentic than they might have liked. On numerous films, such as *The Warriors* and *The Wanderers* (both 1979), street gangs found ways to intimidate and coerce filmmakers into giving them money and/or casting their members. While Francis Ford Coppola was shooting *The Godfather*, widely considered the greatest Mafia film ever made, producer Albert S. Ruddy was forced to bargain with the mob and, again, pay them (by way of the Italian-American Civil Rights League) and cast mobsters. Similarly, *Across 110th Street* (1972) producer Anthony Quinn found himself in a situation where he had to convince Luciano family crime boss Frank Costello to allow his production to shoot on the streets of Harlem. There were also instances where police activity, real-life murders, and other very real crimes impeded the filming of scenes.

It should be noted that the city's crime and state of disrepair weren't the only reasons for the deluge of filmmakers suddenly wanting to shoot there. In 1966, Mayor John V. Lindsay had established a movie coordination organization within his administration to assist filmmakers who wanted to shoot in the city, making the process easier and helping them avoid time-consuming red tape. Lindsay's program proved to be a tremendous success. Within the five years that followed the organization's establishment, more than two hundred films were made in NYC. These included films of all genres, from comedy to drama to horror. It just so happened that the city's decline, both in appearance and crime rate, lent itself to an equally nasty crime genre.

Interestingly, it was my agent, Lee Sobel, who came up with the concept for this book. Since I'd done a lot of writing about the genre, and because I have an affinity for the crime films of the 1970s, the idea appealed to me the moment I heard it. So, what exactly is this book? In *The Taking of New York City*, we'll examine fifty NYC crime films produced during the decade. Additionally, we'll look at the events of the time that helped make New York City the ideal location for these kinds of films.

A number of factors went into the selection of the fifty films discussed here. Most of them are commonsense selections because they're obvious representatives of the gritty crime films the city would become known for; such films as *Taxi Driver*, *Death Wish*, and *The French Connection*. But not every selection is so obvious. For instance, *The Anderson Tapes* (1971) is a far less gritty film. It was selected because it gives the reader a sense of how varied the NYC crime pictures really were. Then there are *The Godfather* and *The Godfather Part II*, which can be seen as more upscale entries. They aren't gritty, but they're certainly violent and feature ruthless criminals. Those films are significant because the Mafia was, for many years, including the 1970s, the driving force in the New York City crime world. The obscure no-budget movie *Massage Parlor Murders* is an interesting example of a film that might seem like a questionable inclusion. But again, it represents a different kind of NYC crime film, and its very creation was as cheap and gritty as anything one could have found on the city's garbage-strewn streets. Additionally, *Massage Parlor Murders* provides one of the best snapshots of 1970s' Times Square as it really was. There is absolutely no glamour in its presentation. Then there are other films included that are primarily seen as horror films, but are, at their core, bleak, ultra-violent New York City crime pictures.

There are films included that were released in every year between 1970 and 1980. It should be noted that 1980 is included because the films that were released that year were actually made in 1979, making them the last of the 1970s' NYC crime films. That same distinction (that they are holdovers from the decade in which they were made) could be made about the films that were released in 1970, but I chose to include them to give the reader a fuller understanding of the 1970s NYC crime film's evolution. While the 1970s' New York City crime film isn't a recognized genre, sub-genre, or cycle, I would contend that it is actually a specific, and often recognizable, sub-genre of 1970s crime pictures, just like blaxploitation and *Poliziotteschi*.

The information presented here was the result of hundreds of hours' worth of research in libraries and on the internet, watching the films and their supplementary materials, and new, original interviews with individuals involved with the films. Tracking down interview subjects was sometimes difficult because many of the key figures involved in the creation of these films are gone. In the write-ups for these films, I will discuss (when possible) the history of the production, provide behind-the-scenes minutia, discuss or list the locations where they were shot, share critical appraisal from the time of their release, and take a look at their legacies (when applicable).

It's my hope that you find this book informative and interesting. *The Taking of New York: Crime on the Screen and in the Streets in 1970s Big Apple* is intended to be a time machine of sorts. So sit back, strap in, and let's go.

1970
Black Film and White Anger

Despite the bad press it received, New York City was not the *most* crime-ridden city in the nation. According to a 1971 Federal Bureau of Investigation crime report, NYC ranked third in 1970 with 5,222 crimes per 100,000 population. Ranking first was Miami with 5,342.8 crimes per 100,000 population. Ranking second was the San Francisco/Oakland area with 5,329.3 per 100,000 population. This is not meant to imply that New York City wasn't a scary place in 1970. There were 1,146 homicides that year. This was a dramatic increase from the 482 homicides that had been reported just a decade before (in 1960).

If New Yorkers believed the news that crime in their city couldn't get any worse, they were mistaken. In April 1970, undercover cop Frank Serpico detailed widespread corruption within the ranks of the NYPD in a David Burnham–penned *New York Times* exposé titled "Graft Paid to Police Here Said to Run into Millions." The piece eventually led to the establishment of the Commission to Investigate Alleged Police Corruption, better known as "the Knapp Commission." Although the commission was set up in June 1970, it would not begin public hearings for another two years. At the end of the year, Mayor John V. Lindsay announced the promotion of a new NYPD commissioner named Patrick V. Murphy. Murphy had a history of fighting corruption with the Office of Law Enforcement Assistance, and later with the Law Enforcement Assistance Administration.

An incident of violence that would become known as the Hard Hat Riot occurred on May 8, four days after thirteen Kent

State students protesting the Vietnam war were shot by cops in Ohio (four of whom died). Jeffrey Glenn Miller, one of the slain protesters, was from Long Island. On the day of the Hard Hat Riots, approximately a thousand demonstrators protested the Kent State shootings in front of the New York Stock Exchange at 11 Wall Street Court in Manhattan, and then later in the day at the Federal Hall National Memorial building at 26 Wall Street. When word of the protest got out, pro-war blue-collar workers became incensed. Around noon, approximately four hundred construction workers left their worksite and made their way toward the protest. On the way, approximately eight hundred office workers joined them. These "hard hat" anti-protest protesters waved American flags and chanted pro-USA jingoism. The two groups clashed and the angry pro-war workers punched and kicked the protesters. The fracas went on for several hours. There were approximately twenty thousand people in the streets, and more than one hundred people were injured, including several NYPD officers. Afterwards, in typical Richard Nixon fashion, the president praised the violent rioters and invited them to meet him at the White House, where they presented him with a hard hat of his own.

On July 14, the South Bronx's Lincoln Hospital was overtaken by 150 activists representing a Puerto Rican group called the Young Lords Organization (YLO). They asserted that the hospital, which served primarily black and Puerto Rican patients, was providing inadequate healthcare. A July 15, 1970, *New York Times* article quoted a hospital employee as likening the place to "a butcher shop that kills patients and frustrates workers from serving these patients." Medical staff at the hospital were responsible for dangerous and sloppy practices such as leaving surgical utensils inside patients' bodies after surgery. Additionally, the infant mortality rate at Lincoln Hospital was three times higher than the national average. Many minority patients believed they were treated without respect or dignity. Members of the Young Lords Party had approached the hospital administration multiple times in the months preceding the takeover but felt their complaints had fallen on deaf ears. Members of the Young Lords, along with representatives from the Heath

Revolutionary Unity Movement and the Think Lincoln Committee, met with hospital administrator Dr. Antero Lecot, a representative from the mayor's office, and members of the Health and Hospitals Corporation to discuss ways the hospital could better serve the community. The activists' demands included that there be no cutbacks of hospital staff, that the construction of the new Lincoln Hospital be expedited, and that the hospital institute a community interaction group to test and care for members of the community for a number of things, including drug addiction. The takeover lasted twelve hours. During that time, two men, Pablo Guzman and Luiz Alvarez Perez, were arrested and then released. The takeover led to the establishment of the Patient Bill of Rights and helped bring about changes in policies that drastically improved healthcare conditions.

Although they had their hands in just about every pot in the city, the Mafia was fairly quiet in 1970. The August 27 New York City arrest of Sicilian Mafioso Tommaso Buscetta on a pending investigation in Italy was the primary story. Because Italy had not requested extradition, Buscetta was released. But the biggest mob-related story of 1970, although no one knew it at the time, was the congressional passing of the Racketeer Influenced and Corrupt Organizations Act, better known as RICO. Although this was national news as opposed to regional news, the bill designed to combat organized crime would have a tremendous impact on New York City because it would, in the years to come, all but destroy the Mafia.

As stated previously, 1969 was, for many reasons, a demarcation line of societal change. One of the many things that would come almost immediately was the emergence of the gritty NYC crime film. The films that were released in 1970 had been made or gone into production in 1969, so there were only a handful of them. So, the only two films we'll discuss here are *Cotton Comes to Harlem* and *Joe*.

Cotton Comes to Harlem and *Joe* are an interesting pair because they are, in a way, related. *Cotton Comes to Harlem* was only the second studio film ever made by a black director (Ossie Davis). It was also the first studio film fashioned for a black audience that made money and proved that audience was financially viable. This is key. *Cotton Comes to Harlem* and the slew of black films that would soon follow came as a direct result of the civil rights victories of the Sixties. Suddenly, black kids were going to school alongside white kids, and black people were finally starting to obtain many of the rights they'd long been denied. These changes angered far-right whites. The film *Joe* tells the story of one such angry white conservative. *Joe* isn't a racist film, but rather a film about a racist character. Although the film (written by liberal writer Normal Wexler) wasn't meant to endorse Joe's views, audience members who related to the character cheered him on. So, *Joe*, by way of the angry far-right whites who inspired it, came as a response to the things that led to the making of *Cotton Comes to Harlem* in much the same way that Donald Trump's 2016 election can be seen as a response to the election of the biracial Barack Obama in 2008.

Cotton Comes to Harlem

Cotton Comes to Harlem is an interesting entry. For a cop film as light as it is, it's been constantly re-appraised. One of the most popular discussions deals with whether or not it qualifies as a "blaxploitation" film. Kansas University film professor and Oscar-winning *Blackkklansman* (2018) scribe Kevin Wilmott says he doesn't believe the film belongs in that category. "There is much debate about this issue, and opinions differ, but so-called blaxploitation often refers to the exploitation of sex and violence as entertainment choices targeted toward a male audience," he says. "*Cotton Comes to Harlem* doesn't make any of those choices, but it is thrown into the genre of blaxploitation in the negative sense because of the time it was released."

Some cineastes have labeled the film a neo-noir, and some academics call it the first "buddy cop" movie. In addition to these things, *Cotton Comes to Harlem* is notable because it was only the second Hollywood film written and directed by a black filmmaker. (The first was Gordon Parks' 1969 film *The Learning Tree*. Parks just beat out *Cotton* helmsman Ossie Davis, as well as Melvin Van Peebles, who became the third black filmmaker to direct a studio picture with *Watermelon Man*, by mere months. These productions were so close that *Cotton Comes to Harlem* and *Watermelon Man*, both of which starred Godfrey Cambridge, were released on the same day—May 27, 1970.)

The film was adapted (by Davis and Arnold Perl, who later adapted 1992's *Malcolm X*) from the 1965 novel of the same title by black expat Chester Himes. The novel was the sixth entry in Himes' "Harlem Detective" series, and it had been named as one of "fifty books that define our times" by *Newsweek* at the time of its release.

Before coming onboard to make *Cotton Comes to Harlem*, Ossie Davis had made a name for himself on Broadway. There he'd excelled as a performer, producer, and playwright, earning two Tony Award nominations. When it came time to cast *Cotton*'s tough-guy cop protagonists, "Gravedigger Jones" and "Coffin Ed" Johnson, Davis naturally hired two former Broadway actors in Godfrey Cambridge, who had appeared in the Davis-penned "Purlie Victorious," and Raymond St. Jacques. The duo proved to have real chemistry, with Cambridge playing the more comedic Gravedigger Jones to St. Jacques' stoic Coffin Ed.

The film shot in the summer of 1969. The production (with the exception of one scene) was shot on location in Upper Manhattan. With assistance from cinematographer Gerald Hirschfeld, *Cotton Comes to Harlem* showcased the streets of Harlem, capturing visuals of the neighborhood's best-known locations, including the Apollo Theater and the since-demolished Loew's Victoria Theater, both located on 125th Street. (Several scenes even take place inside the Apollo Theater.) *Cotton Comes to Harlem* features some great footage of Harlem at night. In these scenes, there are mutlicolored neon signs for Harlem eateries, bars, record stores, and laundromats. The *Village Voice*'s William Paul observed, "By selecting locations for their pleasing appearance and a delicate use of filters, Davis manages to beautify Harlem as he photographs it: even groupings of high-rise, low-income tenements, one of the most desolate sights in New York, are made pretty by the warm, pinkish tones the film lends them. The picture of Harlem that emerges is a spirited, joyful, and often adventurous place to live."

Both Himes' and Davis' works display the artists' genuine affection for the black community, including some of the seedier aspects, such as pickpockets and con men. In *Cotton Comes to Harlem*, the creators seem to take delight in some of the Harlemites' more outrageous schemes.

Selected urban vernacular of the period—terms and phrases like "soul brother," "honky," and "black is beautiful"—are used in the film, and coming from Himes and Davis, sound authentic, as opposed to the forced and tone-deaf usage of such words and phrases in some later "black" films made by white filmmakers.

Claims that *Cotton Comes to Harlem* is neo-noir seem silly considering the picture's light, often whimsical feel. Much of the dialogue, as well as Cambridge's performance, are broadly comical, and each time the film approaches anything remotely gritty, the bouncy, up-tempo music (scored by Galt MacDermot of *Hair* fame) starts to play, keeping the proceedings light.

True to the time and location, the characters express their sense of "otherness"; their world is theirs and theirs alone, existing separate from white America. In one scene, Coffin Ed asks, "What the hell does the Attorney General, the State Department, or even the president of the United States know about one goddamn thing that's going on up here in Harlem?" This otherness is something Gravedigger Jones and Coffin Ed's white commanding officer is well aware of, and it's for this reason he allows them leeway in their decision making. After all, they're far more knowledgeable about the neighborhood and the way things work there than he is. Despite their familiarity with the neighborhood (and the neighborhood's familiarity with them), Gravedigger Jones and Coffin Ed are viewed by a lot of Harlemites as being sellouts. One militant remarks, "The only thing I hate worse than a honky pig cop [is] a nigger pig cop."

The film's plot finds the two cops traveling the Harlem streets tracking Reverend Deke O'Malley, a former convict who now presents himself as a man of God. O'Malley has been raising money intended to help the locals return to Africa. However, the once and former con man has stolen the $87,000 raised from unassuming people in the neighborhood. The plot is contrived and, at times, difficult to follow, and it includes black militants, the Italian Mafia, O'Malley's religious supporters, cops, an old man played by Redd Foxx who seems (until the film's conclusion) to pop up occasionally for no discernible reason, and a mysterious bale of cotton containing stolen loot.

Made on a budget of $1.2 million, *Cotton Comes to Harlem* took in $5.2 million at the box office. It was the twentieth most successful film of 1970, proving that black people could be a viable audience (which studios had previously doubted). Hoping to cash in on the film's popularity, United Artists immediately green-lit a sequel.

Joe

Before becoming a filmmaker, John G. Avildsen worked as a copywriter for an advertising agency. There he met and befriended another highly educated ad man with creative aspirations. His name was Norman Wexler, and he was on the verge of becoming a produced playwright. Avildsen eventually broke into the film business directing industrial films and working as an assistant director on films such as Arthur Penn's *Mickey One* (1965) and Otto Preminger's *Hurry Sundown* (1967). Avildsen made his directorial debut with the 1969 sexploitation picture *Turn on to Love*. He made his second film, *Guess What We Learned in School Today?* (1970), also a sexploitation pic, for Cannon Films. While he was editing the film, Cannon executives came to him and asked if he had anything that could be made quickly. (The studio had raised money for another project, but when the screenwriter turned in his script, they hated it. Cannon didn't want to give the money back to investors, so they decided they'd make another film.) Avildsen suggested a treatment by Wexler called *The Gap* that he'd previously pitched to Cannon that they'd passed on. The studio execs still didn't love the treatment, but they had nothing else, so they green-lit the picture.

The treatment for *The Gap* told the story of a WASP businessman who, after killing his daughter's dope-dealing boyfriend, befriends a crude blue-collar laborer. Although the two men seem nothing alike, they bond over their bigotry, hatred of hippies, and love for Richard Nixon. In the end, the two men murder a group of hippies, and, in the process, the businessman inadvertently kills his own daughter. Wexler's primary inspirations for the story were Vice President Spiro T. Agnew's "silent majority" rhetoric and a *New York Magazine* article by Gail Sheehy about a wealthy father from Connecticut who tracked down his runaway daughter and murdered her drug dealer boyfriend. It should be noted that Harvard alum Wexler did not share the views of his characters. In fact, a couple of years later, Wexler would be jailed for threatening to assassinate Nixon during a commercial flight from New York City to San Francisco. However, Wexler had grown up in Detroit, the son of two factory workers, so he knew about the world of blue-collar laborers. Most importantly, the screenwriter had an ear for dialogue and knew how they spoke. After Avildsen informed Wexler that the project had been green-lit, Wexler produced a full script in a mere eight days.

The first actor cast as beer-guzzling bigot Joe was Lawrence Tierney. "I was there for the auditions," recalls Avildsen's friend and production assistant Lloyd Kaufman, who went on to co-direct *The Toxic Avenger* (1985) and establish Troma Films. "Did you know that Lawrence Tierney was originally supposed to play Joe? The bosses wanted him. He was a name. Avildsen wanted Peter Boyle. Peter Boyle did an improvisation during the audition. I can't remember what the line was supposed to be, but he added, *'And I ain't queer!'* Something to that effect. He improvised a piece like that, and Avildsen fell in love with it. But they were going with Tierney. So later, we were on an escalator in Alexander's, which was a discount store across the street from Bloomingdale's. Tierney was on the escalator, I was on the escalator, there was somebody ahead of me—maybe the costume guy. I felt something tapping on my blue jeans, kind of around the ankle. It was really weird . . . *Lawrence Tierney was peeing on me!* I don't know if it was me, or it was just . . . He had a drinking problem. They got rid of him after that."

After Tierney's departure, Avildsen cast Boyle. Boyle had created a character he would later describe as a "reactionary bigoted kind of guy" while he was at Second City. Because of this, Boyle felt he already knew the character. So he played Joe exactly the way he'd played the character at Second City.

In the secondary roles, Avildsen cast Dennis Patrick as the businessman and a fresh-faced ingenue making her film debut to play the daughter. The actress was Susan Sarandon, who would eventually become a movie star and receive a handful of Oscar nominations, winning for *Dead Man Walking* (1995).

After the one-month shoot, as Avildsen was editing the film, an incident occurred in New York City in which four hundred construction workers walked off a job site to attack college students protesting the Kent State massacre and the Vietnam War. The unruly construction workers injured protesters and bystanders alike, going on to smash windows before marching to City Hall and demanding that the American flag flying at half-mast to honor the Kent State victims be raised. Recognizing the timeliness of the film and the possibility that Joe could become a hero to the "silent majority," Avildsen and Wexler conceived new scenes and recut the existing ones so the film featured more of Boyle's angry character. Because of this, the film was retitled *Joe*.

Of his performance, Boyle would later say in a Television Academy interview, "The picture was such a low-budget movie, so inauspicious, I thought nobody would ever see it. So I just did everything I felt like doing with complete abandon."

Joe opened on July 15, 1970, just two months after the Kent State massacre, to mostly positive reviews. Most critics believed the film accurately captured the way many Americans felt. Gene Siskel of the *Chicago Tribune* praised *Joe* as "a landmark film because of the issues and social norms it justifies. It is a dramatic, if not always sophisticated, documentary of a growing portion of the national mentality." *Los Angeles Times* critic Charles Champlin called the film "an immensely sophisticated piece of filmmaking." He went on to write, "The plot is laced with implausibilities and the movie full of scenes which are heavily contrived but which play well because they are swept along by the plausibility of Joe himself."

While a Times Square theater named The Embassy played the film around-the-clock, twenty-four hours a day, Boyle and a pal slipped into the back of an in-progress screening so he could watch the film in anonymity. Boyle was stunned to see sympathizing bigots cheering for Joe and screaming their approval. But Joe's like-minded fans weren't the only audience members speaking up. Those who were opposed yelled things like *"I'm going to shoot back, Joe!"* For months people approached Boyle on the street, believing he was actually the character. This terrified Boyle, who feared he might be gunned down or stabbed by some nut case confusing him with Joe.

The film enjoyed a twenty-one-week first run in New York City. On January 20, 1971, the film was re-released in theaters. *Joe* wound up making $20 million theatrically, becoming the highest-grossing independent film of 1970 and the thirteenth highest-grossing film overall. Wexler received an Oscar nomination for his screenplay, which was the first he'd ever written. In 1980, Cannon announced that a sequel cleverly titled *Joe II* was forthcoming. Five years later, Cannon ran an advertisement for another promised sequel, *Citizen Joe*. The ad's tagline read: "The man has changed, but the times have not." Despite these declarations, a sequel never materialized.

1971

The Blue Flu, The French Connection, *and* Shaft

In the 1970s, there were lots of crime films made in New York City, primarily because of the visuals of the crumbling city's urban decay. But the films also aligned with America's (and the world's) vision of the city at that time; NYC was now seen as a dark and dangerous place festering with rapists, muggers, and murderers, which made sense because the city's rate of homicides set new personal worst records in 1969 and 1970. Sadly, 1971 would prove to be more of the same with the number of homicides rising to a staggering 1,466. To put this into perspective, World Health Organization data at the time showed that, "in recent years," the city had more homicides than the countries of England, Scotland, Wales, Ireland, Northern Ireland, Switzerland, Spain, Sweden, the Netherlands, Norway, Denmark, and Luxembourg combined. It should also be noted that the combined populations of those countries was roughly sixteen times more than NYC's population. While newspapers around the world chose to focus their attention on the city's ever-increasing murder rate, NYC provided a wide variety of crime-related stories to report on in 1971.

Between January 14 and 19, twenty thousand NYPD officers refused to work. This was done as a form of strike. The officers coordinated their sick days and called in as a way to get around Article Fourteen of the New York State Civil Service Law (known as the Taylor Law), which prevents police officers from going on strike. This action would become known as the "Blue Flu."

Officers made themselves available to take care of major crimes and emergencies but refused to engage in their normal day-to-day patrolling duties. As a result, there were sometimes as few as two hundred cops on the streets covering the entire city. This action came after a lawsuit by the Sergeants Benevolent Association that would have increased pay for police officers and firefighters and granted them back pay going back to the previous contract was dismissed in court. An angry mayor John V. Lindsay threatened to fire the entire police department, but the threat rang hollow since no one believed he would do it. After the cops returned to full duty, the back-pay issue was resolved. The officers were also fined for violating the Taylor Law.

In other NYPD news, two patrolmen, Waverly Jones and Joseph Piagentini, were killed in an ambush in Harlem on May 21. Jones and Piagentini were on foot patrol in the Colonial Park housing complex, located at 159th Street and Harlem River Drive. As they were returning to their cruiser, three men blindsided them and opened fire. Jones was shot in the head and died immediately. Piagentini was shot thirteen times and died while being transported to the hospital. Jalil Muntaqim, Albert Washington, and Herman Bell, all members of a radical group known as the Black Liberation Army, were identified and arrested for the murders.

In March 1971, Colombo crime family boss Joe Colombo was convicted of perjury and was sentenced to two-and-a-half years in prison. The sentence was delayed pending an appeal. So, in the meantime, it was business as usual. After Colombo made an enemy of former Profaci family captain Joe Gallo, Gallo (allegedly) sent a gunman named Jerome Davis to the Unity Day rally in Columbus Circle on June 28 with instructions to kill him. The forty-eight-year-old Colombo was addressing the crowd as head of the Italian–Civil Rights League when Davis fired three shots from the crowd. One of the bullets struck Colombo in the head, rendering him comatose and paralyzed. The gunman was then shot by someone in the crowd. As a result, no one has definitively proven that Gallo was the one who sent him. Other theories posit that Davis was a lone shooter or was sent by Gambino family boss Carlo Gambino.

Specific NYC crime statistics for 1971 showed that one Harlem precinct with 53,351 residents had 105 homicides, or two per week. However, one precinct in Kew Gardens, Queens, which had 162,802 residents, had only one homicide. That year, the homicide rate in Central Harlem was 328 times as high as the homicide rate in Kew Gardens. On the East Side of Manhattan, there were 1,291 robberies reported between 59th and 86th Street, with a rate of 86.5 robberies per 10,000 residents. On the West Side, there were 1,741 robberies, with a rate of 178.7 robberies per 10,000 residents. Greenwich Village reported 2,563 burglaries, with a rate of 459 burglaries per 10,000 residents. This was 31 percent higher than the burglary rates found in eight of the city's "worst slum" neighborhoods. There were 3,466 reported car thefts in South Jamaica, Queens, with a rate of 218.4 car thefts for every 100,000 residents. That rate was double the rate of car thefts in the Ridgewood section of Queens, where there were 97.3 cars stolen for every 100,000 residents.

In May, twenty-one members of the Black Panthers, known as the "Panther Twenty-One," who had been accused of coordinating attacks against two police stations and an education office, were acquitted by a jury after it was revealed that undercover cops had misrepresented the group and their actions to their superiors.

The seven films from 1971 that we'll discuss are an eclectic bunch. Two of them, *The French Connection* and *Shaft*, would become iconic game-changers. While there were already cop films being made, the massive success of *The French Connection* would lead to a seemingly never-ending string of them that lasted throughout the decade. It would also, more directly, lead to four more (vastly inferior) films; first there were *Badge 373* and *The Seven-Ups* (both 1973), which were technically unrelated films depicting further exploits, individually, of Eddie Egan and Sonny Grosso, the cops *The French Connection* was based on; additionally, there were the official follow-ups *The French Connection II* (1975) and *Popeye Doyle* (1986). And while there were other films that played a role in the creation of the cycle now known as "blaxploitation," *Shaft* was the primary progenitor. Like *The French Connection*, *Shaft* not only led to copycats and indirect successors, it also became a cottage industry of official sequels, a television series, and reboots (not to mention novels, novelizations, and comics).

Two of the films discussed here, *Born to Win* and *The Panic in Needle Park*, focused on the city's increasing heroin problem. Rounding out the selections in this section are *The Anderson Tapes*, *The Gang That Couldn't Shoot Straight*, and *Klute*.

The Anderson Tapes

Although his name isn't associated with New York City the way Martin Scorsese's and Woody Allen's are, Sidney Lumet was most certainly a true-blue NYC director. Many of his films, including *The Pawnbroker* (1964), *Serpico* (1973), *Dog Day Afternoon* (1975), and *Prince of the City* (1981), were shot in the city. Another Lumet-directed NYC crime film that doesn't get nearly the acclaim it deserves is *The Anderson Tapes*. While this heist film isn't as gritty as those previously mentioned, it was shot entirely in NYC and stands as an effective time capsule of the period and place where it was made.

The Anderson Tapes first existed as a 1970 epistolary novel penned by fifty-year-old first-time novelist Lawrence Sanders. Sanders, a former journalist and editor, received a paltry $300 advance for *The Anderson Tapes*. Sanders would have the last laugh, however; in addition to receiving the Mystery Writers of America's award for Best First Novel, he would be paid $100,000 for the paperback rights and an additional $200,000 for the film rights.

The story of the film began when producer Robert Weitman read a pre-publication galley. He immediately bid on the film rights and won. He then enlisted *Cool Hand Luke* (1967) scribe Frank Pierson to adapt the novel. After that, Weitman hired Sidney Lumet to direct. Lumet, who had been nominated for a Best Director Academy Award for *12 Angry Men* in 1957, had a reputation for working with his actors to help them give naturalistic performances.

For the lead role of safecracker Duke Anderson, Lumet pushed for Sean Connery, with whom he'd worked previously on *The Hill* (1965). Connery had just stepped down from playing the James Bond character he was known for (although he would return to the character almost immediately for 1971's *Diamonds Are Forever*). *The Anderson Tapes* would be the second of five Lumet/Connery collaborations. (The others are *The Hill*, *The Offence* [1973], *Murder on the Orient Express* [1974], and *Family Business* [1989].)

For the role of "The Kid," Lumet cast a former child actor named Christopher Walken with whom he'd worked years before. "It was Christopher Walken's first film role," Lumet later wrote in *Making Movies*. "I had known Chris for a long time. He was a kid actor along with his brother, who was also a kid actor who had worked with me in live television days. . . . [W]hat's interesting is how beautiful he was. A very sensuous face, a very arresting face. As an actor he never does anything that's cliché in any way, it's always completely original, completely his own. I knew that about his work. I remember he came in and read for the part and I said, 'It's yours.'"

The cast, solid from top to bottom, also included Dyan Cannon, Martin Balsam, Ralph Meeker, Alan King, Conrad Bain, Margaret Hamilton, Garrett Morris, Anthony Holland, and Paul Benjamin. While Balsam's performance as a homosexual robber would raise a few eyebrows and draw ire today because of its broad nature, the character was a progressive addition to the film at the time it was made.

While some scenes were shot on a soundstage at Production Center Studios on West 26th Street in NYC, the majority of *The Anderson Tapes* was shot on location. These locations included the Luxor Turkish bathhouse on 41st Street (for the scene in which Duke Anderson meets "Socks" Borelli for the first time), the Port Authority Bus Terminal at Eighth Avenue and 41st Street, Alan King's home at King's Point on Long Island (for the scene where Pat Angelo meets with "Papa" Angelo), the Convent of the Sacred Heart on 1 East 91st Street (the apartment building the crooks rob), and St. Patrick's Cathedral at Mulberry and Huston Streets (the funeral scene). Other locations include Central Park, the so-called "Millionaire's Row" on Fifth Avenue in Manhattan, and East 10th Street (the location of Tommy Haskins' antique store).

Lumet and his crew had an interesting experience while filming at St. Patrick's Cathedral. While filming the Mafia funeral scene, real-life mobsters tried to shake them down, claiming they were offended by the way their families were being portrayed. At one point, actor Alan King nearly came to blows with the wiseguys. When Lumet heard some of the mafioso threatening to take away the negative, he started breaking off the negative after he shot each scene and having his production assistants carry them off set.

Lumet would later explain that the Mafia wasn't the only group who tried to make money off of filmmakers shooting in New York City; it seems that the NYPD was in on the action as well. "We used to budget for it," Lumet told author James Sanders. "You'd start shooting at seven-thirty in the morning and have to take care of all three shifts; the sergeant who'd stop by in his car, and the cops on the street."

The Anderson Tapes was released on June 17, 1971. Reviews were middling, with most critics complaining about the film bouncing back and forth between attempting to be a serious crime film and a broad comedy; the general consensus was that the more serious aspects of the film worked better than the humorous. Lumet also received criticism for attempting to make a sociopolitical statement about Big Brother watching Americans without fully understanding what it was he wanted to say. Andrew Sarris of the *Village Voice* remarked that *The Anderson Tapes* had "about eleven good minutes in it," going on to report that Sanders' book was better than the film. *Chicago Sun-Times* critic Roger Ebert observed, "The only serious structural flaw in the movie involves the emphasis on electronic surveillance. The original novel, as you probably know, was supposedly based on transcriptions from various public and private spies. That was a literary device, and even too cute for a bestseller. In the movie, it's dead weight. . . . Perhaps Lumet was simply being too ambitious by trying to work anti-bugging sentiment into the film. If he'd thrown out all the hidden mikes and stuck with the heist, *The Anderson Tapes* would have moved with a more confident step in the direction of *Rififi* [1956]."

The Anderson Tapes was produced on a budget of $3 million and earned just under $11 million at the box office. (In case you were wondering, $11 million in 1971 dollars would be approximately $83,597,000 today.) Despite the film's success, it hasn't made much of a dent in terms of legacy. It's rarely discussed, even in conversations about Lumet's crime films of the 1970s. Everyone knows *Serpico* and *Dog Day Afternoon*, but if you mention *The Anderson Tapes*, you'll likely get blank stares.

Born to Win

In the 1960s, David Milton Scott, a member of an avant-garde off-off-Broadway theater troupe called Theatre Genesis, wrote a play titled *Scraping Bottom*. Scott owned a restaurant on 72nd Street (near Needle Park). There he observed the actions and mannerisms of addicts who frequented the place. *Scraping Bottom*, inspired by the drug users Scott had encountered, focused on a down-on-his-luck heroin addict living in Manhattan. Czech-born filmmaker Ivan Passer was an audience member at a production of Scott's play. The director was intrigued by the characters and the story and saw potential for a movie. Passer then optioned the film rights to the play and spent several months with Scott interviewing recovering addicts at the Phoenix House rehabilitation center. While interviewing former junkies, Passer promised many of them he would put them in the movie as extras.

Passer wound up casting George Segal, who would also serve as co-executive producer. Karen Black and Paula Prentiss were cast as Segal's love interests in the film. Although Prentiss only appears in the film for three minutes, she receives second billing to Segal (and above the title billing at that). When asked about this, Passer would later explain that the actress's agent demanded she be billed second. Passer didn't care about this, so he agreed. The cast also included appearances by Hector Elizondo, Robert De Niro, and Burt Young.

Passer and company began shooting in February 1971. The film, shot in and around Times Square, was being made at the same time as another Manhattan heroin-addiction film, *Needle Park* (1971). Some of the locations shown in the film include the 20–23rd subway station (what kind of NYC film would it be without a subway scene?); Howard Johnson's restaurant, located at West 46th and Broadway; the House of Cromwell men's clothing store, located at 669 Lexington Avenue; Childs Restaurant, located between Broadway and Church Street; and the Biltmore Theater, located at 47th and Broadway. As characters make their way through Times Square, a number of film titles are visible on theater marquees; these include an Andy Milligan double feature consisting of *The Body Beneath* (1970) and *Guru, the Mad Monk* (1970).

While the film was in post-production, United Artists lost faith in the picture, so they recut it in an attempt to make it a comedy. In his book *The Films of Robert De Niro*, author Douglas Brode later wrote, "If handled properly, this might have been a black comedy, but that is not the result. At times, the movie turns into a vivid, harrowing case study of an addict and his craving on the order of *The Man with the Golden Arm* [1955]. At other moments, it transforms into a Feifferesque example of edgy humor about a lovable Jewish schnook trying to survive in the ever-more-threatening Manhattan, like *Little Murders* [1971]. Occasionally, it's supposed to be a romantic comedy about a Neil Simonish guy and his girls. We're left with the impression that the filmmakers set out to make one sort of movie, were persuaded to do something else entirely after they had started shooting, then changed their minds a third time when things were clearly not working out and everyone became desperate. When the scenes were finally edited together, the result was a mishmash, a total mess." In addition to the cuts, the studio also changed the title from *Scraping Bottom* to *Born to Win*.

The film was first unveiled at the 1971 New York Film Festival and later released theatrically in December 1971. United Artists unsuccessfully advertised the film as a buddy comedy, and

Born to Win flopped. Reviews were generally unfavorable. *Los Angeles Times* critic Charles Champlin wrote that the film "leaves no doubt that Ivan Presser is a topflight director with a special capacity for handling close relationships and intense private moments. But here . . . his observant eye seems to have watched not American life but movies and TV purporting to be about American life." Nick Yanni of the *Hollywood Reporter* observed that "Passer's direction seems strangely unfocused [so] much of the picture comes off as phony and ill conceived . . . It's unfortunate that a sensibility as fine as Passer's has gotten bogged down in a film that is so cliche-ridden." Roger Greenspun of the *New York Times* wrote that *Born to Win* "is only Passer's second movie, and it is a dreadful disappointment—but not without its reasons, and not, I think, without some honor."

Born to Win would eventually fall into the public domain, leading to its being released in a variety of shoddy VHS editions, most attempting to con potential buyers into believing Robert De Niro was its star. It was also released on VHS as *The Addict*. Despite its problems—mostly the result of interference from United Artists—the film would eventually gain a following. Josh and Ben Safdie would later point to the film as being an influence on their own *Uncut Gems* (2019). On his commentary for *Born to Win*'s 2022 Blu-ray, *Fun City Cinema* author Jason Bailey proclaimed it "one of the unsung New York movies of the early 1970s."

The French Connection

In 1961, two New York City cops named Eddie Egan and Sonny Grosso made the biggest drug bust in US history. They broke up an organized crime ring that had smuggled fifty kilos of cocaine into the country every six weeks for twenty-five years. Egan, Grosso, and company seized an astounding 112 pounds of pure cocaine. In 1969, author Robin Moore chronicled the events leading up to the bust in a book titled *The French Connection: A True Account of Cops, Narcotics, and International Conspiracy.*

Phillip D'Antoni, a producer whose credits had been limited to television before breaking out with the Steve McQueen–starrer *Bullitt* (1968), optioned the film rights to Moore's book. The producer then approached a director friend of his about the would-be project inside a steam room on the Paramount lot. The filmmaker was William Friedkin, who had a few minor features under his belt and, like D'Antoni, had done a lot of TV. Friedkin wasn't overly excited about the project since it wasn't set up at a studio. Nevertheless, Friedkin agreed to meet Egan and Grosso.

When he met with the two cops and learned more about them and their story, he decided he wanted to make the film. It seems that what mostly appealed to Friedkin, who'd never read Moore's book, was the camaraderie and dynamic between Egan and Grosso. It has been said that they balanced each other out; Grosso was cynical, seeing the glass as being half-empty, whereas Egan tended to be more optimistic, seeing things as being half-full. Because of this, Egan nicknamed his partner "Cloudy"—the opposite of "sunny" (Sonny). "I thought they were hilarious," Friedkin later told documentarian Russell Leven. "And I thought their approach to law enforcement was just the absolute right touch for the time. It was like a game to them."

Despite having no studio attached, Friedkin immediately dove into the project and began spending time on the streets with Egan and Russo. The cops took the director along as they conducted drug seizures, questioned informants, and testified in court. In an effort to show Friedkin the kinds of things they saw on a daily basis—things Friedkin was not familiar with—they took him to a place they called the "shooting gallery." This was an abandoned Manhattan apartment building located at 110th Street and Fifth Avenue, where heroin-addicted transients came to shoot up. Since the apartment building was just more than a mile from Friedkin's own apartment, the visit was an eye-opener for him. On another occasion, Randy Jurgensen, a cop who served as a technical advisor, allowed Friedkin to accompany him when he arrested a man who'd just shotgunned his whole family. Jurgensen even let Friedkin handcuff the killer.

1971: The Blue Flu, *The French Connection*, and *Shaft* / 27

Friedkin and D'Antoni commissioned a number of screenwriters to work on the project. *Point Blank* (1967) screenwriter Alex Jacobs, a mutual friend of Friedkin and D'Antoni, was brought in first. Jacobs wrote several drafts, but neither Friedkin nor D'Antoni liked them. The next writer they hired was Robert E. Thompson, who'd written Sydney Pollack's *They Shoot Horses, Don't They?* (1969). Thompson wrote a single draft, which they immediately rejected. The third (and final) screenwriter brought in to work on the project was Ernest Tidyman, a former *New York Times* reporter who had written *Shaft* (1968). The process with Tidyman: Friedkin and D'Antoni sat with him and fed him dialogue comprised of their own improvisation and lines supplied by Egan and Russo. Although Tidyman is the only screenwriter credited and ultimately won the Writers Guild Award for Best Adapted Screenplay, Friedkin insists that no dialogue by the screenwriter actually appears in the film.

The screenplay was shopped around to studios, but they continually passed on the project; some even passed twice. After more than a year of this, Richard Zanuck, the head of production at 20th Century Fox, agreed to make the picture if Friedkin could make it for $1.5 million or less. Friedkin agreed, although he would end up going over budget by $300,000. When Friedkin explained his plan to make the film look as real as possible (a style he called "induced-documentary"), he and D'Antoni were shocked to find that Zanuck agreed.

The director initially wanted Jackie Gleason to play the lead (Popeye Doyle, based on Egan) and even reached out to Gleason (who agreed to play the part), but Zanuck vetoed this. Egan himself requested that Rod Taylor play him in the film because he believed he looked like him. In the end, it was agreed that, in the spirit of making the film look and feel realistic, unknown (or virtually unknown) actors and amateurs would be cast. At some point, *New York Daily News* journalist Jimmy Breslin was auditioned for the lead role. Zanuck eventually pushed for a young actor named Gene Hackman to be cast as the lead. Friedkin didn't like Hackman for the role, but he ultimately gave in. Casting director Bob Weiner suggested Roy Scheider for the

Grosso character (Buddy Russo in the film). Friedkin met with Scheider, liked him, and cast him without an audition. For the third key role, the character known as "The Frenchman," Weiner made a massive faux pas and cast the wrong actor; after Friedkin told him to cast the actor (Jean Sorel) from the Luis Bunuel film *Belle de Jour* (1967), Weiner mistakenly cast Fernando Rey. When Friedkin learned of the mistake, he became enraged, pointing out that Rey (from Spain) wasn't even French. Nevertheless, Friedkin rolled with it, making the movie with two actors he believed were wrong for their parts. Even worse, at one point the studio wanted to change the title of the film; their highly creative suggestions included the titles *Popeye* and *Doyle*. (One can imagine such further "inspired" titles as *Policemen* and *Drug Bust*.) Luckily, D'Antoni and Friedkin put the kibosh on the title-changing.

The first day of shooting (of eighty-six total) was November 30, 1970. Shooting temperatures were so cold that the cameras froze and cast members would go inside stores to find warmth between shots. A major problem arose immediately when Hackman expressed displeasure regarding his unsavory character and bad deeds. The actor wanted to quit, but Friedkin convinced him to stay. Because Hackman believed the Egan-based Popeye Doyle was an unsavory character, and because Egan was on the set almost every day, the actor and the cop clashed. "The character was a bigot and anti-Semetic and whatever else you want to call him," Hackman said in a 2008 interview. "That's who he was. It was difficult for me to say the n-word. I protested somewhat, but there was a part of me also that said, that's who the guy is. You like him or no, that's who he was. You couldn't really whitewash it." In an effort to elicit believable anger and ferocity from Hackman, Friedkin said and did things to manipulate him and make him unhappy.

D'Antoni's film *Bullitt* had made a huge splash with what was, at the time, considered the greatest car chase sequence ever filmed. So, during filming, D'Antoni decided he wanted to duplicate that success by creating a chase scene in *The French Connection* that was even wilder and more impressive. "The chase scene was never in the script," Friedkin told *Deadline*'s Mike Fleming. "I created that chase scene with producer Phillip D'Antoni. We just spit-balled ideas. We walked out of my apartment, headed south in Manhattan and we kept walking until we came up with that chase scene, letting the atmosphere of the city guide us. The steam coming off the street, and the sound of the subway rumbling beneath our feet, the treacherous traffic on the crowded streets."

They decided the chase scene would be largely improvised and shot with real drivers and pedestrians on the streets. Cinematographer Owen Roizman voiced concerns about the dangers of this, but Friedkin did it anyway. According to Friedkin, the shot was "stolen," meaning there were no permits, so it had to be accomplished in a single shot. (The accuracy of this claim is questionable.) Stuntman Bill Hickman (D'Antoni's driver from *Bullitt*) would start at Coney Island around Bay and 50th Street in Popeye Doyle's 1971 Pontiac LeMans, speeding at approximately ninety miles per hour through twenty-six blocks of traffic, jumping over the curb, weaving, and heading into oncoming traffic. During the shot, Hickman sideswiped a real city bus. In addition, the speeding car caused several traffic accidents. But, in the end, Friedkin and D'Antoni achieved their goal—the six-minute sequence is widely considered the greatest chase scene ever filmed.

When selecting locations, Friedkin chose the dingiest, dirtiest places he could find. Friedkin wanted to show the city's underbelly; a part of the city that only the cops and drug dealers saw. In 2018, actor Willem Dafoe, who worked with Friedkin on *To Live and Die in LA* (1985), told documentarian Francesco Zippel, "When you look at *French Connection*, you feel New York . . . You feel it in that time period. It serves as kind of a time capsule." Production assistant Ralph Singleton, responsible for obtaining shooting permits, says he would sometimes have to secure more than one location for use in a single scene. "Billy [Friedkin] kept changing his mind," Singleton says. "It drove me crazy. Billy was not the easiest person to work for. He was very talented, but he was tough, a real hard driver."

Approximately a hundred locations appear in the film. Here are a few of them: when we first encounter Popeye, he is on a stakeout in front of the Oasis Bar & Grill at 914 Broadway in Brooklyn; the two-thousand-seat Rio Piedras Theatre is visible next door; after chasing a suspect on foot, Popeye and Cloudy apprehend him in a vacant lot located at 760 Broadway, where the Woodhull Medical Center stands today; the Circus Cinema and Trans-Lux Theater make appearances as the cops drive through Times Square; they wait for the couple outside Ratner's, a Kosher restaurant that was located at 138 Delancey Street on the Lower East Side of Manhattan; in one scene, the cops drive through Little Italy, passing the Alleva Dairy and its neighbor, the Piemonte Ravioli Co., on Grand Street; Popeye observes Boca carrying the suitcase to 177 Broome Street; and the Bocas are up to no good at Sal & Angie's, a restaurant located at 91 Wyckoff Avenue in Bushwick.

The French Connection was released on October 9, 1971. The reviews were terrific, with *Chicago Sun-Times* critic Roger Ebert hailing it as "a new kind of film." At press-only screenings, critics stood and applauded. *The French Connection* became a massive hit and was the fourth-highest grossing film of 1971 (behind *Billy Jack* [1971], *Fiddler on the Roof* [1971], and *Diamonds Are Forever* [1971]) with $41 million. By the end of its theatrical run, *The French Connection* had earned more than $75 million. The film received eight Academy Award nominations, taking home five statuettes, including Best Picture and Best Actor (Hackman).

The film made enough money that 20th Century Fox ordered a sequel, *The French Connection II* (1975). (That film is not covered in this volume because it takes place in France, not NYC.) With the success of the film, Egan and Grosso each got their own films about their further adventures. These were *The Seven-Ups* (1973), in which D'Antoni directed Scheider playing Grosso ("Buddy"), and *Badge 373* (1973), with Robert Duvall playing Egan ("Eddie Ryan"). Fifteen years after the release of *The French Connection*, Ed O'Neill of *Married with Children* fame attempted to fill Hackman's sizable shoes in the NBC telefilm *Popeye Doyle* (1986).

The Gang That Couldn't Shoot Straight

Jimmy Breslin, the author and journalist dubbed "the voice of New York," who wrote regularly for publications including the *Daily News*, the *New York Herald Tribune*, and *New York* magazine, conceived his novel *The Gang That Couldn't Shoot Straight* while having drinks with some friends at the bar of Gallagher's Steakhouse (at 228 West 52nd Street) in Manhattan. According to Breslin, he, with a beer in hand, announced, "I don't have to keep chasing fires for a living. I'm going to do a book called *The Gang That Couldn't Shoot Straight*." Breslin's novel would take a satirical look at the violent and bloody war that was taking place between the Gallo and Profaci crime families.

Producers Irwin Winkler and Robert Chartoff, who had previously produced the Elvis Presley film *Double Trouble* and the action-thriller *Point Blank* (both 1967), optioned the film rights in February 1969, months before the book was published. After news of the option hit the trades, an agent representing a young filmmaker named Francis Ford Coppola pitched his client to Winkler and Chartoff to direct the film. The producers sat down and screened Coppola's *Finian's Rainbow* (1968) and *The Rain People* (1969). After watching them, Winkler would later admit they "decided there was no reason to think Mr. Coppola could direct a gangster film." When Coppola learned that Winkler and Chartoff had passed on him, he tried a different tack; he wrote a direct pitch. In a bold move, Coppola wrote the pitch in screenplay form as a conversation between he and his mother in which he explained how much he wanted to direct *The Gang That Couldn't Shoot Straight* and why he believed he was the best candidate. While the producers were impressed with this unique method of proposal, they were not moved. The story that took place afterward is one we all know—Coppola went on to direct the mother of all gangster films, *The Godfather* (1972), which became a colossal hit and is widely considered one of the greatest films ever made.

Having recently viewed the Paul Newman/Joan Woodward film *Winning* (1969), Winkler and Chartoff approached and hired the film's director, James Goldstone. To write the adaptation, they hired Waldo Salt, hot off his Academy Award–winning screenplay for *Midnight Cowboy* (1969). Winkler would later share a story about Salt offering to drive him to the airport each Friday for Winkler's cross-country trips to visit his parents. One day the producer told Salt's daughter, Jennifer Salt, how nice her father was for driving him. The actress chuckled and told him that her father just did this to avoid writing the script. After that, Winkler took cabs.

Casting the film would become another interesting story that again involved *The Godfather*, which we'll discuss in a moment. The producers first cast Italian actor Marcello Mastroianni as the lead. Fearing that he couldn't speak English well enough to play the role properly, Mastroianni backed out. Jerry Orbach was then cast as the lead. The rest of the cast included Lionel Stander (in his first American role since he'd been blacklisted in 1951), Leigh Taylor-Young, Burt Young, future *Fantasy Island* star Hervé Villechaize (miscast as an Italian), and a then-unknown actor named Al Pacino.

During rehearsals at the Stanhope Hotel (at 995 Fifth Avenue), Pacino left the film to play the lead in *The Godfather*. MGM, owned by billionaire Kirk Kerkorian and run by James Aubrey, refused to release Pacino. Paramount head of production Robert Evans was adamant that Pacino play the lead in *The Godfather*, although, in truth, he didn't want him either, but did this to appease producer Albert S. Ruddy. Evans turned to alleged mob lawyer Sidney Korshak to get the actor out of his contract. According to Peter Bart, who was a studio exec at the time, Korshak remarked, "No one in this town even knows who this kid is. Suddenly two studios are fighting over a nobody." A little while after Evans spoke with Korshak, MGM chief Aubrey called him, screaming and spewing obscenities. According to Evans, Aubrey said, "*I'll get you for this! The midget's [Pacino] yours!*" Evans then paid $35,000 for Pacino's release, and the actor contractually promised to appear in two more films for MGM. (He never did.) When Evans asked Korshak how he convinced Aubrey to allow Pacino to leave *The Gang That Couldn't Shoot Straight*, the lawyer said he'd told Aubrey, who was building the MGM Grand in Las

Vegas, that if ever wanted to finish building the hotel, he needed to let the actor go.

It should be noted that MGM sued Pacino anyway. "I paid for the lawyers, I paid for everything," Pacino explained to author Ron Base. "I was broke after that, even in debt. But I didn't care. I've been broke before, but from the beginning, I knew I'd have more money [from making *The Godfather*] than I'd ever need."

Once Pacino was gone, Winkler and Chartoff found another future icon to replace him. That actor's name was Robert De Niro. Interestingly, De Niro had also been cast in *The Godfather*. The two actors might have passed each other as they each jumped ship from one movie to appear in the other.

De Niro would always consider this his "first big-deal movie." He was paid $750 a week. "He came into rehearsal seemingly very ordinary," Leigh Taylor-Young would recall in an interview with author John Baxter. "Quiet and mumbly and with a very endearing sweet, shy way about him. His eyes didn't make direct contact for very long." Winkler, who continued to work with De Niro as both producer and director for decades after, immediately recognized that there was something special about the actor. De Niro told the producers he wanted to travel to Sicily for a few weeks so he could study Sicilian speech patterns and perfect his character's speech. When they told him there was no money in the budget for this, De Niro paid his own way.

In an attempt to better acquaint them with their characters, Goldstone, the director, sent Taylor-Young and De Niro out to explore New York City completely in character. The two took the Fifth Avenue bus and got off near the Empire State Building. Taylor-Young would later admit that De Niro's perfect accent intimidated her. When the two performers walked through Macy's department store, De Niro got caught shoplifting some shirts. They attempted to explain to the guards that they were actors trying to act as their characters and that De Niro had stolen the shirts because his character would have done this. After being arrested, one of the cops recognized Taylor-Young from the television series *Peyton Place*. Realizing that they were actually actors, the cops let them go.

Most of the film was shot in the Red Hook area of South Brooklyn. There were problems with the union that caused the producers to consider relocating the production, but they ended up staying in New York City. During the shoot, Orbach and Goldstone clashed repeatedly—primarily about things the California director didn't understand about the city and the people who lived there. According to Orbach, the two had "forty or fifty arguments."

When the film was released on December 22, 1971, it was panned across the board. One of the critics' primary complaints was the film's broad stereotypes and most of the cast's awful accents. The only actor spared from this criticism was De Niro. In fact, most reviewers praised his acting, which stood out among the film's cavalcade of embarrassing performances. In his book *The Cinema of Robert De Niro*, author James Cameron-Wilson perfectly hits the hammer on the head when he calls the film "a chaotic mess of obvious jokes," going on to assess that "the film's humor was as unsubtly broad as the film's title was long." Another favorite is *Time* magazine critic Jay Cocks's assessment: "You don't have to be Italian to hate *The Gang That Couldn't Shoot Straight*, although that gives you a distinct edge. The movie's febrile witlessness easily transcends all ethnic boundaries and comes guaranteed to outrage virtually everybody."

After the movie was released, mobster Joe Gallo, the man Orbach's character was sending up, became close friends with the actor. In fact, Orbach's wife, Marta, was in negotiations to co-author the gangster's autobiography. On April 7, 1972, the Orbachs celebrated Gallo's birthday at the Copacabana nightclub (then located at 617 West 57th Street), which he owned. After the couple had gone home, Gallo moved the party to Umberto's Clam House (at the corner of Hester and Mulberry Streets in Greenwich Village). While celebrating (and presumably eating crabs), Gallo was gunned down in cold blood.

While *The Gang That Couldn't Shoot Straight* isn't a particularly good picture, and despite it not having any sort of cult following whatsoever, it's an important film because it documents (in its own dumb way), and was even a part of, New York Mafia history. Additionally, it played a key role in the lives and careers of iconic actors Al Pacino and Robert De Niro, as well as the lore of *The Godfather*.

Klute

Jane Fonda had become a major star and a sex symbol after the success of her hubby Roger Vadim's 1968 sci-fi flick *Barbarella*. By late 1969, Fonda was becoming interested in the Women's Liberation movement. As such, she wanted to separate herself from the sexpot image *Barbarella* had saddled her with. Recognizing that her long blonde hair was a part of her sexy image, Fonda asked her husband's stylist, Paul McGregor, to chop it off. Around this time, director Alan J. Pakula, who, at the time, was best known for producing *To Kill a Mockingbird* (1962), offered her the lead role in a film called *Klute*. When Fonda read the script, written by brothers Andy and Dave Lewis, about a Manhattan call girl, she liked it and wanted to do it. However, she had reservations, questioning whether a true feminist would play a prostitute. Before making her decision, she solicited the opinion of feminist friend, blues singer Barbara Dane. According to Fonda's 2006 memoir *My Life So Far*, Dane said, "Jane, if you think you have room in this script to create a complex, multifaceted character, you should do it. It doesn't matter that she's a call girl, as long as it's real." In a 2019 interview with Illeana Douglas, Fonda said Dane told her, "That's feminism." So, Fonda agreed to make *Klute* as long as she could keep the shorter hair style.

In order to research the role, Fonda asked Pakula to line up a few call girls and madams for her to meet. The actress then spent eight days with the women, talking with them and observing their actions. "I spent time with call girls who were at the bottom rung who were really strung out," Fonda told Douglas. "It was the underbelly of the city. I would go to the after-hours clubs where they would hook up with their johns at three in the morning . . . And I spent time with very wealthy madams who made money, and who tricked themselves also." The actress observed one call girl purchase and then snort cocaine. Although she didn't partake, Fonda believed watching the girl doing coke helped inform her about her character. The actress ultimately became friends with some of the girls. She would later write that several of them died of overdoses, committed suicide, married wealthy businessmen, or "married into royalty." Fonda's portrayal of Bree Daniel was largely modeled after two of the girls. Pakula also hired one of the call girls to work on the film as a technical advisor.

After visiting with the call girls and discovering that most of them had gone through sexual trauma as children, Fonda decided to portray her character as someone who had been victimized by incest. With this in mind, she read numerous books about sexual trauma and the psychology of prostitutes.

When Fonda accompanied the call girls to after-hour clubs, none of the johns paid her any mind and none of the pimps attempted to recruit her into their stables. As such, Fonda concluded that she wasn't the kind of girl they were looking for, and thus wouldn't be able to play the role of a call girl convincingly. Fonda went to Pakula, telling him he'd made a mistake in casting her and needed to release her from her contract. She told him that her friend Faye Dunaway would be better suited to the role. Pakula just laughed and told her she was being ridiculous. Fonda says the director later shared this anecdote with acting classes as a lesson for them not to doubt themselves.

After ten days of rehearsal, *Klute* went before the cameras in Manhattan in December 1970. Fonda had previously lived in NYC but had been away for many years, living in France and then California. When she returned, she was shocked to see the state of disrepair the city was in. "New York has changed a lot since I lived here," she said in the promotional short *Klute in New York*. "This is the first time I've been back in that length of time, and it's very changed." In that same short, her costar Donald Sutherland remarked, "I think anyone who comes here for the first time is initially appalled. It's impossible to breathe. There are way too many people, and it's compressed too tightly. I was awestruck by the degradation, alienation, and the squalor."

Bree Daniel's apartment was constructed on a soundstage at Filmways Studios in East Harlem. (The apartment building's exterior was shot at 411 West 43rd Street.) Wanting to fully discover the character and become one with her, Fonda asked Pakula to have running water and lighting installed inside the apartment so she could live there throughout the shoot. Pakula agreed. At night, as Fonda lay in her bed inside the apartment, she focused on her character, trying to figure out exactly who she was. It was through these moments of contemplation that she concluded that Bree would own a cat and read books. These things were then added into the film. Because Fonda had become infamous for being an outspoken anti-war activist and, as a result, been labeled as anti-American in some quarters, she awoke one morning to discover that an unknown crew member had hung an American flag over the entrance to the apartment. This angered Fonda, who channeled the emotion into her performance as the strong, take-no-shit Bree Daniel.

Fonda and Pakula collaborated with complete synergy, and he allowed her room to discover her character. He also trusted Fonda and Sutherland enough that he allowed them to improvise. For one scene, Fonda convinced Pakula that Bree should smoke a joint. Then, when they shot the scene, she improvised further, singing a hymn. "There is an improvised scene in *Klute* when, as Bree Daniel, alone in her apartment, sitting at a table, smoking a joint, I started singing softly to myself, 'God our Father, Christ our brother, all who live in love are thine,'" Fonda recalled in *My Life So Far*. "I don't know why I did that—it just came out—and the director, Alan Pakula, always one to appreciate contradictions, left it in."

Fonda asked Pakula to get her access to the city morgue. When she visited the morgue, she was shown hundreds of photographs of dead women who had been battered and bruised by angry men. These photos understandably upset her. Later, when Fonda performed in a scene in which the killer (played by Charles Cioffi) plays audio of Bree's friend being murdered, she recalled images of the dead women, using them to get her into an authentic mental state and simultaneously convey horror and sadness. In other scenes, Bree talks with a psychiatrist. In the screenplay, the psychiatrist was written to be a man. However, Fonda came to the conclusion that the damaged Bree would never open up to a man. Because of this, she convinced Pakula to cast the character as a woman. The director also conceded to Fonda's request to move the shooting of the psychiatrist scenes to the end of the shoot, giving her time to better understand Bree. This worked wonderfully. When they shot those scenes, Fonda improvised most of her lines, giving an outstanding and believable performance.

Lastly, the screenplay for the film had a happy ending with detective John Klute and Bree basically heading off into the sunset together. But Fonda didn't believe there could be such an ending for her character, who was scared to be loved and had a habit of destroying everything good in her life, so she and Pakula rewrote the ending, shooting something darker in tone and ultimately ambiguous.

Filming of *Klute* wrapped in March 1971. The film premiered in New York City and Los Angeles on June 23, 1971. Two days later, it was released nationally. Most critics praised the film. Charles Champlin of the *Los Angeles Times* wrote, "*Klute* is visually stunning, full of surprises, bewildering and suspenseful, faultless in its time . . . Like the best mysteries, *Klute* offers more than its diversions and redeems its sordid materials by understanding them and finding them worth pity, not amusement." Gene Siskel of the *Chicago Tribune* wrote, "More interesting than the mystery is the character of Bree . . . the nicest part of her character (due to the script and Miss Fonda's fine performance) is that this prostitute doesn't have a heart of gold. She's a hung-up little broad who, when cornered by violence or tenderness, will scratch and bite." The *New York Times*' Roger Greenspun wasn't as impressed, writing, "Pakula, when he is not indulging in subjective camera, strives to give his film the look of structural geometry, but despite the sharp edges and dramatic spaces and cinema presence out of *Citizen Kane*, it all suggests a tepid, rather tasteless mush. The acting in *Klute* seems semi-improvisatory, and in this Jane Fonda, who is good at confessing, is generally successful. Everybody else merely talks a lot, except for Sutherland, who scarcely talks at all. A normally inventive actor, he is here given precisely the latitude to evoke a romantic figure with all the mysterious intensity of a youthful Calvin Coolidge."

Made on a $2.5 million budget, *Klute* earned $12.7 million at the box office. The film received numerous awards and nominations, the most significant being Jane Fonda's Academy Award win for Best Actress. *Klute* also received a second Oscar nomination for Andy and Dave Lewis' screenplay, which lost out to Jeremy Larner's script for *The Candidate* (1971). Pakula and Fonda (along with cameraman Gordon Willis) would collaborate again on the films *Comes a Horseman* (1978) and *Rollover* (1981).

In 1985, the *Chicago Reader*'s Dave Kehr called *Klute* "as close to a classic as anything New Hollywood produced."

The Panic in Needle Park

In 1968, renowned writer and New Journalism pioneer Joan Didion read a novel by *Life* magazine associate editor James Mills titled *Panic in Needle Park*. Mills' bleak novel focused on a couple of junkies in New York's Sherman Square (at the intersection of Broadway and Amsterdam Avenue), known as "Needle Park" because of the abundance of junkies, pushers, and prostitutes who hung out there. Didion liked the book and believed it would make a fine film. She then spoke to her husband, John Gregory Dunne, also an acclaimed journalist, and his older brother Dominick Dunne, who worked in television. The Dunne brothers read Mills' book and agreed with Didion's assessment.

The brothers sat down to dinner with Mills, hoping to option the film rights to his book. Mills, however, only wanted to talk about politics. When the Dunnes were finally able to get the subject around to Mills' novel, the author agreed to sell the rights. The Dunnes optioned the rights for $1,000 a year against $17,500 and 5 percent of the net profits. It was then decided that Didion would write a treatment. Recognizing that the material was oppressively dark and would likely be a tough sell, Didion conceived the idea to pitch the project as "Romeo and Juliet on junk." Dominick Dunne, working as producer, then secured a deal for the film at Avco-Embassy, the small studio that had found success with *The Graduate* (1967). John Dunne and Joan Didion moved into the seedy Almanac Hotel next to Needle

Park to write the script, hoping to find inspiration and soak up the atmosphere. However, the socialite couple was out of their element; Dunne and Didion left the drug-infested neighborhood each day to have lunch at the upscale La Cote Basque on West 55th Street. Didion quickly grew tired of staying in the rundown hotel and went home. Dunne, however, stayed behind and finished the script, adding dialogue to Didion's treatment.

Dunne had the idea to cast The Doors frontman Jim Morrison to play Bobby, the male lead. The Doors were at their peak at the time, and the idea sounded good to everyone involved with the film. Didion got a magazine assignment to cover The Doors, whom she'd dubbed "the Norman Mailers of the Top Forty," and she planned to use the opportunity to assess whether or not Morrison would be a good fit for the film. When Didion visited a Doors recording session for the band's album *Waiting for the Sun*, her Morrison experience was not a positive one. Morrison was late for the session, and when he finally showed up, he was stoned and had two young girls in tow. When he spoke, he was nearly incomprehensible, and he tossed lit matches at Didion. Didion and the Dunnes crossed the rock star off their casting list.

Avco-Embassy soon dropped the film, and Dominick Dunne would have to negotiate with studios again. This time he secured a deal for *The Panic at Needle Park* at 20th Century Fox.

Dominick Dunne hired a former *Vogue* fashion photographer named Jerry Schatzberg to direct the film. He'd been impressed with Schatzberg's photography work, and Schatzberg had just directed a film called *Puzzle of a Downfall Child* (1970), starring his girlfriend, Faye Dunaway.

Schatzberg suggested an actor for the male lead—a young man he'd seen in a play titled *The Indian Wants the Bronx*. The actor's name was Al Pacino, and he hadn't done any film work. When Schatzberg mentioned him to Dominick Dunne, it turned out that Dunne had seen him in a play titled *Does a Tiger Wear a Necktie?* and thought he was great. When they reached out to Pacino, they learned that he'd been offered nine film roles but had turned them all down. These films included Otto Preminger's *Tell Me That You Love Me, Junie Moon* (1970) and Mike Nichols' *Catch-22* (1970). Pacino had actually wanted to make

Catch-22, but Paramount would only allow his casting if he signed a multipicture deal, and the young actor didn't want to be tied down. Pacino had also turned down a Broadway run of *Zorba the Greek*. Despite all of this, he agreed to appear in *Panic in Needle Park*. Twentieth Century Fox chieftains Richard Zanuck and David Brown didn't want to cast Pacino, instead wanting someone taller, less Italian, and already a star. Dominick Dunne fought them and somehow won, and Pacino was signed to make the film.

Schatzberg and Dunne found another stage performer they liked for Helen, the female lead. The actress, Kitty Winn, had been named "discovery of the season" after performing in an American Conservative Theater production of *Saint Joan* in San Francisco. Again, Zanuck and Brown disapproved of Winn, instead wanting Mia Farrow. Humorously, they thought Winn was too young at twenty-five, despite the fact that Farrow was only a year older. In the end, Schatzberg and Dunne got their way, and Winn got the part.

Pacino and Winn researched their roles by hanging out in Needle Park so they could fully understand the atmosphere and the junkies' desperation. Things got weird one day when a group of angry junkies accused them of being narcotics officers. Pacino and Winn also visited drug treatment facilities and spoke with addicts about their lives and experiences. Pacino also had addicts teach him the mechanics of shooting up heroin. One day while sitting in on a methadone session, Pacino was outed as an actor and ordered to leave.

The ten-week shoot began in mid-October 1970 with a budget just north of a million dollars. Schatzberg would joke throughout the shoot that the budget was so small that they couldn't afford to actually purchase heroin. On the first day of the shoot, Pacino was so nervous that his breakfast consisted of a single glass of wine. Rookie film actor Pacino fought Schatzberg's leadership for the first two weeks of shooting but ultimately conceded to his instructions.

Schatzberg allowed the actors to improvise as long as they stayed close to the script. He also instructed the actors to mimic some of the mannerisms of the real addicts they'd met. When

Winn suggested that one scene might work better without a lengthy monologue, Dominick Dunne, perhaps protecting his brother's dialogue, told Winn and Schatzberg to perform the scene as it was written. However, Schatzberg instructed Winn to do the scene without the monologue, and that's the version that ended up in the finished film.

As *The Panic in Needle Park* was still filming, the studio executives viewed the dailies and became concerned. "The studio head—no names—watched dailies and sent a request for a phone call," cinematographer Adam Holender recalled in an interview with author Jason Bailey. "They said, 'I didn't see New York! I didn't see the Empire State Building!' We sat down with the producer for ten minutes at lunch and said we were after something different. 'We're not looking for landmarks, but the texture of life on the streets of New York.'"

Another concern was Pacino's reluctance to do nude scenes. Before filming a scene in a prison shower alongside other actors, Pacino hesitated to strip, nervously pointing to a script girl and asking Schatzberg, "Is she going to be there while we take our pants off?" But this wasn't just about being nervous and shy; Pacino also questioned the purpose of a sex scene with Winn, reminding Schatzberg that no one ever kissed in a Shakespeare play, and that included *Romeo and Juliet*. In the end, Pacino saw that the scene was important to the story and did it.

One day, between takes, Pacino drew the attention of a real drug dealer, and the two engaged in a long, angry stare-down. On another day of shooting, Winn injected herself with a needle for a scene. Of course, she injected herself with sugar water rather than heroin, but she insisted on the injection to make the scene appear authentic.

"The role was hard because it had to do with physical exhaustion, which I did not feel until I had completed the film," Winn told *Teen* writer Fiona MacDougall. "It was such an emotional role. There was one scene where Bob and Helen are fighting and Helen becomes hysterical. We filmed that for about five hours! By the end of it I felt as if the top of my head was going to come off. It was a very unnatural kind of experience which gave me nothing back, really. When I got home that night I had to go to sleep right away because I felt so drained."

Shooting wrapped on December 22. According to Pacino, the rage he'd felt as the character made him feel like he needed to be locked in a sanitarium by the time he finished the shoot.

The Panic in Needle Park had its first screening at the Cannes Film Festival on May 21, 1971. The film was nominated for the coveted Palme d'Or but ultimately lost to Joseph Losey's *The Go-Between* (1971). However, Kitty Winn won the award for Best Actress.

Critical reception for the film was divided, but it did receive a good amount of praise. The *San Francisco Bay Guardian*'s Margo Skinner wrote, "Compassion is the hallmark of *Panic in Needle Park*. . . . Its dingy, tawdry Manhattan West Side settings and sad, anesthetized people are completely believable." Arthur Knight of *Saturday Review* wrote, "Never before have two characters deteriorated so gradually, yet so convincingly, before our eyes, with every step of their descent shooting out fresh stabs of pain. It is a masterful accomplishment, for both the director and the performers, and makes *The Panic in Needle Park* one of the most affecting pictures in years." *Esquire*'s Jacob Brickman raved, "The entire cast, especially Al Pacino and Kitty Winn in the leads, create intensely real people. Their brand of realness feels close to documentary." On the flip side, *The New Republic*'s Stanley Kauffmann called the film "rotten." Arthur B. Clark of *Films in Review* complained, "It fails to depict all of it; proffers no explanation as to *why* the girl or youth become addicted; avoids most of the racial aspects of the NYC 'drug scene'; shows little of the addicts' physical and mental deterioration; and, in a subtle way, accepts the couple's 'stooling' on each other and the girl's whoring to get money for drugs."

Shaft

Shaft, like many iconic works of art, was conceived out of sheer desperation and financial need. (See also: *The Godfather* [1972].)

In this case, the artist was a writer named Ernest Tidyman. The Ohio native had worked as a journalist for numerous publications, including the *Cleveland News*, the *New York Times*, and the *New York Post*, and had penned two books that were considered duds. Tidyman was in financial straits with an ex-wife suing him for alimony. So, when his literary agent suggested he take a meeting with a mystery editor from Macmillan, Tidyman agreed. The editor was interested in commissioning Tidyman, a white writer, to create fiction about a black hero. Seeing dollar signs, Tidyman jumped at the opportunity. He then pitched the idea of a black detective in the mold of Philip Marlowe or Sam Spade. The editor liked Tidyman's idea but felt he should be tougher, perhaps throwing a criminal out of a window in the first chapter. Tidyman liked the idea and ran with it, allowing that no-bullshit characterization to define his protagonist. And thus, John Shaft was born.

When Tidyman passed pre-publication galleys of his book around in Hollywood, the project drew interest from Columbia by way of producer Leon Mirell, who envisioned Yaphet Kotto in the role. Shortly after that, the *Hollywood Reporter* announced that Tom Gries would be directing an adaptation with Kotto playing Shaft. That never panned out, and MGM stepped in and purchased the rights to the novel in April 1970. That same month, the novel appeared in hardback and became an instant hit, selling almost half-a-million copies. MGM then restructured Tidyman's contract, making it a three *Shaft* picture deal. The writer also inked a deal with Bantam to write two more John Shaft novels and a novelization of the impending film. Early on, rumors circulated that Harry Belafonte, and then Sidney Poitier, would play Shaft. Producer Stirling Silliphant approached director Ossie Davis, fresh from the successful *Cotton Comes to Harlem* (1970), about making the film. Davis wasn't interested. New MGM chief James Aubrey then approached noted *Life* magazine photographer Gordon Parks about directing. At the time, Renaissance Man Parks' only directorial credit was the 1969 adaptation of his novel, *The Learning Tree*, so he was far from a sure bet. Even Parks was unsure of his filmmaking skills. Nevertheless, he signed on.

Screenwriter D. F. Black was brought in to rewrite the script. Black brought more elements of black culture to the story. He also (at the behest of Parks) changed the name of Shaft's nemesis, Knocks Persons, to "Bumpy Jonas," as a reference to real-life gangster Bumpy Johnson. MGM would ultimately attempt to credit Black as having written the screenplay. This, as one might expect, rankled Tidyman since most of the shooting script came from his drafts. Tidyman challenged the matter through Writers Guild mediation and wound up with credits for both story and screenplay.

When it came to casting the lead, the filmmakers knew that literally everything was on the line. They had to have the *perfect* John Shaft for this to be the hit they believed it could be. With Kotto now out of the picture, they auditioned several actors, including Raymond St. Jacques, Billy Dee Williams, and Bernie Casey. In the end, however, the role fell to a talented twenty-nine-year-old stage actor named Richard Roundtree. Roundtree had only one screen credit, for *What Do You Say to a Naked Lady?* (1970). But whatever he lacked in credentials, he more than made up for with talent and presence. Although Parks recognized Roundtree as the perfect John Shaft the moment he laid eyes on him, the actor was nonetheless coached heavily and given a daily workout regime to fully make him the John Shaft the producers envisioned.

When we think of *Shaft*, we associate the character with NYC. The location is almost as important a character as Shaft himself. However, the pairing almost didn't happen. Just a couple of days before the cameras were to begin rolling, MGM tried to relocate the production to California. Parks and the film's producers knew the importance of maintaining the NYC location and argued their case. Thankfully, the studio ultimately stepped aside and allowed the production to move forward in New York City.

"All you have to do is look at the [later] *Shaft* television movies that were set in Los Angeles to get a sense of how much of a potential mistake it would have been to take the character out of New York," *Shaft* comic book writer David F. Walker explains. "There is a profound difference between New York and LA, both culturally and aesthetically, with New York feeling more like a character. And it's not just *Shaft* where the city is a supporting character—we see it in films like *The French Connection* [1971], *Taxi Driver* [1976], and *Midnight Cowboy* [1969]. At best, if *Shaft* had been shot and set in LA it would feel like director Ivan Dixon's *Trouble Man* [1972], but with that film there's no true sense of character in the location."

Although there are scenes shot all over in the city, most of the film takes place in Manhattan. At the start of the film, as the credits roll, Shaft is shown striding through traffic on Seventh Avenue. Stills of that scene have since become *the* iconic *Shaft* images we see most often. John Shaft's office (165 West 46th Street) and his apartment (on the corner of 55 Jane Street and Hudson Street) are both located in Manhattan. The primary location outside Manhattan that appears in the film is City Hospital, a former prison hospital that was located on Welfare Island. (It has since been demolished.)

Filming began on March 1, 1971, and would wrap on March 18. Once shooting wrapped, editor Hugh Robinson began cutting the film. During the editing period, funk singer Isaac Hayes, who had also auditioned for the role of Shaft, went to work recording the film's now iconic score. The album and the film's theme song in particular ("Theme from Shaft") would become massive hits that play a significant role in the continued success of the film. "Theme from Shaft" rose to number two on the Billboard Soul Singles chart and number one on the Billboard Hot 100 chart.

The film debuted on June 25, 1971, and, despite mixed reviews, became a huge hit. *Time* magazine called the $13 million the film earned on a budget of $500,000 "astonishing." While the successes of *Cotton Comes to Harlem* and *Sweet Sweetback's Baadasssss Song* (1971) played a significant role in setting the blaxploitation film craze into motion, it was primarily the cultural phenomenon of *Shaft* that convinced studios that films made for primarily black audiences could be box-office earners. In addition to these successes, *Shaft* would also receive two Academy Award nominations, both for Hayes (one for Best Dramatic Score and another for Best Original Song). Hayes ended up losing in the score category but took home the Song Oscar for "Theme from Shaft." Hayes' win is significant because it marked the first time a black performer won an Oscar in a non-acting category.

The character John Shaft has since become a cultural icon. The film was followed by two sequels, *Shaft's Big Score!* (1972) and *Shaft in Africa* (1973). It also spawned a television series that ran for a single season between 1973 and 1974. Tidyman penned six more novels (*Shaft Among the Jews*, *Shaft's Big Score!*, *Shaft Has a Ball*, *Goodbye, Mr. Shaft*, *Shaft's Carnival of Killers*, and *The Last Shaft*). Dynamite Entertainment produced a six-issue *Shaft* comic book series in 2014. The film has also spawned two reboot/sequel films, both titled *Shaft* (2000, 2019).

On the continued popularity of *Shaft*, David Walker believes the film's location plays a vital role. "*Shaft* endures in large part due to the aesthetics of the film that is rooted in it being shot on location in New York," he says. "It wasn't the first film to be shot on location, but so many of the films shot during that time in New York stood in stark contrast to the slick (and sometimes sterile) films shot in LA. *Shaft* is a solid film, and part of what makes it so effective is the city itself, which in turn is part of why it endures."

1972

Grass Eaters and Meat Eaters, Charlie Chop-off, and **The Godfather**

By 1972, New York City had fully become the dark, scary place we envision when we talk about NYC in the 1970s. Pimps and prostitutes had overrun Times Square; an abundance of muggers and rapists made Central Park a dangerous no-man's-land; the graffiti 1970s New York would become known for had begun to flourish, covering subway trains and buildings in rundown urban areas; crime on subways was dramatically increasing; in addition to all of this, homeless people were starting to appear on the streets *en masse*.

In 1972, police commissioner Patrick V. Murphy touted the fact that there was an 18 percent decline in "serious crimes." While that statement sounds great on the surface, it glosses over the fact that murder, rape, and felony assault had all increased. Murder was up 14.7 percent with 1,691 murders reported, with an average of five murders per day. Rape was up 35.4 percent with a startling 3,271 rapes reported. The 18 percent decrease in serious crimes Murphy touted was the result of decreases in robbery (including muggings and holdups), burglary, larceny, and auto theft. That 18 percent decrease brought the total number of serious crimes down to its lowest level in six years. While some members of the media questioned the accuracy of these statistics, Murphy insisted they were accurate.

But what was leading to the rise in murders? Police studies at the time indicated that guns were a major contributor. According to these studies, guns had been involved in only 25.1

percent of the city's homicides a decade before. But by 1972, they were involved in 51.4 percent of the homicides.

The year's biggest bombshell was the release of the Knapp Commission's final report. Compiled after a thirty-one-month investigation, the report asserted that "well over half" of the New York Police Department was corrupt. The report explained that there were two kinds of police officers accepting pay-offs—the "grass eaters" and the "meat eaters." According to the committee's definition, the grass eaters, which made up the majority of the cops in question, routinely accepted ten- and twenty-dollar bills to look the other way. These cops, the report said, did not actively pursue these payments. The meat eaters, which the commission said made up only a small portion of the force, aggressively sought out situations they could exploit for financial gain. The commission's report also concluded that "organized crime is the single biggest source of police corruption, through its control of the city's gambling, narcotics, loan-sharking, and illegal sex-related enterprises like homosexual after-hours bars and pornography, all of which the department considers mob-run." The report said the second largest source of graft money came from legitimate businesses trying to circumvent the system and avoid bureaucratic red tape.

While the Knapp Commission's report painted the NYPD in a bad light, Robert McKiernan, president of the police union, unequivocally dismissed the report as being "a fairy-tale, concocted in a whorehouse and told by thieves and fools." When two hundred pounds of heroin was stolen from police evidence lockers later in the year, one had to wonder if the thieves McKiernan was referring to were the cops themselves. Maybe not, but that heroin certainly didn't steal itself. It was, of course, never found.

Just two days into the new year, Samuel Nalo and Robert Comfort orchestrated and helped pull off a $3 million robbery (the equivalent of $27 million today) at the Pierre Hotel (Fifth Avenue and 61st Street). The robbery was allegedly bankrolled by the Lucchesi crime family. Nalo and Comfort were professional robbers who'd already pulled off major heists at the Drake Hotel, the Carlyle Hotel, the Sherry Netherland Hotel, the St. Regis, and the Regency. On this particular night, Nalo,

1972: Grass Eaters and Meat Eaters, Charlie Chop-off / 51

Comfort, and six other men, dressed in disguises, took control of the hotel. The robbers handcuffed the staff for two-and-a-half hours while they looted the hotel's vault. No one was killed or injured in the course of the robbery, which the *Guinness Book of World Records* identifies as being the most successful hotel robbery in history. Nalo and Comfort were later convicted and each sentenced to four years in prison.

The Black Liberation Army (BLA), a militant offshoot of the Black Panthers, were suspected to have been involved with more than seventy incidents of violence between 1970 and 1976. On January 27, 1972, three members of the BLA ambushed two NYPD officers on foot patrol near Avenue B and East 11th Street. It was likely that the victims, rookie officers Gregory Foster and Rocco Laurie, never saw their attackers, who came up from behind and shot them repeatedly in the back. After the officers were down and dying on the ground, the attackers stood over them, shooting out Foster's eyes and shooting Laurie in the testicles. After that, they took the officers' pistols, and one of the gunmen danced a jig over their bodies. The BLA later took responsibility for the murders, saying they were retaliation for prisoners killed during the September 4, 1971, riot at the Attica Correctional Facility. Although the murders were never officially solved, the police had three suspects, two of whom died in unrelated police shoot-outs in New York City and St. Louis.

On April 7, Joseph Gallo, the former Colombo crime family captain who had allegedly tried to assassinate Colombo family boss Joe Colombo ten months before, was gunned down while celebrating his forty-third birthday at Umberto's Clam House in Little Italy. Joseph Luparelli, a member of the Colombo family, told police that he and four other mobsters had shot Gallo, but the police dismissed the claim. Frank Sheeran, a mobbed-up labor union official, later claimed to have killed Gallo on orders from Pennsylvania mobster Russell Buffalino.

Throughout the year, a serial killer who murdered black and Puerto Rican boys roamed the streets of Manhattan. The media nicknamed the killer "Charlie Chop-off." The killer murdered four children—three black and one Puerto Rican. One of the children was eight years old, and the other three were nine. The killer stabbed three of the children repeatedly (he stabbed two of them exactly thirty-eight times) and slashed another with a straight razor. The killer also sliced and/or cut off three of his victims' penises. After failing in an attempt to kidnap a Puerto Rican boy the following year, a man named Erno Soto confessed to being the killer. However, due to his mental instability and a claim by Manhattan State Hospital officials that Soto was in their custody during one of the murders, Soto was never charged.

There were many films shot in NYC that were released in 1972. Here we will discuss seven of them: *Across 110th Street, Come Back Charleston Blue, The Godfather, The Hot Rock, The Last House on the Left, Shaft's Big Score!* and *Super Fly*. While *The Last House on the Left* is generally labeled a horror film, it is also a crime film. *The Last House on the Left* raised the bar for cinematic violence and the way it is presented. The film's grit, darkness, and unflinching attitude personifies the kind of casual violence we now associate with 1970s' NYC.

There are three blaxploitation films included (as well as a fourth film, *Across 110th Street*, that's occasionally labeled as blaxploitation), making apparent the number of black films Hollywood was now making. When you consider the fact that the majority of blaxploitation films were filmed in Los Angeles, the number of them made in NYC gives you a good idea of the cycle's popularity.

But, despite the existence of, and intended-competition by, all of these films, the only crime movie that really mattered in 1972 was Francis Ford Coppola's *The Godfather*. *The Godfather* not only became the biggest moneymaker of 1972, but it goes well beyond the simple "crime movie" classification. It may well be *the* greatest American film ever made. *The Godfather* went on to influence all facets of popular culture from then to now, and it is also said to have influenced organized crime itself.

Across 110th Street

Across 110th Street, one of the grittiest crime pictures of the 1970s, started as a novel (simply titled *Across 110th*) written by a television news cameraman named Wally Ferris. Ferris had never been a professional writer, but he wrote the novel at his kitchen table in his spare time. When the novel was finished, Ferris had no idea what to do with it. Since he knew Maurice Woodruff, a writer who published books about astrology, Ferris asked him for help getting a publisher. Eventually, *Across 110th* was published by Harper and Row. *Publishers Weekly* called it "a tough, convincingly realistic crime novel," going on to say that it "packs a whale of a punch." The novel was a hit, and Ferris quickly sold the film rights in a deal that also paid him to write a draft of the screenplay. He was flown to Los Angeles to write his draft, but producers disliked it and jettisoned it, then hiring scripter Luther Davis (*Lady in a Cage* [1964]) to adapt the novel.

At some point, actor Anthony Quinn got a hold of the screenplay. Believing he was one of the few Hollywood players with enough clout to get a rough-and-tumble film with a predominantly black cast made, he decided to executive produce the picture. Quinn wanted to cast the film with Hollywood's most well-known black actors. These included Sidney Poitier, Sammy Davis Jr., Harry Belafonte, and Bill Cosby. For the role of Frank Mattelli—the film's biggest role for a white actor—he approached John Wayne, Burt Lancaster, and Kirk Douglas, all of whom passed. While it's not clear why Quinn was unable to cast the black actors on his wish list, one would assume it had to do with budgetary concerns. As for the role of Mattelli, Quinn wound up taking the role himself.

Barry Shear was hired to direct. Shear was one of the most experienced television directors at the time, having worked on such series as *The Donna Reed Show, The Man from U.N.C.L.E.*, and *Hawaii Five-O. Across 110th Street* was the third of four features Shear would direct in his career. Jack Preistley would handle camerawork on the film. Savvy readers might recognize that Priestley also worked on the NYC crime classics *Born to Win* (1971), *Contract on Cherry Street* (1977), and *The First Deadly Sin* (1980).

Yaphet Kotto, an actor who had done lots of television work but had done only a few films, was cast as Lt. Pope. This was the role Quinn had envisioned Poitier playing. Barry Shear had worked with actor Anthony Franciosa on a number of projects prior to this, including the series *Fame Is the Name of the Game*, from which Franciosa was fired for (alleged) bad behavior. Despite this, Shear (and possibly Quinn, who'd worked with the actor on 1957's *Wild Is the Wind*) brought Franciosa onboard to play hit man Nick D' Salvio. The cast, which also features Paul Benjamin, Richard Ward, Antonio Fargas, Gloria Hendry, and an early cameo by Burt Young, was solid from top to bottom.

Across 110th Street was shot on location in Harlem at a time when the neighborhood was the prime spot for NYC crime films, due in large part to its seedy, rundown appearance. Harlem was a haven to all types of criminal activity at the time in which these films were made, giving them an air of authenticity. On his commentary for the film, cinema historian and author Matthew Asprey Gear explains, "*Across 110th Street* is a kind of snapshot of New York City in the early 1970s. A very difficult time for the city. We see a lot of focus on its decaying spaces and crumbling infrastructure. We see a city plagued by racism, drugs, violence, corruption, [and] brutality. In that sense, it has something in common with a number of other films, several released in 1971: *Klute*, *Panic in Needle Park*, and *The French Connection*."

According to Quinn, he had breakfast with Luciano family mob boss Frank Costello each morning at Rumplemayer's cafe and ice cream parlor (50 Central Park South, now closed). Quinn later explained that Costello played a key role in obtaining permission to shoot *Across 110th Street* in Harlem. Later, when the film went a million dollars over budget, Costello offered to loan the sum to Quinn, who wisely declined the offer.

This film was the first to utilize the (then) new Airflex 35 BL camera, which was light and portable, allowing the crew to shoot in tight spaces. The film's heavy use of the handheld camera gave it a documentary feel, adding to the "New York realism" Quinn and Shear wanted. Muted colors used throughout the film, as well as filling the picture with haggard-looking characters, also played a role in achieving the gritty, authentic aesthetic. Approximately sixty locations were used to make *Across 110th Street*, and many interior scenes were filmed inside condemned buildings.

When the filmmakers sought to hire Bobby Womack (and his band Peace) to write and record new music for the film, the studio was reluctant. In the end, however, the producers won out and the singer was hired. Womack stayed awake for the better part of two weeks, writing and recording the songs while on tour. He ended up contributing five new songs, including the film's title song. Interestingly, Womack would later record a new and catchier version of the song, releasing it as a single. Filmmaker Quentin Tarantino would use the song twenty-five years later in *Jackie Brown* (1997).

The film was released on December 12, 1972. The reviews were lackluster, which is a shame because *Across 110th Street* is a great film. Is it blaxploitation? Is it neo-noir? Who cares? Whatever you want to call it, *Across 110th Street* is a fantastic picture and one of the most criminally underrated crime films (see what I did there?) of the era.

Come Back Charleston Blue

After the success of 1970's *Cotton Comes to Harlem*, Warner Bros. decided to make a sequel. After all, that's what Hollywood does—if something makes money, then well, hell, it *obviously* needs a sequel, right? Or two, or three, or ten. While it's an objective truth that sequels almost always pale in comparison to their predecessors, it almost seems like producer Samuel Goldwyn Jr. was doing everything he could to make sure this one would be mediocre at best.

Ossie Davis originally planned to return, but Goldwyn Jr.'s decision to create a new story instead of adapting another Chester Himes novel caused Davis to walk away from the picture. Screenwriters Ernest Kinoy and Peggy Elliott were then hired to come up with a plot for the film, which would be titled *Come Back Charleston Blue*. Mark Warren, a director who'd never directed a feature and had cut his teeth helming episodes of *Rowan and Martin's Laugh-In*, was hired to replace Davis.

It was apparent that the project was doomed from the start. Making matters worse, Godfrey Cambridge, an actor who had struggled with his weight throughout his life, reported to the shoot *considerably* heavier than he'd been in *Cotton Comes to Harlem*. In fact, he almost looks like a completely different person. (Sadly, Cambridge's reported food addiction would ultimately lead to his suffering a heart attack and dying a few years later on the set of *Victory at Entebbe* [1976] at the age of forty-three.) Additionally, Raymond St. Jacques looked significantly older, despite there being just a two-year gap between the films.

Like the first film, *Come Back Charleston Blue* showcases a number of Harlem locations. There are copious shots of neighborhood churches and liquor stores. The corner of 125th Street and Lenox Avenue figures prominently in the story, and the Apollo Theater, just down the street, once again makes a cameo. Perhaps the most interesting real-life location that appears in the film is the legendary National Memorial African Book Store on West 125th Street. The bookstore, opened and operated by Lewis H. Michaux, was a well-known landmark. (Sadly, the store closed its doors two years after the film was released.) *Chicago Sun-Times* critic Roger Ebert observed, "The movie has been photographed lovingly on location in Harlem, and shows this as a place of beauty and ugliness, pride and corruption, community building and drug pushing, all side by side." Ebert's description (and the film's presentation of the neighborhood) is in keeping with Davis and Himes' love for, and unblinking depiction of, the good, bad, and ugly in the community.

One NYC location worth mentioning is the Cypress Hill Cemetery on Jamaica Avenue in Brooklyn, where the funeral shoot-out sequence occurs. Why, you might ask, is this location significant? Backstory: a few years before this production, a photograph of a cemetery was featured in a prominent publication. Because the magazine didn't have clearance from the deceased's relatives, they were successfully sued. After that, producers and film studios were gun-shy about putting real cemeteries in their films because they didn't want to get sued. So, when second assistant director Ralph S. Singleton was instructed to find a cemetery where the filmmakers could shoot the sequence, he had a difficult task ahead of him. "I went into the project and I looked and looked and looked," Singleton says. "I spent a lot of time in the four boroughs, aside from Staten Island because there was little to nothing there at the time. I finally found a place called Cypress Hill Cemetery, which was the largest cemetery in the boroughs. I scouted the cemetery, and I found this meadow in the cemetery. I said to the director of the cemetery, 'Listen, if we put fake tombstones in here, with all the [real] tombstones around in the cemetery, you would believe that it's all part of the same place.' And he says, 'Damn right, you would. You could do anything you want here.'" After securing the location, the crew constructed a mausoleum made of plywood and surrounded it with painted Styrofoam tombstones. "It worked," Singleton recalls. "We shot the whole shoot-out sequence and the chase sequence there." After filmmakers discovered that the Cypress Hill Cemetery had this open space and was open to filming, it became a popular film location in the 1970s. (It's also the cemetery where Charles Bronson's character buries his wife in 1974's *Death Wish*.)

Come Back Charleston Blue's ridiculous plot finds mobsters and drug dealers being killed off by an unknown figure, whom everyone believes to be the ghost of a long-dead Harlem gangster named Charleston Blue. And the ridiculousness doesn't stop there. The film's shenanigans include a deadly bomb-throwing henchman who dresses like a nun, a junkie named Earl J who will do anything he can to be arrested and go to jail, a group of beret-wearing revolutionaries led by a drug dealer, a Mafia chief who holds court inside a flower shop, a crazy fortune teller who believes her dead boyfriend Charleston Blue will return for her any day now, a dwarf gangster, and a nonsensical scene in which mobsters in sloppy blackface are gunned down in a cemetery by the attendants of a faux funeral (including the minister and the corpse, who pops up out of the coffin). There's also an asinine storyline in which Gravedigger Jones and Coffin Ed fake their deaths and somehow convince everyone to play along with the charade.

The scene featuring the cops' fake demise created a significant problem for the filmmakers. "They decide to fake their own deaths," Ralph S. Singleton explains. "So they go into this building, and the building blows up. So what's my assignment? Find a building in New York that I can blow up. So I go to the city, and they say, 'No. No. No. We're not going to give you a permit to do that.' So I do a little more research, and I found out there is a way that I can do it. I talk to the city people again. And this is not Mayor John Lindsay, he's just the mayor. I'm not blaming him. But I am going to blame the real estate division in 1972 for this. 'If you meet me on a street corner with a brown paper bag filled with money, you'll get your permit.' So I went back to see [production manager] Stanley Neufeld and Sam Goldwyn. I said, 'This is the deal, guys. If you want it, you've got to pay for it. I want you to know that's going to happen. *I'm* not going to do it. It's not *me*. It's *us*. We're all doing this together, right?' They said, 'Okay, we'll do it.' So I met a guy on a street corner, gave him the money, and we got the permit."

If *Come Back Charleston Blue* had been a stand-alone film, it would have been remembered (or forgotten) as simply being a run-of-the-mill, mediocre crime picture. But it was the sequel to a well-made landmark film. As such, it fails miserably and comes nowhere close to the quality of *Cotton Comes to Harlem*.

The Godfather

If not for Mario Puzo and Francis Ford Coppola both having gambling debts and the financial desperation that comes with that, *The Godfather*, arguably the greatest American film of all time, would never have been made.

Hell's Kitchen novelist Mario Puzo wanted to write serious literature. The only problem was, his first few novels hadn't sold particularly well. Puzo was down on his luck and deep in debt due to his gambling addiction. Remembering that an editor had once suggested he focus more on the mob in his novels, the writer decided to "sell out" and go for the easy money. He did his due diligence, studying turncoat Mafioso Joseph Valachi's personal writings, as well as transcripts of the 1950 Kefauver hearings on organized crime. The author then produced a ten-page outline for what he called his "Mafia novel." Puzo managed to finagle a meeting at G.P. Putnam and Sons, where he landed a contract and a $5,000 advance. Puzo then managed to sell his still unwritten novel (again based on the outline) to Paramount Pictures for $12,500.

When the 448-page novel was published in 1969, it became a smash hit and stayed on the *New York Times* bestseller list for sixty-seven weeks. Fawcett purchased the paperback rights for an unprecedented $410,000. *The Godfather* sold more than nine million copies in two years. Interestingly, Puzo's novel was also popular in mob circles. It was also influential; the real-life gangsters began to emulate the characters Puzo had created.

Burt Lancaster's production company, Hecht-Hill-Lancaster, offered $1 million to make the film with Lancaster playing the Godfather. But this wasn't to be. Seeing the potential the film adaptation had, Paramount head of production Robert Evans began production. There are varying reports as to how much Evans initially budgeted for *The Godfather*, but it was somewhere between $2.5 million and $6 million. Soon Al Ruddy, a producer with little more than the TV series *Hogan's Heroes* to his name, persuaded Evans to hire him as producer. Evans and Ruddy's first order of business was to hire Puzo to adapt the novel. For this, the author would be paid $500 a week and given an office on the Paramount lot.

Then came the task of finding the right director. Richard Brooks, Costa-Gavras, Arthur Penn, Peter Yates, and Otto Preminger were approached, and all passed. Sam Peckinpah and Sidney J. Furie both wanted to make the film, but Evans and Ruddy didn't think their directing styles suited the material. They then decided that the director should be Italian-American. The search led Ruddy to a young director named Francis Ford Coppola. Neither Evans nor Coppola himself liked the idea of Coppola directing *The Godfather*. Coppola, like Puzo, saw himself as an artist and believed making the film would be selling out. But also like Puzo, Coppola had a considerable amount of debt. In the end, Ruddy would convince Evans that Coppola was the right choice, and Coppola would sign on for monetary reasons. He received $175,000 to come on board to co-write and direct.

The casting process would be a wild one. Evans and Paramount liked Laurence Oliver for Vito Corleone (aka The

Godfather). After angrily protesting similarities between himself and the Johnny Fontane character (as written in the book), Frank Sinatra expressed interest in playing Vito. Perhaps the silliest Vito candidate was Danny Thomas, who actually considered buying Paramount just so he could have the role. Coppola, Puzo, and Ruddy couldn't envision any of those actors in the role. The actor they all wanted was Marlon Brando. But Brando had made several flops and had earned a reputation as being a pain in the ass, so Evans and Paramount adamantly insisted that Brando not be cast. Eventually, through a long and complicated chain of events, Coppola would win out and be allowed to cast the forty-seven-year-old actor.

Just like Vito, there were many names bandied about for the role of Michael Corleone. Evans wanted either Ryan O'Neal or Robert Redford. Then forty-six-year-old Rod Steiger requested to play the twenty-five-year-old character. Martin Sheen, Dean Stockwell, David Carradine, and James Caan all did screen tests. Among the many actors Coppola considered were Dustin Hoffman, Warren Beatty, and Alain Delon. But when Coppola tested Al Pacino, he knew immediately that this was the guy. The only problem was that Evans and the studio thought Pacino was too short and refused to consider him. Again, it would take *a lot* of convincing before Coppola was finally allowed to cast Pacino. (By this time, the actor had taken a role in another film, *The Gang That Couldn't Shoot Straight* [1972], requiring behind-the-scenes maneuvering by Robert Evans to free him from his contract. Interestingly, Robert De Niro jumped ship from *The Godfather* to go to *The Gang That Couldn't Shoot Straight*.)

Before the role of Michael's wife, Kay, went to Diane Keaton, a slew of other actresses were considered. These included Karen Black, Blythe Danner, Tuesday Weld, Michelle Phillips, Jennifer Salt, Jill Clayburgh, Jennifer O'Neill, and Genevieve Bujold. After seeing John Cazale perform in an off-Broadway play, casting director Fred Roos asked Coppola to meet with him. Coppola did, and Cazale was cast as black sheep son Fredo. James Caan, who'd read for the part of Michael, was eventually cast as Michael's brother Sonny. Coppola had envisioned

Robert Duvall as family consigliere Tom Hagen from the start, so Duvall got the part with ease.

The Godfather faced backlash from the Italian-American community because they felt it depicted Italians in a negative light before the cameras had even begun rolling. A political advocacy group calling themselves the Italian-American Civil Rights League began protesting and stirring up problems for the production. Humorously, the advocacy group itself was established and fronted by Joe Colombo, a well-known mob boss. The actual purpose of the group appears to have been a means to collect donations from the Italian community and to bully the filmmakers into casting gangsters and gang-affiliates in the movie. The filmmakers made this concession and Colombo backed off.

Soon after, there was an assassination attempt on Colombo on June 28, 1971, in which he was shot three times. "We were up in the hotel room for a scene where Al Pacino is with Kay and they're having dinner," Pacino's stunt double, Anthony Caso, recalls. "This was near Columbus Circle. Joe Colombo, the mob boss, was shot in Columbus Circle while we were shooting Godfather up in the hotel. There was a commotion. We were looking down. 'Oh my God!' The Italian-American [Civil Rights] League were having a nice rally, and then this guy came through the crowd and shot him. We were shooting The Godfather, and outside was the real thing!"

There were many interesting occurrences during the making of The Godfather, including Brando missing his first day on set. Also, Robert Evans had a spy on the set, reporting Coppola's every move. There was constant talk of Coppola being fired, and behind the scenes, Evans and others tried to get rid of him.

"My history of The Godfather was very much the history of someone in trouble," Coppola told documentarian Jeff Weiner. "I found [the movie] very tough to do and very tough to finally pull off. I was a young director. I hadn't really done a lot of work and I had an opportunity to do this novel.... I knew, as the book became more popular and more successful, I realized that, in a sense, it was beginning to outclass me in that I wouldn't have gotten the job five months after the book had become the sensation it was. And even in the early, early weeks of production I knew they were not happy with what I'd done; the kind of classic style that I chose in rushes maybe didn't impress them. I just wanted to survive it."

While filming, Coppola had the actors carry items in their pockets, true to the period of the story, that their characters would have carried, such as lighters, flasks, knives, and rosary beads. Even though these items would never be seen on camera, the idea was that the items would add a sense of authenticity, helping the actors better understand and become the characters they were playing. Also of note, *Chinatown* (1974) writer Robert Towne was brought in by Coppola to write a single scene featuring an interaction between Vito and Michael Corleone, for no credit and no pay.

There were reportedly 120 New York locations shot in sixty-seven days. These include Radio City Music Hall, Polk's Model Craft Hobbies (at Fifth Avenue and 31st Street), Times Square (primarily Jack Dempsey's Broadway Restaurant), Bellevue Hospital (462 First Avenue), Best & Company (51st and Fifth Avenue), and Louis Italian-American Restaurant (3531 White Plains Road), where Michael guns down Sollozzo and McCluskey. (Coppola had originally wanted to shoot the scene in Patsy's, a well-known restaurant located at First Avenue and 117th Street, but the restaurant's owners wouldn't allow him to film there.) After scouring New York City for the perfect Corleone family home, Coppola selected a house in Staten Island. After the New York shoot was finished, Coppola and a skeleton crew shot a couple of days' worth of scenes with Pacino in Sicily.

The Godfather was released theatrically on March 24, 1972. The film became a massive critical and box-office success. It was the highest grossing film of 1972; shot on a $6 million budget, the film earned more than $136 million in the United States and $270 million worldwide. *The Godfather* was nominated for eleven Academy Awards, winning three (Best Picture, Best Screenplay, and Marlon Brando for Best Actor). When the Academy Awards were held on March 27, 1973, Brando sent a Native American activist named Sacheen Littlefeather (real name Maria Louise Cruz) in his place to decline the award in protest of Hollywood's portrayals of Native Americans. This gained Brando and

Littlefeather much notoriety and angered many, including John Wayne, who reportedly tried to get to the stage to accost her.

The film has since been re-released to theaters a number of times and has appeared on just about every list of the greatest American films fashioned since its creation. In 1977, *The Godfather* and its sequel, *The Godfather Part II* (1974), were edited together into a television miniseries (which also included scenes cut from the original films) titled *The Godfather Saga*. Mario Puzo published a sequel novel titled *The Sicilian* in 1984, an author named Mark Winegardner published two more sequels titled *The Godfather Returns* and *The Godfather's Revenge* in 2004 and 2006, and a third author named Ed Falco published *The Family Corleone* in 2012. Coppola filmed two cinematic sequels, *The Godfather Part II* and *The Godfather Part III* (1990). In addition, there has been a *Godfather* video game and a 2022 television series called *The Offer*, chronicling producer Al Ruddy's experiences on the film.

The Hot Rock

Donald Westlake published his heist novel, *The Hot Rock*, in 1970. The novel featured the first appearance of the popular literary character John Dortmunder. Westlake had originally intended to write the novel as an entry in his "Parker" series, which he'd been publishing under the pseudonym Richard Stark since 1962. However, he decided the story's plot was too comical for the stoic, hard-bitten Parker, so Westlake rewrote it, leaning into the comical situations and adding humorous supporting characters.

The novel was optioned by producers Hal Landers and Bobby Roberts. The duo then hired screenwriter William Goldman. To Westlake's amazement, Goldman included him in the adaptation process. Goldman was an unabashed fan of Westlake's work, and in 1990 Westlake referred to Goldman as "the best living screenwriter." Westlake praised that, "nobody on earth could have made a movie out of *All the President's Men* [1976], and he did." Goldman immediately impressed Westlake by calling him after he'd been hired to adapt *The Hot Rock*, telling him, "I want to take you to lunch and I want you to tell me everything you know about those characters that you didn't put in the book." Westlake told *Sight and Sound*'s Patrick McGilligan that, much to his chagrin, the screenwriter removed the only scene from the novel that Westlake had considered an ideal movie scene. "[It was] a scene where [the thieves] have stolen a locomotive from a circus because they have to break into an insane asylum," Westlake said. "It's a complicated scene, but that seemed to me like a movie scene. Bill explained to me why he couldn't use it and he was right. Every once in a great while—I don't think in terms of movies if I'm writing a book and I think anyone who does is crazy—I'll look back at something I've written and say, *'That's* a movie scene.' And if the movie rights are sold, that scene is never used."

For director, the producers turned to English director Peter Yates, who had helmed the massively successful (and widely respected) Steve McQueen actioner *Bullitt* (1968). Additionally, the first feature Yates had directed was a heist film, 1967's *Robbery*. While that film wasn't a hit, it was a critical favorite and proved that Yates had the directorial skills to make *The Hot Rock*. In an interview with the *Chicago Tribune*, Yates said he ultimately made the film because it was more upbeat than most of the other films that were being made at the time. He also observed, "The point of the film is not that the characters are criminals, but they are likable, and that they, like many people, plan things all their lives and never have it work out." Westlake, in his interview with McGilligan, assessed that neither the producers nor Yates "gave a damn" about the film. Scanning Yates' respectable career credits, one can safely assume that Westlake's assertion is false. Nevertheless, it's clear that Westlake was not a fan of the film. He has also stated that changes were made to Goldman's original script, which he believed to be far superior to what made it into the finished film.

Robert Redford, whose previous films included *Barefoot in the Park* (1967) and *Butch Cassidy and the Sundance Kid* (1969), which had also been written by William Goldman, was cast as the lead. (*Butch Cassidy* and *The Hot Rock* were the first two of five films written by Goldman and starring Redford. The others are *The Great Waldo Pepper* [1975], *All the President's Men*, and *A Bridge Too Far* [1977].) George Segal, Ron Leibman, Moses Gunn, and Zero Mostel—all fine actors—were in support of Redford. Comic actor/director Christopher Guest also made his film debut in a "blink-and-you'll-miss-him" appearance as a police officer.

While playing Spot the NYC Locations, one can easily identify a handful, mostly in Manhattan. Kelp's (Segal) key shop is situated at 682 Columbus Avenue and West 43rd Street. The Brooklyn Museum (200 Eastern Parkway) makes an appearance. The prison scenes were shot at Nassau County Jail on Carman Avenue (located in East Meadow, Long Island), which is now Nassau County Correctional Center. A scene in which Murch (Leibman) drives his car into the back of a tractor trailer was filmed on Hempstead Turnpike, also in East Meadow. The bank where the safety-deposit box resides is located at 399 Park Avenue. Perhaps the most significant NYC location appearance occurs during the helicopter scene; in that scene, both of the World Trade Center buildings appear. At that time, the south building was still under construction.

When *The Hot Rock* was released on January 26, 1972, it was met with little fanfare; the critics were ambivalent, finding it too mediocre to muster up any enthusiasm one way or the other, and it failed to find an audience, earning back only half of its $5 million budget. In 2015, *New York Times* writer Daniel M. Gold wrote, "It's never been clear why *The Hot Rock* . . . didn't get more love at its 1972 release." He went on to speculate, "Maybe [it's] because the city was simply an unfunny tableau of urban decline, not yet the object of nostalgic affection it would become." *The Hot Rock* did, however, snag an Academy Award nomination for Best Editing.

Director Yates would later tell *Boston Globe* reporter Michael Blowen that he thought *The Hot Rock* was a better film than his cult favorite *Bullitt* because he believed he'd pulled off a genuine feat by convincingly mixing comedy and suspense. "I thought I had a hit with *The Hot Rock*. It was an interesting story, and we had Robert Redford and George Segal for the leads. [But] nobody went to see it."

The Last House on the Left

A friend told Wes Craven about a building at 56 West 45th Street that housed several documentary production companies. One filmmaker working there, Sean Cunningham, was looking for someone to sync up dailies. Searching for an entry into the film world, Craven applied for the job and landed it, and the two men immediately became friends. The film Cunningham was making was a faux documentary called *Together* (1971). The film was financed by Boston theater owners who funded their own second-bill pictures. When the film was finished, the financiers liked the resulting product and asked Cunningham to make a second film. This time, however, they wanted a horror film with a lot of sex scenes.

Knowing Craven wanted to make his own films, Cunningham asked him to write, direct, and edit this sex/horror project with Cunningham producing. Craven jumped at the opportunity. Wanting to make something different from the horror films he'd seen, Craven decided to lift part of the plot from Ingmar Bergman's 1960 film *The Virgin Spring* and use that as the framework for his film. His primary interest was *The Virgin Spring*'s exploration of innocent people driven to kill. Craven found further inspiration when he and Cunningham watched one of Sergio Leone's "Man with No Name" pictures. In this instance, inspiration didn't come directly from the film or its story, but as a reaction to it. In Leone's Western, the two men saw what they believed to be a detached approach towards murder and violence. They felt Leone's film depicted murder with a complete disregard for life. Vietnam was in full swing at the time, and Craven was constantly exposed to footage of the war on television that showed a different side of violence and death than what he saw in films like Leone's; he concluded that real-life violence was sadistic, horrific, and disturbing. Because of this, Craven decided he would make a film that depicted the ugly nature of real-life violence and murder.

With these ideas swirling around inside his head, along with a self-imposed goal to break every cinematic barrier he could, Craven went away to Long Island to write the script. He hammered out the first draft in two days. The script was titled *Night of Vengeance* and featured several scenes depicting hardcore sex. Craven and Cunningham were both pleased with the script, and they believed they could make the film with a $50,000 budget, the idea being that they would make the film for $40,000 and pocket the remaining $10,000. But then, to their surprise, their Boston benefactors gave them $90,000 to make the film.

When they set out to cast the film, a number of actors turned down the project because they found the screenplay revolting and overly graphic in its depictions of rape and violence. Actor Fred Lincoln would later recall that early drafts of the script had scenes containing cannibalism and necrophilia.

Casting Lincoln proved to be a boon since his involvement led to the casting of two key roles. First, Lincoln's agent convinced him to introduce one of his other clients, Sandra Peabody, to Craven and Cunningham. As a result, Peabody landed the role of Mary. Lincoln then introduced the filmmakers to his friend Jeramie Rain, suggesting her for the role of Sadie. Because Rain was only twenty-one and Sadie was written to be age forty, they were skeptical. When Rain read for the part, however, she convinced them that she was the right actress for the role. When Rain read the rest of the script, she balked. She would later recall a scene where Sadie was supposed to cut a woman's breast off and eat it. Wanting her in the film, Craven and Cunningham cut the scene.

Actor Marc Sheffler, who plays Junior, visited his manager, Dick Towers. When Sheffler entered the office, Towers told him about Craven and Cunningham's movie. Towers told Sheffler to leave his office and hop on a bus to read for them. Sheffler did as he was told and read for the filmmakers. He then returned to Towers' office to learn that Craven and Cunningham had, in the amount of time it had taken him to travel back to the office, called Towers and offered Sheffler the role. Towers himself would also be cast in the film as Mari's dad, Mr. Collingwood.

Perhaps the most important role in the film would be the head villain, Krug. If he wasn't scary and intimidating, the film would be dead in the water. Craven and Cunningham first offered the role to Martin Kove (best known today for playing

John Kreese in *The Karate Kid* [1984]), but Kove wasn't interested. Instead, he took the comedy relief role of the deputy. But Kove told them he knew just the guy—the *perfect* Krug! Kove's sister was living with a friend of his named David Hess. Kove immediately went to Hess and told him that he needed to meet the filmmakers. Despite Hess's large stature, Kove didn't think he was large enough for the role, so he made him wear several layers of sweaters. The only problem was that it was summertime and Kove's station wagon had no air conditioner. Nevertheless, Kove and Hess climbed into the hot car and headed for Craven and Cunningham's office. By the time they arrived, Hess was so overheated and cranky that he stormed into the filmmakers' office and yelled at them. Recognizing that Hess was perfect for the role, they cast him on the spot.

Before filming began, Fred Lincoln convinced the filmmakers that the script was solid enough to stand on its own without sex scenes. After considering this, the filmmakers decided to cut out the sex.

The shoot lasted four weeks and was split between New York City and Connecticut. The thrifty filmmakers used guerilla filmmaking tactics, stealing shots and locations without permits. They used a seven-man crew and used a station wagon to haul their equipment from location to location. The cast stayed together at Cunningham's house for much of the shoot. One cast member would liken the experience to being at summer camp. Various locations in Cunningham's home were used as locations in the film. These included his backyard, his mother's bedroom, her kitchen, her swimming pool, and the inside of her car.

One extremely important aspect of *The Last House on the Left*'s effectiveness was Craven's decision to shoot the film like it was a staged documentary, using long takes—sometimes as long as nine minutes without cuts. This, he hoped, would make the audience feel like they were watching raw footage of a real-life horror. Craven also allowed the actors to improvise heavily in the hopes that the fresh, in-the-moment dialogue would make the conversations feel more realistic.

There was a negative aspect to the shoot that also added to the film's sense of realism. Sandra Peabody was ostracized from the other cast members. Since David Hess remained in character, Peabody was constantly afraid for her life. She was manhandled and terrorized by members of the cast throughout the shoot. Craven later concluded that Peabody may have believed she was starring in a snuff film. It's difficult to understand exactly why the cast treated her the way they did. It's perhaps even more difficult to understand why she was so afraid of her fellow cast members. But one thing is clear: the fear Peabody exhibited on screen was authentic.

Several alternate titles were used in advance screenings. These included *Krug & Company* and *The Sex Crime of the Century*. But these titles failed to put asses in theater seats. In the end, it was an ad man named Lee Willis who suggested the title *The Last House on the Left*. It had nothing to do with the contents of the film, but when the film was screened with that title in Indiana, people came out in droves to see it.

When the film officially opened in New York City on August 30, 1972, there were lines of people around the block waiting to see it. The film proved to be so successful in terms of Craven's goal to stir up viewers' emotions that many audience members were angered by it. Jeramie Rain remembers a viewer at the film's premiere demanding that she refund their money. Both Wes Craven and David Hess found that people treated them differently after watching the film. While Craven was at a group dinner, someone announced that he'd directed *The Last House on the Left*, causing several people to stand up and walk out. Craven also noted that his friends no longer wanted him around their children. Perhaps Hess had it the worst, because people recognized him as the sadistic Krug and believed he was actually the character, angering and/or frightening them.

Theater owners around the country made their own edits to the film, cutting scenes they didn't want to screen. Censors in many countries around the world demanded cuts be made before they would allow the film to screen within their borders. *The Last House on the Left* was initially banned in both England and Australia. Even now, it's only available in a heavily censored form in England.

What is it about *The Last House on the Left* that makes it so effective? How can a low-budget film made with amateur actors and featuring scenes shot in the producer's backyard work so well? Craven summed this up while speaking to documentarian David Gregory: "Because it's primal. It doesn't look away from a very ugly truth. It literally does not look away; it does not cut, it does not fade to black. It just stays until the act plays out, then you see all of the after-effects unblinkingly. I think many, many people depend on films to blink at a certain point. *Last House on the Left* does not blink."

Shaft's Big Score!

Without yet knowing how popular *Shaft* (1971) would or wouldn't be, MGM announced that they would be producing a sequel months before the film's release. The first draft of the sequel screenplay was written by B. B. Johnson (whose real name was Joe Greene), author of the popular "Superspade" book series (about a black private eye named Richard Abraham Spade). In this early draft of the screenplay, the film was simply titled *Shaft #2*. That script, which found John Shaft in the Caribbean, was rejected. Ernest Tidyman, Shaft's creator, wrote a script of his own that was also rejected. (That script eventually became the 1974 novel *Shaft's Carnival of Killers*, the sixth installment in Tidyman's Shaft book series.) Tidyman then wrote a rejected treatment for a film based on his already-completed second Shaft novel, *Shaft Among the Jews*. (This novel would be released in 1972.) Producers Stirling Silliphant and Roger Lewis then wrote a draft of the script themselves titled *Shaft Gets It On*. Tidyman hated, hated, hated the script and convinced the producers to ditch it. Tidyman himself then embarked upon a script that would change titles (*Gang Bang*, *Shaft's Triple Cross*, and *Bury Me Deep, John Shaft*), as well as locations (at least one Tidyman draft relocated the detective to Chicago). In the end, the producers would move forward with a Tidyman script titled *Shaft's Big Score!*

Now that the producers had screenwriter Tidyman attached, they set out to sign the other key players from the first film: director Gordon Parks, composer Isaac Hayes, and, of course, the most important of the bunch, Richard Roundtree. (Really, what would a Shaft film have been without Roundtree, who was by then immortalized as the character?) Parks seems to be the only one of these three who returned without issue. Although Parks vowed upfront that this would be the last "black action movie" he would make, he liked the idea of making Shaft films. Parks would tell *Chicago Sun-Times* critic Roger Ebert on the set of *Shaft's Big Score!* "People come up and ask me if we really need this image of Shaft the black superman. Hell, yes, there's a place for John Shaft. I was overwhelmed by our world premiere on Broadway. Suddenly, I was the perpetrator of a hero. Ghetto kids were coming downtown to see their hero, Shaft, and here was a black man on the screen they didn't have to be ashamed of. Here they had a chance to spend their three dollars on something they wanted to see. We need movies about the history of our people, yes, but we need heroic fantasies about our people, too. We all need a little James Bond now and then."

Roundtree had received only $12,000 for the first film. Recognizing that he now had leverage, he held out until he received a reported $50,000 for the sequel. The producers considered recasting, but Parks threatened to leave the production if Roundtree wasn't signed.

Isaac Hayes, who had won an Academy Award for his work on the first film, haggled with the producers. Hayes wound up contributing a single song ("Type Thang"). He was slated to score the entire sequel but pulled out of the project two weeks before *Shaft's Big Score!* was supposed to be completed. As a result, Parks was forced to score the film himself, adding yet another talent to his already impressive resume.

Actors Moses Gunn and Drew Bundini Brown returned to reprise their roles from the first film. Joining them as *Shaft* newcomers were Joseph Mascolo, Julius Harris, and Joe Santos. Cinematographer Urs Furrer, art director Emanuel Gerard, and set decorator Robert Drumheller also returned. Shooting began in

January 1972 and lasted until April. None of the film wound up being shot in either the Caribbean or Chicago. Instead, Parks and company shot entirely on location in New York City. Shooting locations included the Brooklyn Navy Yard and Cypress Hills Cemetery, both of which would be popular filming locations throughout the 1970s. Scenes were also shot at LaGuardia Place and Bleeker Street.

During filming, Roundtree performed most of his own stunts. "He racked himself up against a stone wall once, but he kept driving," Parks told Ebert. "That made it easy for us. We could get close with our helicopter shots because you could see it really was Roundtree and not a stunt driver. We spent twelve days on that chase, and wrecked four cars, two boats, and a mock-up chopper."

Shaft's Big Score! was released theatrically on June 21, 1972, to mixed reactions from audiences and critics. Clyde Jeavons of *The Monthly Film Bulletin* opined, "It's efficient, exciting in a predictable, routine way, and excessively violent (with the emphasis on pyrotechnics, beatings, and messy bullet-holes); but plot-wise, it's patently absurd, with Shaft's invulnerability attaining supernatural proportions in the climax, as he makes life as easy as possible for his murderous opponents by scampering about suicidally in front of their machine guns, which he survives with nary a scratch." Both Roger Ebert and Gene Siskel, years before the two would become a TV collective, gave the film three out of four stars in their respective Chicago papers. *New York Times* critic Roger Greenspun wrote that "the new Shaft follows a new and glossier and tidier image, an image that is much more James Bond than Bogart." He went on to observe that "Gordon Parks keeps improving as a technician, and *Shaft's Big Score!* is far more ambitious and professional than the original *Shaft*. But it is also more mechanical and more exploitative of the material. And so it becomes less responsible, less detailed, less personal, less serious, and less fun."

David F. Walker, writer of the *Shaft* comic book series, believes the sequel is superior to the original film. "I like *Shaft's Big Score!* more than *Shaft* for a few reasons, not the least of which is that it is bigger in scope, but also because Gordon

Parks Sr. and Richard Roundtree are more assured in what they are doing; especially Parks. The first film is a traditional private detective story, with nominal action, and the direction, cinematography, and editing are a bit low-key, especially compared to the second film."

The first *Shaft* was made on a budget of $500,000 and raked in approximately $12 million at the box office. For the second film, Parks was allowed a $2 million budget. While *Shaft's Big Score!* was a hit, earning $10 million, it was less profitable than its predecessor.

While not as good as its predecessor, *Shaft's Big Score!* helped make John Shaft the cultural icon he is today. It also opened the door just a little bit wider for the novels, films, television series episodes, spin-off films, and comic books that would follow.

Super Fly

Through the successes of *Cotton Comes to Harlem* (1970), *Sweet Sweetback's Baadasssss Song* (1971), and *Shaft* (1971), Hollywood learned that films that were geared toward black audiences were capable of making money. Suddenly, studios and film producers were scrambling to make black films. One man who began to consider black filmmaking was a New York advertising agent named Phillip Fenty. Fenty was interested in writing a script about a drug dealer. Since Fenty's friend Nate Adams, who ran an employment agency on 125th Street in Harlem, had connections and knew what was happening in the streets, Fenty asked him for help. Adams shared everything he knew with Fenty, and the screenwriter took notes. Adams then introduced him to street-level coke dealers and pimps. Wanting to learn more about these hustlers, understand their motivations and perspectives, and get a better idea of the ways they operated, Fenty began hanging out with them.

The script Fenty was writing would be a story about the things he saw around New York City, both in terms of the street life it depicted and the creatives who lived there. "New York in the late Sixties and early Seventies was unbelievable," Fenty recalled in *Super Fly: One Last Deal* (2016). "It was an incredible place to be. There was tremendous creative energy."

Once Fenty had fashioned a short forty-five-page screenplay titled *Super Fly*, his friend Gordon Parks Jr. came onboard as director. Since Parks' father, noted author, photographer, and film director Gordon Parks, had just directed the hit film *Shaft*, the savvy Fenty no doubt recognized the money- and interest-raising potential of his friend's name. After Parks was attached, Fenty approached a producer and distributor named Sig Shore. At the time, Shore was theatrically distributing foreign films such as Francois Truffaut's *The 400 Blows* (1959) and *Black Jesus* (1968). Shore was interested in finding American films he could produce, and he was well aware of the current interest in black films, so he signed on to find financing.

When Shore showed the script to possible financiers, he was often met with laughter, eye-rolling, and rejections. "Anybody who would read the script and see that it had a drug dealer as a hero thought I was insane," Shore said in 1990 on the Stanford news show *The Exchange*. But Shore would have the last laugh. He didn't raise *a lot* of money, but he raised *enough* money. The film would be made with a budget somewhere in the neighborhood of $60,000. Shore got $53,000 of that money from a couple of black dentists who lived near him in Stanford. Additionally, Gordon Parks Sr. contributed approximately $5,000. It seems appropriate that Shore had to hustle to raise the funds to make a film about a hustler.

When it came time to cast, Parks Jr. called on a friend he'd gone to school with in Cleveland named Ron O'Neal. The thirty-one-year-old O'Neal was a classically trained stage actor with one film credit (*Move* [1970]) and an appearance on the television series *The Interns*. O'Neal signed on to play the drug-dealing lead character, Youngblood Priest. The other top-billed roles were filled by Carl Lee, Sheila Frazier, Julius Harris, and Charlie McGregor. McGregor was fresh out of prison, and his knowledge of the streets allowed him to assist the filmmakers as a technical advisor.

A Volkswagen was used as the "crew car" in the making of the film. The filmmakers went from location to location all over Harlem and East Village, "stealing shots" without permits. Because of the film's limited budget, Parks Jr. had to limit the number of takes he shot. The filmmakers occasionally ran out of money, so Shore would have to raise more so they could continue filming. During filming, the crew was occasionally harassed by street gangs trying to shake them down for shooting in their territory.

The filmmakers needed a score. When they made a list of musicians they would most like to work with, Curtis Mayfield was one of their top selections. They took the script to Mayfield and showed him what they were working on, and Mayfield loved it. So, he scored the film. That score would become a smash hit and is generally acknowledged as one of, if not *the*, greatest soundtracks of the blaxploitation cycle.

When the film was later released, it would be applauded for its authenticity. Shore would credit the lack of studio interference for the filmmakers' ability to capture the street vibe of the time. Fenty liked a real-life pimp named K.C.'s tricked-out Eldorado, so he convinced him to let them use the car in the film. According to Fenty, the pimp initially believed he was being duped by con men. Once K.C. gave him consent to use the car, they also allowed him to appear in the film, adding to *Super Fly*'s Harlem authenticity. Nate Adams, who had originally introduced Fenty to the real-life hustlers, was brought in to handle the film's costume design because of his keen eye for fashion. Sheila Frazier wore her own clothes in the film, including the pricey white mink. But Adams dressed most of the other characters. He convinced stores and fashionable people he knew to give or lend him clothes to use.

When *Super Fly* was completed, Shore took a print of the film to California to try to sell the project to Warner Bros. Looking at the film's miniscule budget and the profit they would likely make from it, Warner Bros. snatched it up. When the studio screened the film for preview audiences, the first screening was in Westwood at a "white theater." Because that was not the film's target audience, it was not a success there. The second screening was at the Fox Theater in Philadelphia, Pennsylvania, where it played back-to-back with *Shaft*. The film was a huge success there.

When *Super Fly* opened on August 4, 1972, it received mostly positive reviews despite media figures taking the filmmakers to task for perpetuating stereotypes. But *Super Fly* would be a massive success. In New York City, there were lines down the streets waiting to get into screenings. At one Times Square theater, the crowd broke down the door and forced their way in to see the film. *Super Fly* also proved to be a crossover sensation, just as *Shaft* had been. "*Super Fly* has played to an awful lot of white people," Ron O'Neal said in a 1972 interview with James Earl Jones. "It's the only way you can do $19, $20 million. We've been in Boston seventeen weeks. We ran out of black people in three weeks in Boston." In the end, the film's box-office take would be about $30 million, which was a tremendous profit for a $60,000 production.

Novotny Lawrence, Iowa State associate professor and co-editor of the book *Beyond Exploitation*, explains the film's significance: "*Super Fly* was controversial after its release, as some people believed it promoted drugs. The title was the street name for cocaine at the time, and given how cool Youngblood Priest is, I understand some of the concerns. At the same time, that has always been the dilemma of the gangster film. The characters engage in illegitimate activities, acquire wealth and status, and for a time, live the 'American Dream.' Consequently, there has always been a danger that some viewers would identify with the gangster and potentially view having it all for a short time and meeting a terrible fate, as better than never having had anything at all.

"While it is easy (and fair) to focus on those things, *Super Fly* was actually very influential," Lawrence says. "It depicted a black gangster who is unapologetically black and successfully navigates a society that marginalizes him. In addition, the 'one last score' narrative has become a standard in cinema thanks to *Super Fly*, and as such, its influence lives on. Curtis Mayfield's soundtrack is iconic, and along with the tremendous success of other blaxploitation soundtracks, it helped usher in the practice of using soundtracks to sell films. That was a standard marketing practice during the ensuing decades. Importantly, the soundtrack also helped standardize the use of R&B, and other genres of popular music, in cinema. Hollywood and other media industries also continue to use songs from the *Super Fly* soundtrack in their creations. *Super Fly* was also highly successful at the box office, demonstrating that black actors could helm lucrative films and that black moviegoers were a viable demographic. *Super Fly* also helped save Warner Bros. from going bankrupt. In conjunction with *Cotton Comes to Harlem*, *Sweet Sweetback's Baadasssss Song*, and *Shaft*, *Super Fly* helped start the blaxploitation movement. Finally, *Super Fly* and other blaxploitation films continue to have a tremendous effect on rap and hip-hop music in the form of samples, aesthetics, and themes, among other aspects."

1973

Cop Movies, Blaxploitation, and Mean Streets

Watergate was in the news in 1973. The Supreme Court legalized abortion, and President Nixon announced that a peace accord had been reached in Vietnam. In New York City, the mayoral election saw the sitting mayor, John V. Lindsay, replaced by comptroller Abraham Beame. The year would also see New York State governor Nelson Rockefeller enact some of the nation's strictest drug laws. After the Rockefeller laws went in to effect, opposing critics expected the state's prison population to double in size within a year. However, the number of drug-related incarcerations remained roughly the same. (In fact, two years later the number of drug incarcerations in the state would drop substantially.)

On the evening of January 19, 1973, four African American Sunni Muslim men (Shulab Abdur Raheem, Dawd A. Rahman, Yusef Abdallah Almussadig, and Salih Ali Abdullah) robbed John and Al's sporting goods store, located at 927 Broadway in Brooklyn, on the edge of the Bushwick and Bedford Stuyvesant neighborhoods. The robbers, all in their twenties, were trying to acquire weapons. They claimed the weapons were for self-defense as a reaction to the Hanafi Muslim Massacre, which had occurred the day before in Washington, D.C. When police officers from the 90th Precinct arrived on the scene, a shoot-out occurred, leaving one officer dead. This was followed by a three-day standoff in which the robbers took twelve hostages. Eventually, hostage negotiators convinced the robbers to release the hostages. The four robbers were ultimately found guilty on forty-two counts, including assault, robbery, and kidnapping.

Three months later, an undercover cop named Thomas Shea shot and killed ten-year-old Clifford Grover, whom he suspected (along with his stepfather) of having just committed a robbery. When the boy became afraid, believing he was in danger, and ran for safety, Shea fired on him, hitting him at least twice. Shea and his partner, Walter Scott, would later claim the boy had been carrying a firearm, although no such gun was ever found. Immediately following the incident, rioters took to the streets of the South Jamaican neighborhood to express their anger at what they saw as a racially motivated killing. Shea was then tried for murder, becoming the first NYPD officer to be tried for a murder committed in the line of duty. Shea was later acquitted in 1974, resulting in another riot in which cars were overturned and private property was damaged and destroyed.

There were a few significant Mafioso deaths in 1973, some natural, some the result of bullet holes. Former Luciano family boss Frank Costello died peacefully in a Manhattan hospital. Bonanno family boss Natale Evola also died of natural causes. A couple of mob-related murders are significant because of the men who killed them; the infamous Roy DeMeo, a Gambino family captain whose crew is believed to have killed about two hundred people, put two bullets in the head of porno kingpin Paul Rothenberg. Future Gambino family boss John Gotti, along with two others, walked into Snoopes Bar (94 Sharpe Avenue, Port Richmond) in Staten Island, disguised as cops, and gunned down James McBratney after McBratney had attempted to kidnap a Gambino associate.

1973 was also a big year for NYC crime movies. Here we'll look at nine features. These are *Badge 373*, *Black Caesar*, *Cops and Robbers*, *Hell Up in Harlem*, *Massage Parlor Murders*, *Gordon's War*, *Mean Streets*, *Serpico*, and *The Seven-Ups*. Four of these are cop films, which had become all the rage following the success of *The French Connection* (1971). Three of the films are blaxploitation pictures, which were also extremely popular. The obscure cheapie *Massage Parlor Murders* might seem like an odd selection, but the film, while not particularly good, is included because it remains one of the best displays of 1970s NYC grittiness.

Badge 373

Robert Duvall's character Eddie Ryan in *Badge 373* is based on Eddie Egan, one of the real-life cops responsible for the famed 1961 "French Connection" bust. Judging from the film, Egan must have loved saying the word "spic," because the epithet appears in the film about as frequently as the word "God" appears in the Bible. (Although the word is actually only used twenty-nine times, it *feels* like 129.) Not surprisingly, because of the excessive use of the slur and the film's negative depiction of Puerto Ricans, a group calling themselves the Puerto Rican Action Coalition protested the film for being "racist" and "insulting and degrading," demanding that Paramount Pictures withdraw the film from release. The studio refused.

After the success of *The French Connection* (1971) two years earlier, as well as Robin Moore's book of the same title, it stands to reason that the film's real-life subjects would use their newfound fame to cash in. Separate films based on the exploits of the two NYPD officers (*Badge 373* by Egan and *The Seven-Ups* by Sonny Grosso) were released in 1973. Egan's film beat Grosso's to the box office by five months. Both Egan and Grosso had appeared in *The French Connection* and had also worked as technical advisors. Since both men found work after that as actors, it's safe to say they'd been bitten by the movie bug.

The film's associate producer, Lawrence Appelbaum, was friends with Egan before *Badge 373*. "Do you want to know what kind of guy Eddie Egan was?" Appelbaum says. "Eddie was the kind of guy who was in the Marine Corps. He was one hell of a cop. He was very flamboyant. He sang 'God Bless America' every night. I opened a bar with him called Eddie Egan's Fort Lauderdale Connection. He entertained every fireman [and] every cop who ever went through the area. He was an American hero in my book because of the things he did. But he was also a pain in the butt! But you would expect that from a guy like that."

Appelbaum would occasionally hire Egan to handle security on the films he produced in order to keep local gangs from interfering with the shoots. "At that time in New York City, any time you were shooting in their territory—mostly Harlem—the gangs would shake the productions down to get a piece of the action," Appelbaum explains. "But we didn't have to pay on *Badge 373*, even though we did shoot in Harlem. A few of the gangs tried to shake us down at first, but then, lo and behold, they found out that the cops were involved with us, and they left us alone after that."

While William Friedkin's *The French Connection* had taken some liberties with its story, *Badge 373* seems to be almost entirely fictional. As *Chicago Sun-Times* critic Roger Ebert wrote at the time of the film's release, "I can believe ... that Egan really did set out to the find the killer of his partner. But I somehow doubt that their final confrontation came hundreds of feet in the air on a crane in the Brooklyn Navy Yard, and that the killer had a machine-gun as well as several philosophical points to make about the Puerto Rican experience." Interestingly enough, both Egan's and Grosso's "biopics" told the story of cops tracking down their partner's killers.

To describe the events portrayed in *Badge 373* as being ridiculous would be an understatement. Not only are they unbelievable, but they are so over-the-top sensationalized that they're laughable. In one such scene, Ryan (Egan) is confronted on a dark street, alone, by seven or eight armed gang members (who cares about the specific number? It's absurd either way.) who wish to cause him harm. Without even having to use his gun, Ryan manages to escape unharmed by using impressive hand-to-hand fighting moves and a couple of evasive spins. But wait. Believe it or not, that's not even close to being the most ludicrous aspect of this sequence. After the defeated gang members give chase through the streets, Ryan hijacks a bus to get away. This leads to an insane and, again, wholly unbelievable car and bus chase. Many critics accused the film of trying to outdo *The French Connection*'s chase scene here. And maybe it does, but at least the chase scene from Friedkin's film was believable. The car and bus chase in *Badge 373* is like something out of a Jason Bourne movie.

Badge 373 was Robert Duvall's first leading role. He put on weight for the part and stayed in character even when the cameras weren't rolling. "He was a pain in the ass," Appelbaum recalls. Duvall's performance is over-the-top at times, but everyone else (especially the real Egan) is subdued and seem to be sleepwalking through the film. By now, we all know Duvall's immense talent as an actor, so there's no reason to go down that rabbit hole. Let's just say that Duvall had given a truly impressive Oscar-nominated turn in *The Godfather* (1972) the year before, so it's clear that *Badge 373*'s director, Howard W. Koch, was lacking when it came to getting performances from actors. Certainly, Koch was no Francis Ford Coppola.

For reasons unknown, Koch seemed to believe the film would benefit from multiple scenes featuring the balding Duvall with the little bit of hair he still had on top standing upright as if by static electricity. These scenes only serve to make Duvall look goofy.

The script by journalist Pete Hamill (and supposedly Egan) doesn't do Duvall or anyone else any favors. The script is horrible, and it's at its worst when Hamill tries to put cutesy tough-guy witticisms in Duvall's mouth. "I hope you're circumcised, because your freedom comes down to a matter of inches." This is followed by "Send him to the Circumcision Division and charge him with a violation of the penis code." Another doozie is, "You've got more tracks than a Long Island railroad." In another scene, after being offered a drink, Ryan quips, "Thanks, but I'm driving to Ireland." Yes, that one is completely nonsensical, but it's rivaled by "You're the funniest thing since sneakers." Then there's the tough-guy talk that's not supposed to be humorous, but sounds forced, like "Stick the mayor up your ass!" and "If you touch me again, I'll turn this place into a fuckin' garage!"

Badge 373 was shot in fifty-three New York City locations. In one scene, Ryan drives past Nathan's Famous on 1025 Boardwalk West in Brooklyn. The BQE (Brooklyn-Queens Expressway) is visible in another, and at one point, Ryan walks under the Brooklyn Bridge in the rain. Scenes shot at the Brooklyn Navy Yard were filmed in zero-degree temperatures. While the entirety of the film seems to have been shot in the city (mostly in Brooklyn), *Badge 373* doesn't put a lot of landmarks on-screen. The film seems more intent on telling its story, even if it's a mediocre one, than showing off locations to prove its authenticity.

When *Badge 373* was released on July 25, 1973, it became both a critical and box-office flop. To say that critics hated the movie would be an understatement. While the film would be substandard by any measure, most critics compared it to *The French Connection*, which it couldn't possibly have stacked up to. Gene Siskel of the *Chicago Tribune* remarked that the film felt like a *MAD* magazine parody of Friedkin's film. Comparing the two films, the *Washington Post*'s Gary Arnold wrote, "Duvall's cop is a little cruder than Hackman's, and he also seems less capable. The lack of any original characterization is a little embarrassing; *Badge 373* seems to think it's different because Duvall insults Puerto Ricans, whereas Hackman insulted Negroes." Roger Greenspun of the *New York Times* summed it up best when he wrote, "Howard Koch's helpless direction to the dumpy performances by all the cast—unless you care to hate Puerto Ricans (or Irish cops), I don't see how this movie can have anything for you."

Black Caesar

By 1973, the so-called "blaxploitation" cycle was in full swing. Low-budget producers saw that they could make a quick buck working in this new genre, but they were always on the lookout for ways to increase their chances of making a hit film. *The Godfather* (1972) had been the highest-grossing film of the previous year by a wide margin. In fact, the film was so popular that it dominated the box office for much of the year; after the film's March 24 release, it became the number one film in the nation for an astounding twenty-six weeks straight. After being knocked out of first place by *Butterflies Are Free* (1972) on August 30, *The Godfather* resumed the top spot for another three weeks. So it was inevitable that someone would craft a Mafia/blaxploitation hybrid film.

Enter screenwriter/director Larry Cohen. Though he'd directed only one film (1972's *Bone*) prior to this, he had amassed an impressive number of writing credits, mostly in television. When American International Pictures (AIP) asked Cohen if he had anything that could be made as a blaxploitation film, he told them he had a preexisting script that would work perfectly. The script, *Black Caesar*, told the story of a gangster's rise and fall in New York City. Cohen had envisioned the film to be similar to the classic Edward G. Robinson and James Cagney gangster films of the 1930s.

"*Black Caesar* is not any different from those Warner Bros. films like *Little Caesar* and *The Public Enemy* [both 1931]," Larry Cohen says. "It really is the same kind of a story about the rise and fall of an American gangster. It's not really your typical black exploitation film, where the black hero wins every fight, wins the woman, and gets everything. In *Black Caesar*, he loses everything and ends up in the gutter. He loses the woman who betrayed him, and he loses his entire empire. So, in that aspect, it's really more like *Public Enemy* or *Little Caesar*."

Cohen had originally envisioned a slightly different film. The lead role had actually been written for Sammy Davis Jr. "Sammy was a little guy," Cohen explains. "But so was Edward G. Robinson and James Cagney. They were great as gangsters, and I felt we could do a black gangster movie. The rise and fall of a Harlem gangster."

After AIP green-lit the project, Cohen cast former football star Fred Williamson, who brought a more contemporary feel to the film. "Fred Williamson brought something different to it," Cohen observes. "He brought glamour to it. Fred was a good-looking guy. You know, he wore the clothes beautifully."

Black Caesar stood out from the blaxploitation pack from the start. For starters, it had a solid screenplay, which many of the films did not. The film also dealt with police corruption, which was, of course, topical at the time. (While Cohen's film beat *Serpico* to theaters by eleven months, the real Frank Serpico and the Knapp Commission had been in the news a great deal. Additionally, journalist Peter Maas' book *Serpico* hit shelves just a month before *Black Caesar* arrived in theaters.) One of the best things

Black Caesar had to offer was the presence of Fred Williamson. While Williamson may not be Laurence Olivier, he does a fine job, and his natural charisma more than makes up for whatever he lacks as an actor.

Williamson believes *Black Caesar* and the entire blaxploitation cycle were important in a historical context. "You have to look at the whole picture," Williamson told David F. Walker in 2004. "The total picture is important. You have to understand that in the early 1970s and late 1960s, they were still siccing dogs on black people. More than eight people, more than ten blacks on a corner constituted a riot, so it was time to call out the dog squad. So there was no way for the black public to fight back. They had no way to fight back without getting themselves into serious trouble. So what we brought them at the time was a guy who won the fight. When the smoke cleared, we were still standing. There wasn't no butlers. There wasn't no porters. There wasn't no shoeshine guy. And when I did do a shoeshine guy in *Black Caesar*, I was killin' somebody with the shoeshine box. So we had images that were needed and necessary for that particular time and that particular era."

Aside from the quality of the film's screenplay, there was another aspect of *Black Caesar* that was different from other films at the time; Cohen's film had a lurid rape scene in which Williamson's Tommy Gibbs overtakes his girlfriend, played by Gloria Hendry. "[It was] shocking," Hendry recalls. "I don't think a rape scene had been the thing to do at that time, except between a husband and wife. Not that kind of rape. This had never been addressed. This was something different. I don't remember another movie where they addressed a rape scene between a husband and wife prior to that. I think this was one of a kind."

Most blaxploitation films are criticized for being about black people while being written and directed by white filmmakers. But Cohen allowed Williamson to tell him when he felt something was wrong, and he listened to his input, making the film more authentic. Williamson recalls, "[Cohen] had to convince me to do it because I wasn't sure I wanted to be in this kind of movie until I came up with my idea of Caesar from Edward G. Robinson and knew how I was going to play the role. I wasn't depending on Larry Cohen's script to carry me through because I knew he didn't understand black motivation. We had this discussion saying, 'I'll do what I feel is right and I will discuss it with you, and if I don't think something is right, I'll discuss it with you and I won't do it. It's that simple."

Cohen managed to snag James Brown to perform the film's entire soundtrack. This is significant because Brown crafted only two film scores, the other being *Slaughter's Big Rip-Off* (also 1973). The eleven original songs Brown created for *Black Caesar* are at times strangely literal. For instance, the singer wrote and performs the song "Mama's Dead" when Tommy's mother dies. In other songs, Brown sings about a black man rising to the top in New York City. The soundtrack, as one might expect, is exceedingly funky and is vastly superior to the majority of blaxploitation soundtracks, which is a feat considering these films are generally known for having qualitative soundtracks.

Black Caesar is a film where New York City itself, or, more specifically, Harlem, is as much a character as anyone in the film. While some interiors were shot in Los Angeles (including scenes shot inside Cohen's house), most of the film was shot in Harlem. As such, a number of recognizable businesses and locations pop up. There is a scene that takes place inside the now-legendary Latin Quarter club (511 Lexington Avenue). The Apollo Theater (253 West 125th Street) makes a couple of cameos. Lewis Michaux's famed National Memorial African Book Store (Adam Clayton Powell Jr. Boulevard at West 125th Street) shows up briefly, which is interesting because the store shuttered their doors before *Black Caesar* was even released. Rufus' church is said to be located at 145th Street and Amsterdam Avenue. Tommy Gibbs purchases a gift at Tiffany & Company (727 Fifth Avenue) before being shot and stumbling in front of Van Cleef and Arpels (744 Fifth Avenue). In another scene, Tommy strangles a man on a park bench across the street from the now-defunct Flagg Bros. Shoes (Gage and Pacific Boulevard in Los Angeles).

The film was released on February 7, 1973. Its reviews were middling to good and were better than most blaxploitation films and American International Pictures (AIP) outings. The film performed well enough that Cohen and Williamson made a sequel, *Hell Up in Harlem* (1973), which was released the following December.

Cops and Robbers

With constant news stories about rampant police corruption and films about renegade cops who shot first and asked questions later (such as *Dirty Harry* [1971] and *The French Connection* [1972]) putting up big numbers at the box office, author/screenwriter Donald Westlake believed audiences were primed for a movie about cops who doubled as robbers. Having already written two failed screenplays, Westlake wrote a third titled *Cops and Robbers*. The script was quickly optioned and went into production.

The film follows two NYPD patrolmen who, as Henry David Thoreau once wrote, "lead lives of quiet desperation." These cops, Tom (Cliff Gorman) and Joe (Joseph Bologna), struggle through the daily grind of their torturous and thankless job, each day dealing with the dregs of society. "What are you gonna do?" Joe laments while stuck in traffic on the Long Island Expressway. "You gotta take the good with the bad, right? You get up, you go in, you do your job, you make a buck and you go home. What the hell's the use of complaining?" After Joe tells Tom about his having robbed a liquor store and how it not only improved his financial situation but also his sex life, the two begin to scheme so they can make some real money. Original artwork for the film depicts Tom and Joe carrying bundles of cash, but this is misleading. Did the artist even watch this movie? (Probably not.) Tom and Joe will instead attempt to steal $10 million worth of bearer bonds, for which the Mafia will hand them a cool $2 million.

Actor Joseph Bologna spent time riding along in a squad car with his cop brother-in-law to prepare for his role. "My dad said he would talk to the cops as they were walking into the station, and once they were dressing in the locker room, the moment their uniforms were on, they were totally different people," Bologna's son, Gabriel, who also appears in the film, explains.

"Their chests kind of puffed with pride and they walked with a gait. He was fascinated by that. They were just average Joes until they put their uniforms on. My dad said he carried that with him when he played the role—that sense of pride."

While Westlake's script leaned heavily into comedy, director Aram Avakian's film was sillier than Westlake had envisioned. While Westlake liked the resulting movie, he didn't *love* it. Believing his original story was superior to the film, Westlake decided to adapt his screenplay into a novel. While adapting a script into a novel is a rare occurrence—it usually happens the other way around—this was the second script Westlake had refashioned into a novel. (The first was his unproduced kidnapping script *Who Stole Sassi Manoon?*)

In a 1974 *Take One* interview with journalist Albert Nussbaum, Westlake challenged the "auteur theory," which was popular at the time. (The auteur theory is the notion that the director is the sole artist responsible for the creation of a motion picture, or, to put it in simple terms, the filmmaker is the painter and the film is his painting.) In doing so, Westlake painted a picture of his own highlighting the creative restraints he had on the film while inadvertently providing a peek behind the moviemaking curtain. "I am responsible for the novel *Cops and Robbers* in a way I could never be responsible for the movie version. . . . In *Cops and Robbers*, I am responsible for most, but not all, of the storyline; however, I wind up responsible for very, very few of the details along the way. In one scene in *Cops and Robbers*, two mobsters are being interrogated by cops at typewriters. The emphasis was on one of the mobsters who was being introduced as a major character; however, the other mobster and the cop interviewing him were not ordinary actors, no sir. The cop was a real honest-to-god New York City plainclothes detective, and the guy playing the mobster was a real-life Cadillac dealer and no stranger to the bent life. They brought a choreography in that scene that I couldn't have invented and the director couldn't have invented, either. And it was somebody else entirely who thought to have the mobster give his occupation as 'wholesale meat,' so the cop could look at him and say, 'A butcher?' And I'm talking here about the secondary characters in the scene; so, in that three-minute segment, who's the auteur?"

Avakian was a director open to ideas. Art director Gene Rudolf recalls an instance where Avakian implemented one of his suggestions. "When Cliff Gorman and Joe Bologna are driving in the car, there's always a problem in the traffic," Rudolf recalls of the film's repeated gag of having Tom and Joe jammed up on the Long Island Expressway. "I said to Aram, 'One time, it has to be all the traffic is moving, so they get to go. But then *they* have a problem with *their* car!' And Aram Avakian said, 'Oh, that's good!' So they put that in with the two of them stuck with a flat tire, and they have to work on their car while all the rest of the traffic is in motion."

I cannot verify the accuracy of this story, but Joseph Bologna liked to tell a tale about the filming of the Central Park chase scene. "There was an extra who raised his hand when the First AD said, 'Whoever wants a line, we'll give it to them if they do a stunt,'" Gabriel Bologna explains. "This guy was literally begging to do this stunt. He had to dress up as a policeman and jump off the bridge onto the police car that my dad was driving. My dad said, 'This guy's not a stuntman. I don't think this is a good idea!' So the guy did the stunt, and he landed and broke his leg. As the extra was being carried off on the stretcher, he asked, 'Do I still get my line?' He couldn't care less that he'd broken his leg."

Filmed in various locations around Manhattan, *Cops and Robbers* showcases a decaying New York City. "What's interesting about the movie is that I can honestly say it didn't feel like a movie," Gabriel Bologna explains. "When you see movies that take place in the Seventies in New York, it's too clean. There are too many colors. You could spend the entire day without ever seeing a color. That's how it looked when I think of New York City growing up as a child. So if you look at *Cops and Robbers*, you see the real New York of that era. There was soot on the streets. There was soot on the buildings. There were dark cars. Dark suits. Even the dresses that women wore. It wasn't the splash of color that people think of the Seventies, at least in New York. Look at a movie like *The Godfather*, look how dark the colors were. You see Mafia movies today, you see splashes of color. That's just not how the Seventies looked."

Cops and Robbers was released in New York City on August 15, 1973, and then nationally two days later. The reviews were largely favorable, but *Cops and Robbers* failed to make a dent at the box office and disappeared. It has been released on DVD and Blu-ray but has never achieved the cult status that many of the films in this volume have, which is a shame.

Hell Up in Harlem

An unnamed reviewer on the website Teleport City perfectly sums up this follow-up to *Black Caesar* (1973): "While they were certainly responsible for their share of cinematic flotsam, American International Pictures can also be credited with creating a few good films that are today considered genre classics, as well as some films that are extraordinary solely for the fact that, given the circumstances of their production, they were even made at all. As far as AIP's ventures into the blaxploitation arena go, *Black Caesar* definitely falls within the former category, while its sequel, that same year's *Hell Up in Harlem*, serves as a perfect example of that last-mentioned type of film."

The story behind the sequel's production is a strange tale even for low-budget exploitation pictures, and the film's existence is a testament to the never-say-die persistence of writer, director, and producer Larry Cohen. AIP wanted a sequel ASAP, but Cohen and the film's star, Fred Williamson, were tied up working on other projects during the time *Hell Up in Harlem* needed to be made in order to be finished by the end of the year. Cohen was in production on the horror film *It's Alive* (1974), and Williamson was on the other side of the country making *That Man Bolt* (1973). Most filmmakers would have recognized this as an insurmountable obstacle, but not savvy showman Cohen. It's difficult not to think of Dustin Hoffman's over-the-top movie producer in *Wag the Dog* (1997), saying, *"This? This is nothing!"* each time he's confronted with a game-changing hurdle.

Since *It's Alive* was shooting only five days a week, Cohen opted to use the film's crew to shoot *Hell Up in Harlem* on weekends. But what about a script? What about locations? Since there was no script and no locations cleared, Cohen made the film's story up on the fly, shooting on the streets of Harlem without permits. But even with these problems solved, Cohen still faced the most extreme of the production's many issues: he had no star! *"This?"* Cohen might have said. *"This is nothing!"* Cohen used a body double to stand in for Williamson whenever and wherever possible.

"We shot all of the reverse shots of Fred out in California," Cohen says. "You have to know exactly what you're doing when you make a picture like that. You have to know exactly what every shot is going to look like, and what every cut is gonna look like. I carried the whole picture in my head so I could do it. I don't think I would recommend this to other people. But I did it, and I made it work."

Williamson, however, was less than pleased. "Fred didn't like the double," Cohen says. "He thought the double's ass was too fat. He was pissed off. He said, 'Where'd you get the fat ass on that guy?' I said, 'Look, Fred, no one knows it's not you. Just cool it. Nobody will ever know.'"

Williamson did manage to come to New York for a couple of days while *That Man Bolt* wasn't shooting. While Cohen and Williamson were filming guerilla-style on the street somewhere in Harlem, they ran into Lew Wasserman, head of Universal Pictures. Since Williamson was currently under contract to be working on *That Man Bolt*, which was a Universal film, this could have been a major problem. However, Wasserman apparently believed the film was one of Universal's. In an attempt to distract him from figuring out what was happening, Cohen offered the studio chief a role in the film as a gangster. But Wasserman declined and went on his merry way without ever asking what film Cohen and Williamson were shooting.

Another interesting anecdote from the shoot involves D'Urville Martin, who plays Rev. Rufus. Martin continually clashed with Cohen, so Cohen filmed an impromptu shot of the actor lying dead on the ground. When a confused Martin asked the director what the shot was for, Cohen told him it would be part of a death scene that would enable Cohen to write him out of the film if he continued to challenge him. After that, Martin behaved.

Since James Brown's soundtrack from the first film had been highly qualitative and much loved, Cohen planned to hire him to record a soundtrack for the second film. But there had been a problem with Brown's soundtrack on the first film. As Cohen explains, "Unfortunately, if the scene was five minutes long, James wrote seven minutes' worth of music. If the scene was six minutes long, James wrote nine minutes' worth of music. If it was a one-minute scene, he wrote two or three minutes." Despite this, Cohen and his editor, George Folsey Jr., had trimmed the music to make it work. So, when it came time to make *Hell Up in Harlem*, then titled *Black Caesar's Revenge*, Brown agreed to record new music. However, once he'd made the songs, AIP wouldn't allow Cohen to use them. Brown then released the music he'd made for the film as an album called *Payback*, which became a huge hit. Without Brown's funky music, Cohen then had to settle for what he would later call "a second-rate Motown score" by Edwin Starr.

Hell Up in Harlem was released just in time for Christmas 1973. The reviews were generally poor. Reviewers labeled the film as being "dull" and "implausible." Critics at the time had no idea what had transpired during the film's production, but the shoddiness was apparent. Sequels are rarely as good as the films that precede them, but *Hell Up in Harlem* missed the mark by a wide margin.

Massage Parlor Murders

After making two short films, 1970's *First Class* (in which mime Marcel Marceau plays fourteen different characters) and something called *Waiting for Monday* (year unknown), and also suing chess master Bobby Fischer for $3 million for stopping him from filming Fischer's "Match of the Century" against Russian Boris Spassky, Broadway press representative Chester Fox decided to try his hand at feature filmmaking. The feature would be a blood-soaked horror picture made for the drive-in circuit about a madman slaying prostitutes in New York City.

According to its credits, *Massage Parlor Murders* was co-directed by prolific stuntman and *Sesame Street* cast member Alex Stevens, although it's possible that he directed only a handful of additional scenes the following year. Interestingly, only Fox is named in trade paper announcements of the film, and only Stevens is named as director in a 1974 article in *Genesis*.

The origin of the screenplay (and even the concept) is unknown, as the film doesn't credit a screenwriter. The film's production team of Chris Nolan and Bert Cohen may be of note, although like most things having to do with *Massage Parlor Murders*, little is known about them. Nolan claimed to be a former massage parlor manager, and Cohen is possibly the same Bert Cohen who later became the senior vice president of International Sales at Worldvision Enterprises Inc. Did Fox and Stevens write the script? Maybe Nolan and Cohen? Maybe all of them in some kind of screenwriting orgy? No one seems to know.

This small grindhouse film was shot entirely on location in New York City and would ultimately feature a couple of "known" actors; following her teary-eyed terrified turn in *Last House on the Left* (1972), Sandra Peabody was cast. Character actor George Dzunda, who would later make a splash when he appeared in *The Deer Hunter* (1978), makes his screen debut here.

Production began on *Massage Parlor Murders* in early 1973. Its production title was *Seven Deadly Sins*. Filming ended (at least so far as the primary shoot is concerned) in the following summer. The film was submitted to the Motion Picture Association of America (MPAA) at that time, receiving an R-rating. The cut that was submitted was approximately seventy minutes long. The film would be released in New York City in August 1973. The version released would run about eighty minutes long. After the film performed poorly, six minutes were excised by the distributor, Film Ventures International, and the film was re-released with the title *Massage Parlor Hookers*. This incarnation of *Massage Parlor Murders* did significantly better, and the film (which had a bigger and better advertising campaign) played in drive-ins for the next seven years as a second bill tacked on to such films as *A Touch of the Other* (1970), *Hillbilly Hooker* (1971), and *The Bod Squad* (1971), among others.

Actress Anne Gaybis, who shared a scene with Chester Fox that was cut from the film and later restored, was understandably surprised to learn that the film had been repackaged and re-released as *Massage Parlor Hookers*. Additionally, she had wondered for many years why her scene had been cut. "It didn't play at any theaters that I knew of, and there was no premiere," Gaybis says. When a fan sent her a copy of the DVD (which restored her scene) for her to sign, Gaybis finally saw *Massage Parlor Murders*. "That was the first time I'd ever seen it. When I watched my scene, I thought, 'What was wrong with that?' Because after I saw the rest of the movie, my scene was like Academy Award material! I'm kidding, but it's not a great movie."

NYC locations that appear in the film include 42nd Street and Times Square, Royal Pizza at 592 Third Avenue, and the Horn & Hardart automat located at Lexington Avenue and 45th Street.

Brett Gallman of *Horror Reviews* perfectly sums up the film: "All of that atmosphere has to compensate for tons of incompetence. *Massage Parlor Murders* barely functions as a movie, much less a hard-boiled police procedural. Scenes are loosely strung together, and the movie seems to have been edited together with duct tape and crazy glue." Another telling after-the-fact internet review (there don't seem to be any print reviews to be found from the film's theatrical release) by Michael Hauss of Theatre of Guts proclaims, "This film is odd. It is so unbalanced and bizarre that it jolts your sensibilities at times. It has scenes that lead nowhere, it has some good acting performances, and some downright awful acting at times, badly framed and edited shots, murky camera work, but, the bottom line is it is a dirty, gritty, sleazy, funky, fun romp."

Massage Parlor Murders fell into obscurity for several decades and didn't get a DVD release until 2013. It's a sleazy exploitation picture that no one would ever deem a cinematic treasure, but it does a fine job of encapsulating the grunge and grime of 1970s

NYC. In 2015, *Massage Parlor Murders* was listed as one of Flavorwire's "50 Films That Capture the Dark Side of New York City."

Gordon's War

The blaxploitation film era, or "The Black Film Revolution" as it has been called, was a glorious period of black filmmaking. Even though most of the films were written and directed by white men, the films provided a lot of black actors work and inspired black actors and filmmakers to pursue careers in film. The era produced some good, a lot of bad, and quite a few downright ugly films. *Gordon's War* tends to fall more solidly into the "bad" category than any other. How exactly producer Edgar J. Scherick convinced a filmmaker as talented as Ossie Davis to make this film is a mystery. (It's likely that there still weren't many options for a black filmmaker at the time the production began in 1972.) *Gordon's War* isn't terrible, it's just qualitatively beneath someone as talented as Davis.

The script for *Gordon's War*, which has been referred to as the "anti-*Superfly*," was written by Howard Friedlander and Ed Spielman. Friedlander was known for having done some television. Spielman had no credits, although he would later become known for creating the TV series *Kung Fu*. The storyline for *Gordon's War* finds a black G.I. named Gordon Hudson (Paul Winfield) coming home from Vietnam to find that his community and his wife have fallen victim to the drug epidemic. Righteously pissed, Gordon recruits three of his war buddies to assist him in going to war against the neighborhood pushers.

Filming began on January 8, 1973. There aren't a lot of details available about the production. One thing that is known is that producer Scherick fired the original soundman after a single day of filming. After watching the first day's dailies, Scherick commented to Robert Schafel, another producer, that the audio sounded terrible. When Schafel told Scherick that the soundman didn't like shooting in the freezing cold and was spending a lot of time upstairs in his apartment, Scherick demanded to see the soundman. When the soundman came down, they got into a heated argument, and Schafel fired him. In response to his termination, the soundman declared, *"I'll never work for a Jew again!"* Schafel chuckled and said, "Well then, what business are you going into next?"

Grace Jones wrote in her 2015 memoir that she auditioned with Ossie Davis for the small role of Mary. (The role had only one line of dialogue.) Davis liked Jones' read and handed her the role. Jones was overjoyed but was then called by the producer (which producer isn't specified) and told that final casting approval was his decision. Jones was then flown from New York to Los Angeles to meet him. When Jones arrived at the producer's home, he answered the door wearing only his robe. He invited her inside, where she discovered soft music and champagne awaiting her. After the producer reminded her that the final casting decision was his, he attempted to kiss her. Refusing to participate in this obvious casting couch ploy, Jones smashed her champagne glass into his face and stormed out, sure she'd lost the role. However, the next day she was sent flowers and an apology letter from the producer telling her the role was hers.

While working on *Gordon's War*, Paul Winfield, the film's lead, learned that he'd just been nominated for a Best Actor Academy Award for his turn in *Sounder* (1972). When he found out the other nominees that year were Marlon Brando, Laurence Olivier, Peter O'Toole, and Michael Caine, the actor gushed, "I'm overwhelmed! What a thrill to be competing with four of the world's greatest living actors."

While *Gordon's War* was filmed all over Harlem, it didn't ring particularly true. One of the primary complaints by locals was that there weren't any cops anywhere in the film, including Lenox Avenue, where the police maintained a constant presence at the time the film was made.

Filming ended in March 1973, and *Gordon's War* was released on August 9, 1973. The film did poor business, its $1.6 million budget producing a mere $823,282 return in the United States and $1.25 million worldwide. Reviews for the film ranged from mediocre to poor. *New York Times* critic Howard Thompson wrote, "The picture is tough, fast, moves in a straight line with no fiddling but with pungent humor and vividly jabs the crime-ridden underbelly of Harlem. The sharp direction of Ossie Davis catches the argot, the flavor and the sinister ambiance of the area. . . . But the picture is inconclusive, far from profound, and the urgency of the theme has been overly simplified to fit the action." *Variety* was not impressed even a little bit: "Often incoherent and predominantly tedious . . . Cinematic car-motorcycle chase does not so much realize the film's goals as distend it further; the eighty-nine-minute length seems interminable."

Mean Streets

With two films in this book and several later projects that fit the bill, director Martin Scorsese is the king of the New York City crime film. The first of these incredible features was *Mean Streets*, which focuses on one man's struggles in balancing his street life with what his religion requires of him.

Scorsese and an NYU classmate named Mardik Martin spent much of the late Sixties working on a script titled *Season of the Witch*. The concept had been Scorsese's, and he had begun the process by crafting an outline. After that, Mardik Martin (in his words) "worked out the structure." Once the two had the framework of the film firmly in mind, Scorsese worked on adding dimension and depth to the characters. He also tossed out, retooled, revamped, and added scenes. Much of the writing in the early drafts took place while Scorsese and Martin drove around Manhattan in Martin's Plymouth Valiant.

In writing the script, Scorsese drew heavily from the "personal" filmmakers who had influenced him, including the French New Wave, the Italian Neorealists, and John Cassavetes (particularly *Shadows* [1959]). With this project, Scorsese wanted to create a film that was largely based on events and occurrences he'd either lived through or witnessed in his own life. Growing up, Scorsese had been a small and sickly boy often confined to his home. Certainly he was no gangster. But when he could, he ran with a group of boys who were. With *Season of the Witch* focusing heavily on religion, he envisioned it as the third installment in a trilogy that dealt with religious conflicts. The previous projects were Scorsese's unfilmed screenplay *Jerusalem, Jerusalem* and his 1967 student film *Who's That Knocking at My Door?*

Scorsese's earliest efforts to secure financing for the film failed miserably. First, he took a fifty-page outline to the American Film Institute (AFI), which had just established a program to produce feature films. Scorsese would later admit that the version of the story he'd shown the AFI had been lacking and in need of more development. Next, he took the project to the distributor who had released *Who's That Knocking at My Door?* but he was again turned away. In 1968, Scorsese flirted with what he saw as a likely financier, so he wrote another draft. And again, he encountered rejection. While *Season of the Witch* never left Scorsese's mind, he set it aside and moved on to work on other things.

In 1971, exploitation producer Roger Corman handed Scorsese his first break, hiring him to direct the Depression-era crime-romance *Boxcar Bertha* (1972) for American International Pictures. Scorsese made *Boxcar Bertha* the best film anyone could possibly have made with the budget and script he'd been given, but middling reviews and a harsh appraisal from his mentor John Cassavetes led him to walk away from the realm of low-budget exploitation films. (Corman had asked Scorsese to follow *Boxcar Bertha* with another film and had offered him the choice between a gladiator picture or a project called *I Escaped from Devil's Island*.)

Scorsese returned his focus to *Season of the Witch* and went to work on yet another rewrite. Scorsese's then-girlfriend, Sandy Weintraub, was a tremendous influence on the new draft. She encouraged him to eliminate some of the heavy religious symbolism and add more personal anecdotes from his own life. The title of the project also changed; *Season of the Witch* was dropped in favor of *Mean Streets*, which had been suggested by Scorsese pal (*Time* magazine critic) Jay Cocks. Scorsese would later admit to not liking the title, initially using it as a placeholder to be changed later. Thankfully, later never came. If it had, we might now be discussing a crime film with another title as painfully awkward and ill-fitting as *Season of the Witch* had been.

When Scorsese finished his latest draft, he pitched it to Roger Corman. Corman agreed to make the film with a $150,000 budget, but with a substantial caveat; Corman would fund the picture if Scorsese agreed to make it as a blaxploitation film. "He came to me with the idea and I liked it, but at that time the black films were really very successful," Corman says. "I'd been thinking that I wanted to make a black film and I thought, this film would really work as a black film." Desperate to make the film, Scorsese briefly considered the offer but ultimately passed. He could envision his characters as black men, but try as he might, he couldn't imagine a black lead struggling with the tenants of Catholicism in the way Italian men in Little Italy did. In the end, this was a film that needed to be made the way it had been written. Scorsese then gave his friend Francis Ford Coppola a copy of the script. Coppola read it and passed it along to Al Pacino, but nothing came from it.

Things took a turn when Jay Cocks introduced Scorsese to a rock road manager named Jonathan Taplin, who was interested in producing movies. "We met and he showed me some of his student films, and I loved them," Taplin says. "Particularly a short called *It's Not Just You, Murray*. That's the one that really caught my eye. I just thought it was really original. Then he gave me the script for *Mean Streets* and I decided to finance it. I didn't know enough not to go forward and put my own money into this." Taplin found a second investor named E. Lee Perry who agreed to invest his $175,000 inheritance into the project. Then Taplin secured a deferment from Consolidated Film Industries. Between all of these things, *Mean Streets'* working budget climbed to $300,000. Unsure whether or not *Mean Streets* could be made on this budget (half of the budget of *Boxcar Bertha*), Scorsese hired Paul Rapp, who had been his assistant director on the Corman film, as his production manager. Rapp assessed that *Mean Streets* could be made on the meager $300,000 budget, but only if portions of it were shot in Los Angeles. In the end, six days and nights of exteriors (of the film's full twenty-day shooting schedule) were filmed in New York City with a skeleton crew of NYU students. On the subject of shooting in both cities, the director would later remark to film historian Richard Schickel, "De Niro fired the gun at the Empire State Building in New York and it hit a window in LA."

Scorsese had written the lead role specifically for Harvey Keitel, with whom he had worked on *Who's That Knocking on My Door?* However, box-office considerations led to him instead casting Jon Voight, who had been nominated for an Oscar for his turn in *Midnight Cowboy* (1969). But Voight ultimately dropped out of the project, and Keitel then stepped back into the role. Scorsese then met a young New York actor named Robert De Niro at a party. Although they'd never met, the two recognized each other from hanging out at Manhattan dances with mutual acquaintances. The two quickly hit it off, and Scorsese offered De Niro his choice of roles, promising him anything but the lead. De Niro initially tried to convince both Scorsese and Keitel that he should play the lead role of Charlie but eventually settled for the secondary role of Johnny Boy.

The shoot went relatively smooth because of Scorsese's preparedness as a director. "The cool thing about Marty was that he was so organized," Taplin recalls. "He'd wanted to make the movie for so long that he had literally drawn every single shot in the storyboard. He had five books of storyboards. Every single shot, every pan, every movement, the thing where Harvey Keitel is moving through the bar, all of it. He'd already figured it all out. So he was able to be efficient—he would have like thirty setups a day—that it was just scary. He was so prepared that he could spend time with the actors."

On this first of ten Scorsese/De Niro collaborations (to date), the artists developed a dream working relationship. "They can shorthand stuff," Taplin explains. "They know each other so well that they can just say two or three words or just one sentence, and the other will understand it. They've worked out the way to communicate with one another." Because of this, Scorsese gave De Niro the freedom to make suggestions. This led to De Niro's suggesting the Abbott and Costello–inspired Joey Scala/Joey Clams discussion that appears in the film. In addition to this, Scorsese himself came up with a couple of other new scenes during filming.

Despite having interiors shot in California, *Mean Streets* is very much a New York picture; it does a superb job of depicting Little Italy with a feeling of authenticity. For a scene in which

Charlie and Johnny Boy talk inside a cathedral, Scorsese returned to the Old St. Patrick's Cathedral at 264 Mulberry Street, where he'd once been an altar boy. Other exterior locations include 23 Cleveland Place, 394 Broome Street, Grand Street, Kenmare and Grand (which had been a hangout spot for a teenage De Niro), the Brooklyn Bridge, and Staten Island, where Scorsese filmed the beach scene.

Regarding the film's depiction of Little Italy, Scorsese told Schickel, "That's the world I was in. The violence is always in the background. I'd go into a place, even in a movie theater, I always had my antennae out all the way, because I had to watch if somebody said something wrong to somebody else. . . . [M]y experience is that there are certain groups of people who were aligned with certain families. I didn't know they were called families at the time, but there were certain people with power, and if somebody hits somebody, or does something, not just on the street level, not just kids, the settling up is done, usually, in the old way, between the different groups."

According to Taplin, the filmmakers faced a significant problem after editing was finished. (It was actually edited by Scorsese himself, despite the fact that, due to Directors Guild rules, Sid Levin is credited.) "Marty had all this music he wanted in the movie," Taplin says. "And literally no one had ever licensed that much music in a movie before. When we were budgeting at the beginning, we had no idea that Marty was going to put all this music in the rough cut. The music was brilliant though, and once you heard it and saw it that way, you realized you couldn't make the film without those songs." This led to negotiations (with occasionally changing rates) with a number of bands. The end result was a budget that soared to somewhere in the range of $500,000. (The exact amount is difficult to pinpoint.) Warner Bros. saved the day, purchasing the film for $750,000.

Mean Streets debuted at the New York Film Festival the first week of October 1973 to generally positive reviews. *The New Yorker*'s Pauline Kael, who would later declare *Mean Streets* the best American film of the year, called the film "a true original of our period, and a triumph of personal filmmaking." She went on to write: "This picture about the experience of growing up in

New York's Little Italy has an unsettling, episodic rhythm and it's dizzyingly sensual. The director, Martin Scorsese, shows us a thicker-textured rot than we have ever had in an American movie, and a riper sense of evil." The film also garnered positive reviews for Keitel and glowing reviews for De Niro. It no doubt stung for Keitel to have De Niro steal both the spotlight and his position as Scorsese's number one go-to collaborative partner.

Serpico

New York City police officer Frank Serpico, the man *New York Times* film critic Vincent Canby would later call "The Saint Francis of Copdom," refused to take graft money. "People ask me, 'Why didn't you take the money?'" Serpico says. "Take the money? Why would I take the money? I'm not a crook." Serpico reported the widespread corruption to his superiors, as well as the police commissioner and the mayor's office. But Serpico couldn't get traction; everyone looked the other way. "These cops weren't stupid," he says. "They had college degrees. At least one of them retired as a millionaire." Fed up with the system's failure to acknowledge the problem, let alone deal with it, Serpico told his story to *New York Times* reporter David Burnham. The resulting front-page expose drew attention to the issue and eventually led to the formation of the Commission to Investigate Alleged Police Corruption (better known as the Knapp Commission).

Because he spoke out, Serpico was shunned by his fellow cops. Many of them had already viewed him as an outsider because of his quirky behavior, long hair, and hippie-style clothing. But now Serpico wasn't just seen as being weird—he was a threat. "I had to not only watch the criminals, but also the ones that were wearing the uniform," he says. Serpico remembers another undercover detective asking him, "'Do you think you're the only honest cop?' This was the shit I had to put up with every day. No, I didn't say I was the only honest cop. But I know who the fucking crooks are, and I know who the jackasses are that don't have the smarts to put two and two together."

On February 3, 1971, the situation came to a head. While attempting to make a bust, Serpico, unaware he was being set up by fellow cops, was shot in the face. The shooter was later identified as a cop named Edgar Echevarria. (Echevarria would eventually be convicted of attempted murder.) "The two guys who came in the radio car to pick me up [after I'd been shot] didn't know who I was," Serpico recalls. "I heard one of them say, 'I think he's a narc.' Later, one of them would say, 'If I had known it was Serpico, I would have left him there to fester.'" Much to the chagrin of the cops who'd set him up, Serpico survived. With bullet fragments lodged in his brain, he was left with hearing problems and chronic pain. Eight months after the shooting, he testified in front of the Knapp Commission. The commission's findings and suggestions would ultimately lead to the end of the collective payoff distributed among cops known as "the pad."

At one point, fellow cop and ally David Durk attempted to get a movie version of Serpico's story (and his, with Durk presenting himself as an equal participant in these events) made. Durk invited Serpico to have lunch with Paul Newman. "I didn't know behind my back they were planning to make a movie," Serpico explains. "It was going to be Robert Redford and Paul Newman. I hear Robert Redford and Paul Newman and I'm like, 'You mean like *Butch Cassidy and the Sundance Kid* [1969]?'" The situation angered Serpico, who stood up and walked out.

Serpico never set out to become a star; he'd simply exposed the crooked cops because it had been the right thing. Journalist Peter Maas eventually convinced Serpico to co-author a book about his experiences. The book would prove to be a success, and producer Dino De Laurentiis optioned the film rights for $400,000 before it was published. Director John G. Avildsen of *Rocky* (1976) fame was hired to make the film. He and Serpico became close friends. Avildsen even considered casting Frank Serpico to play himself. One day, Avildsen called Serpico and told him he'd been fired. This angered Serpico, who had only agreed to make the film because he trusted Avildsen. "I said, 'You know what? Fuck them. Fuck the whole project,'" Serpico explains. "'I don't need it.'" Producer Martin Bregman called Serpico and reminded him that he'd signed a contract, and the film would be made with or without him. Adding to the sour taste Serpico had in his mouth regarding the project, his then-girlfriend, Amy Levitt, whom Avildsen had cast in a role, was also let go.

Sidney Lumet was hired to replace Avildsen. By 1973, Lumet had established himself as a talented filmmaker, having already made such films as *12 Angry Men* (1957), *The Pawnbroker* (1964), and *The Anderson Tapes* (1971). Al Pacino was cast in the lead. The previous year, Pacino had delivered an iconic, Oscar-nominated performance as Michael Corleone in *The Godfather* (1972). *Serpico*'s screenwriters Waldo Salt and Norman Wexler were also hot at the time, with Salt having won a Best Screenplay Oscar for *Midnight Cowboy* (1969) and Wexler having been nominated for *Joe* (1970).

Serpico immediately found himself at odds with Lumet, who took liberties with his life story. Serpico observed the filming of a scene in which his character flushes a man's face in the toilet. "I yelled, 'cut!' And he said, 'What are you doing?' 'What am *I* doing? What the fuck are *you* doing?' He says, 'I'm trying to make a movie here.' I said, 'A movie about who?' He said, 'It's about you.' I said, 'Well, I don't remember that scene.' And he says, 'Well, it happened in my life!' And I said, 'If you make a movie about your life, put it in there, but leave it the fuck out of mine!'" Angry and disheartened, Serpico left the set and never returned.

The $3 million film was shot and completed for Paramount Pictures in a relatively short time. The first day of shooting was on July 4, 1973, and it was completed and released to theaters five months later on December 5.

Serpico was shot in four of the five boroughs of New York City (all but Staten Island) in 104 locations. I'm not going to list all of the locations, but I'll point out a fair number of them. When Serpico graduates from the Police Academy, he poses for a photograph. This was filmed behind the Manhattan Center for Science and Mathematics at 280 Pleasant Avenue. He relocates from Brooklyn to Greenwich Village. When he does this, he travels across the Williamsburg Bridge to his new apartment, located at 5–7 Minetta Street. On his first day as a police officer, Serpico reports to 653 Grand Avenue in Brooklyn, which is made to look like the 83rd Precinct police station. At the beginning of his career, while responding to a rape call, Serpico and his partner shut off their lights and park in front of the Manhattan Center for Science and Mathematics, standing in for Brooklyn. When Serpico chases and catches one of the rapists, they appear to be running toward the Interstate 278 Brooklyn-Queens Expressway (known as "the BQE"). However, they are actually running towards the Franklin Delano Roosevelt East River Drive (known as "the FDR"). When Serpico later apprehends the two remaining rapists, he does this at Thomas Jefferson Park at East 114th Street, which is presented as Brooklyn.

Serpico enrolls in courses at New York University in Greenwich Village. He later attends the opera at the New York State Theater (now the David H. Koch Theater) at Lincoln Center Plaza at 150 West 65th Street at Broadway. Scenes featuring the shoe shop owned by Serpico's family were filmed at 688 Tenth Avenue. In one scene, Serpico and his friend Bob meet to discuss their situation at the since-demolished Adolph Lewisohn Stadium at 136th Street and Convent Avenue in Manhattan.

Serpico has multiple subway station scenes, including Dittmar Boulevard, Astoria, in North Queens, at the end of the Broadway local line and the 57th Street Station. When Serpico goes undercover and arrests the loan shark, Casaro, he does this at the Red Triangle Building, 14th Street at Ninth Avenue.

Anthony Caso, Pacino's stunt double in the film, praises Lumet as "a New York director." "What he filmed—*that* was New York. The grittiness. The cops. The undercover detectives, when they meet in the park . . . He captured New York," Caso says. "When I saw the movie, I said, 'Wow.' The streets, up in Harlem, you name it. Everything he did, he captured New York. What you see on the screen, *that* is New York."

Critics were divided. Many complained that Serpico's motives were overly vague, and others disliked the film's omission of many real-life figures' names. Janet Maslin of the *Boston Phoenix* accused the film of being "aimed at the lowest-common denominator crowd." She also wrote, "Lumet has a pretty good eye for New York settings. But he does much better with buildings than with actors; by the time Serpico starts naming names, we are hard-pressed to remember who anybody is." The *Village Voice*'s Andrew Sarris questioned Serpico's apparent naivety in the film: "I can't imagine that audiences which groveled before *The Godfather* in open-mouthed admiration for its baroque violence are now prepared to march on City Hall to avenge the persecution of Serpico. This is New York after all, and is there anyone who grew up on these grimy streets who can truly express shock at the sight of police corruption? Ay, there's the rub. Serpico himself grew up on these streets. Did he never even suspect what was going on? I prefer to believe that he is more street-smart than that."

Nevertheless, *Serpico* was a box-office success, taking in somewhere around $25 million (an exact figure is unavailable). Pacino received an Academy Award nomination for Best Actor, and Salt and Wexler were nominated for Best Adapted Screenplay. An Italian film, *The Cop in Blue Jeans*, inspired by *Serpico*, was released in 1976. That same year, an NBC television series based on Serpico's exploits aired. (The series, which starred David Birney, ran for sixteen episodes between 1976 and 1977.) Then there was the television series *Baretta*. "*Baretta* was another total rip-off, except they called it *Baretta* and made a new fucking series!" Serpico says. "But they did it right down to my cockatoo!"

In the years to come, *Serpico*'s stature would grow considerably, with most online film review sites praising the film as a classic. The "character" Frank Serpico would rank number forty on the American Film Institute's 2003 "100 Years . . . 100 Heroes & Villains" list. *Serpico* would later rank at number eighty-four on the AFI's 2006 list of "Most Inspiring Films."

The Seven-Ups

Immediately after shooting concluded on *The French Connection* (1971), producer Philip D'Antoni pitched an idea for a pseudo-sequel titled *The Seven-Ups* to 20th Century Fox chieftain Elmo Williams. Williams expressed interest in the project, and he and

D'Antoni began to discuss possible directors. When neither of them could agree on a suitable filmmaker, Williams suggested that D'Antoni direct the picture. At this point, D'Antoni had produced the hit actioners *Bullitt* (1968) and *The French Connection*, but he'd directed zero films. D'Antoni would later say that he believed he'd been subconsciously considering directing, because he immediately pounced on Williams' suggestion. The other suits at the studio were far less enthused about the prospect of first-time director D'Antoni making the film, but his enormous successes with the aforementioned films gave him enough credibility to lead *The Seven-Ups* into production.

Going into the shoot, D'Antoni quickly realized the difference between the responsibilities of a producer and a director. Before, when there were problems, he'd been able to confer with collaborators Peter Yates and William Friedkin. But now, with himself serving as both producer and director, his ass was squarely on the line and in the spotlight. To prepare, he gathered every book about filmmaking and filmmakers he could get his hands on and read them all cover to cover. While this was great, D'Antoni would later admit that he learned a valuable lesson while making *The Seven-Ups*—the only way a person can actually learn to direct is in the trial-by-fire process of actually directing a movie.

Following *The French Connection*, almost everyone involved did their best to milk the film's success. Twentieth Century Fox went to work on the official sequel, *The French Connection II* (1975). Eddie Egan and Sonny Grosso, the cops the film had been based on, each went to work making films that purported to be based on their solo exploits. Egan's film would be *Badge 373* (1973), and Grosso's would be *The Seven-Ups*. D'Antoni convinced Roy Scheider to reprise his Grosso-inspired role (using only the character's first name). The supporting cast included Tony Lo Bianco, Larry Haines, Richard Lynch, and stuntman Bill Hickman.

Once the cast and crew were set, D'Antoni scheduled two weeks of rehearsals to "relate to the material and the milieu of New York City and its police." Before the shoot began, D'Antoni's pal Friedkin advised him to exercise and get in shape because directing a film was mentally and physically exhausting. Because *The Seven-Ups* would be shot entirely on location (no soundstages, only exteriors and natural interiors), with more than sixty locations, D'Antoni, who would spend most of that time on his feet, would quickly understand what Friedkin meant.

D'Antoni and his crew shot the film in the middle of a freezing-cold Gotham winter over a span of thirteen weeks. He would later write in the September–October 1973 issue of *Action*, "Being a native New Yorker is invaluable in filming a location picture in that town. Even so, one can be very surprised at stumbling upon a 'new' neighborhood which provides a totally different frame of reference in a film. It's a very exciting place to make a movie." While shooting in the busy NYC streets, D'Antoni would often employ hidden cameras with a minimal crew so that pedestrians and drivers would behave normally. While shooting one scene in downtown Brooklyn in which two men pretend to be cops and drag a pedestrian into their car, two actual NYPD officers saw the pretend kidnapping and ran into the frame to try to stop them. The actors then convinced the real cops that they, too, were police officers, and the cops stepped back and allowed them to continue. D'Antoni was so happy with the footage that he used it in the film.

As with *Bullitt* and *The French Connection*, which had both been praised for their high-octane chase scenes, D'Antoni included a chase scene in *The Seven-Ups*. Shooting this scene was not without problems. The script called for one sequence where the drivers would cross the George Washington Parkway Bridge. Uncredited assistant director Ralph S. Singleton, tasked with obtaining shooting permits, went to Port Authority officials, armed with sketches and models to show them how the scene was supposed to work. He told them, "'These bank robbers have knocked off this place and now the police have closed off the roads so they can't escape. But they break through these barriers and get on top of the George Washington Bridge and go all away across the bridge and onto the Garden State Parkway and stop.'" The officials agreed to let the crew enact the scene. Part of the filmmakers' detailed plan was that all of the traffic from both the east and west would be converted to the lower level of the bridge. When it came time to shoot the scene, a Tactical Police Force sergeant decided the crew couldn't film there. The filmmakers reminded him that they had been given permission, but he wouldn't budge. Singleton then went around the sergeant to the officials who had granted the permit, as well as the mayor's office, and the crew was allowed to film the sequence.

When it came time for the fleeing robbers' Pontiac to crash through the parked police cars, the car was unable to break through the barrier. The crew then had to use a second car to reshoot the scene. This time the car crashed its way through and onto the George Washington Bridge, but it crossed over onto the Palisades Parkway and through the toll gates. This was unplanned. The Palisades police had been notified that there was going to be a movie shooting on the George Washington Bridge, but not the Palisades. As a result, police cars arrived with their horns blaring and lights flashing. Not knowing what was happening, the cops aimed their guns at the actors. The film crew then had to explain that they were part of a film crew and that the helicopter circling overhead was filming the scene. The Palisade cops weren't pleased, but they eventually allowed the actors and crew members to go.

The Seven-Ups was shot primarily in Manhattan. Several scenes were filmed on various Madison Avenue locations. The Commodore Hotel on East 42nd Street, rechristened today as the Grand Hyatt New York, is featured prominently. The Lucia Brothers Funeral Home at 589 East 184th and Hoffman Streets rears its head. As mentioned previously, the George Washington Bridge figures prominently in the film's chase sequence.

By the time the Sonny Grosso–inspired *The Seven-Ups* was released to theaters on December 14, 1973, Eddie Egan's *Badge 373* had already been out for five months. Neither film made much of a splash. Combined, the two films earned less than $4 million. When compared to *The French Connection*'s $51.7 million box-office take, these numbers are embarrassingly poor. Released two years later, *The French Connection II* would fare better with a $12 million take, but that still fell far short of its predecessor.

Reviews for the film were deservedly mediocre. Predictably, most critics seemingly took it to task for not being *The French Connection*. Never one to mince words, *New York Times* reviewer Vincent Canby wrote, "*The Seven-Ups* . . . is a vicious, mechanical, clumsy thriller. It mindlessly uses the violence that in *The French Connection* could be seen as a manifestation of general urban rot. *The Seven-Ups* has no such thoughts in its head. It treats its vigilante cops with respect, not because of anything they might feel or believe in, but because of what they can do." Taking his criticisms a step further, Canby added, "The characters have even less individuality than performing bears." *Cleveland Press* critic Tony Mastroianni wrote, "The obligatory chase sequence lasts fifteen or twenty minutes, or maybe it just seemed that way. It's fast, well-staged, but it really looks as though it's there because someone figured it had to be, not because it meant that much to the story. There's action in *The Seven-Ups*, but it tends to be meaningless action, unlike *The French Connection*, which had minimum dialogue and maximum action, the action saying more about the characters than words." Perhaps *Films in Review* critic Roy Frumkes summed the film up best in his discussion of the chase scene: "There is, in the middle of the film, what may be a D'Antoni trademark, or what may be something he was compelled to do in order to secure funding on a first directorial effort—a car chase. Like the film, it has hardly the classic feel of his others, and yet it is very good."

After hearing repeated criticism that the film celebrated cops taking the law into their own hands, D'Antoni told journalist Mike Baron of the *Boston Phoenix*, "I wasn't trying to make any kind of statement on police abilities and the law, but I believe that the police are hampered by some of these laws. And you can ask any policeman in the country about his work. He'll tell you that the police are hindered by laws protecting criminals."

Today, the film is fairly difficult to find (at the time of this writing, it's not streaming anywhere) and rarely discussed. When it is brought up, it's almost always the chase sequence that's discussed. Although the scene has its fans, most discussions of the chase scene center around it not being as good as the chases in *Bullitt* and *The French Connection*.

1974

Murder Is Down, But NYC Has a Death Wish

Statistically, 1974 was an interesting year in terms of New York City crime. It was the first year in a long time in which the number of reported homicides was less than it had been the year before. There were 1,554 murders. Either way, that's significantly less than the 1,680 murders the year before. Still, that number is way higher than the 637 homicides that had been reported in the city just a decade before. Queens was the only one of the five boroughs that saw an increase (of 8.7 percent) in homicides.

Despite this single bright spot, the city saw an increase in every other category of serious crime. There were 519,825 serious crimes reported, which was an increase of 43.970 percent from the previous year. But, it should be noted that while the number of major felonies in New York City increased in 1974, that rate was lower than in most other major cities. In fact, a study by the Census Bureau for the Law Enforcement Assistance Administration that studied the thirteen largest cities in the United States determined that NYC had, statistically, less crime than any of the other cities. So, despite the city's haggard look and reputation for being a dangerous cesspool, the study concluded that New Yorkers had a far less chance of being raped, robbed, or assaulted. Additionally, it should be noted that three other cities in the United States (Detroit, Chicago, and Philadelphia) had a greater average of homicides per 100,000 residents. While it has been argued that those numbers reflect only the crimes that were reported, and that victims may have chosen not to call the police because they didn't believe it would do any good, that same line of thinking could be applied to every one of those cities.

So, did New York City really deserve its reputation as being the most dangerous city in the United States in the 1970s? No, probably not. And while it's easy to point a finger at the media and blame them for either erroneously portraying the city's crime issues or, at the very least, blowing it out of proportion, NYC's reputation was further sullied by the discovery that much of its police force was dirty. Then, on top of that, there were politicians such as Governor Malcolm Wilson badmouthing the city for their own political purposes. For example, where chief of detectives Louis C. Cottell had publicly concluded that many New Yorkers had turned to crime to support their families during this period of high unemployment, Wilson assessed that it was actually the other way around—the criminals were "running jobs out of town." All of this leads to the question: which came first, the gun-toting chicken or the victimized egg?

In 1974, the streets weren't the only place where New York City crime was thriving; it was also alive and well on cinema screens. We'll take a look at eight pictures shot in NYC that were released that year. Three of these entries (*Death Wish*, *The Godfather Part II*, and *The Taking of Pelham One Two Three*), each very different, are legitimately iconic films. Of those three, *Death Wish* is the film that's most emblematic of the 1970s NYC crime film. While the vigilante picture played up the rest of the country's notion that New York City was a vile, nightmarish hell-scape where murderers hid in every shadow, it also served as wish-fulfillment for New Yorkers who were fed up. Maybe New York wasn't *the* most dangerous city in the United States—maybe it wasn't even one of the top twelve most dangerous cities—but for New Yorkers, the crime there was more than enough. So, for *Death Wish*'s ninety-three-minute running time, they were allowed to act vicariously through vigilante Paul Kersey, doing things they would never actually do in real life.

The films covered from 1974 are *Crazy Joe*, *Death Wish*, *The Education of Sonny Carson*, *The Gambler*, *The Godfather Part II*, *The Super Cops*, *The Taking of Pelham One Two Three*, and *Three the Hard Way*.

Crazy Joe

After the monstrous success of *The Godfather* (1972), every exploitation producer in Hollywood was looking for a Mafia-related film to make. *The Valachi Papers* (1972), *The Don Is Dead* (1973), and *Capone* (1975) were just a few of the films that were released in the wake of *The Godfather*. Italian producer Dino De Laurentiis, whose homeland successes included such classics as *Bitter Rice* (1949), *La Strada* (1955), and *Nights of Cabiria* (1956), had found great success with *The Valachi Papers* and was looking for a similar property to cash in on. His attention eventually landed on *Crazy Joe* (1974), which, like *Valachi*, was based on a true story. The subject of De Laurentiis' newest mob movie would be "Crazy" Joe Gallo, the rogue capo who'd been gunned down in Little Italy in 1972.

De Laurentiis called on Carlo Lizzani, who had been nominated for an Academy Award as a screenwriter for *Bitter Rice*, to direct the picture. The screenplay would be written by Lewis John Carlino, who had previously written the organized crime pictures *The Brotherhood* (1968) and *Honor Thy Father* (1973). Carlino's script evolved from a "story" by Dino Maiuri, with whom De Laurentiis had previously collaborated on *Danger: Diabolik* (1968), that was based on a series of articles about the mob wars by *New York Times* journalist Nicholas Gage (who would later produce 1990's *The Godfather Part III*). De Laurentiis turned to *The Valachi Papers* cameraman Aldo Tonti to lens the film.

Selecting the right actor to play Joe Gallo would be extremely important. De Laurentiis and Lizzani wound up casting Peter Boyle, who was still a hot commodity following his acclaimed turn in *Joe* (1970). While Boyle would never become the household name he deserved to be, he would become synonymous with gritty 1970s' crime pictures; these include *Joe*, *The Friends of Eddie Coyle* (1973), *Crazy Joe*, and *Taxi Driver* (1976). Interestingly, Boyle was not Lizzani's first choice; he had originally approached Robert De Niro, whom he'd enjoyed in *Bloody Mama* (1970). Also interesting is the fact that Martin Scorsese was initially attached to assist Lizzani on *Crazy Joe*. Of course, neither De Niro nor Scorsese wound up working on *Crazy Joe*, but it is interesting to consider what might have been and, on the flip side of that, what might *not* have been.

While the real-life story of Joe Gallo served as the jumping-off point for Carlino's script, the film would take many artistic liberties. While the character Joe Gallo is named and presented as Joe Gallo, many of the other people involved in the real-life story were amalgamated or outright deleted from the storyline. For instance, the character Richie, played by Rip Torn, was actually based on two of Gallo's brothers, Larry and Albert. Also, Joe Profaci, founder of the Colombo crime family, was given the name "Falco." Similarly, the character representing Colombo family chieftain Joe Colombo was named Vincent Coletti. Why did Carlino (and De Laurentiis and Lizzani) do this? It's difficult to know if the filmmakers did this for legal reasons or simply to avoid offending the mob and being riddled with bullets. Not that anyone asked, but my bet is on the latter.

Ralph S. Singleton, who would later win an Emmy for directing an episode of TV's *Cagney and Lacey*, was a DGA (Directors Guild of America) trainee assisting first assistant director John Nicolella on *Crazy Joe*. While Singleton doesn't have many memories of the film, he did share one humorous anecdote with me: "Here's a thing that I find amusing," Singleton says. "John Nicolella and I went scouting for locations with the director and the cinematographer on a survey, as you do. You always do a tech survey whenever you start a movie with all the department heads. So we got in the van and surveyed the various locations. One of them was Rahway State Prison, where one of the principal characters is in maximum security. So we got Rahway, and we go to all of these other locations. What usually happens is all the keys, like the cinematographer, the art director, are with the director and the producer and the production manager, and they're talking and going over things as they see the locations to make notes. But the unfortunate situation was, the cinematographer and the director were both Italian. The producer of the movie is Dino De Laurentiis. So the whole survey is conducted in Italian. As they talked out the locations, I was thinking this is no problem, because John Nicolella is Italian. We got back from the survey and I said, 'Okay, John, what do we do?' He said, 'Ralph, I don't know.' I said, 'Why?' He said, 'I don't speak Italian.'"

Filming of *Crazy Joe* began on June 25, 1973, and the film was shot entirely on location in New York City on a modest budget of $250,000. The film, an American/Italian co-production, was released theatrically in Italy on February 8, 1974, and in the United States a week later on February 15, 1974.

Reviews were lukewarm, as was the box-office take. In *Time* magazine, Steve Vineberg wrote, "I doubt that anyone was looking forward to another post-*Godfather* Mafia bloodbath, but I had a hunch that *Crazy Joe* might be worth seeing because it was directed by Carlo Lizzani, who has a reputation in some film circles as the director of the rarely seen gangster melodrama *The Violent Four* [1968]. It's easy to see, inside of ten minutes, if Lizzani is going to do anything with *Crazy Joe* it would have to be to transcend it—but after another half hour, it becomes apparent that he isn't going to. *Crazy Joe* is directed well enough, but that's hardly a compliment to Lizzani. The movie is so repulsive that solid direction can only be a confirmation of its repulsiveness." Andrew Sarris of the *Village Voice* was equally unimpressed, writing, "There is not too much to say about *Crazy Joe* as a movie. Dino De Laurentiis does another documentary fantasy number in the manner of *The Valachi Papers*, which is to say the real persons are the models for the cartoon characterizations.... With no compelling central performance and no style around the edges, the mind is left free to wander among a great many peripheral topics."

Death Wish

The seed for a vigilante story planted itself in NYC author Brian Garfield's brain after an assailant mugged his wife on the subway. The idea might have faded away like so many ideas do (who has time to write them all?), but then Garfield experienced a second incident. This time, the author's car was vandalized and looted. This caused him to once again consider a vigilante tale—these violations had summoned something primal within him. Soon after, Garfield completed his novel *Death Wish*.

The novel, released by David McKay Publishing in 1972, received little to no fanfare. There were a few reviews published here and there, but the book was not a hit. Despite this, film producers Hal Landers and Bobby Roberts (*Monte Walsh* [1970]) optioned the film rights (as part of a two-book option that also included *Relentless*). The producers invited Garfield to write the screenplay, but Garfield wasn't interested. In truth, he didn't think the novel could be adapted to film.

Screenwriter Wendell Mayes, who had previously received an Oscar nomination for his work on *Anatomy of a Murder* (1959), was then hired to write a script. The screenplay was good and restructured the story so it would work as a film, but there wasn't much studio interest. United Artists was attached to the project for a while but eventually walked away. Sidney Lumet considered directing Jack Lemmon as the vigilante. But soon Lumet became distracted by *Serpico* (1973) and went off to make that instead.

Eventually, Brit Michael Winner was brought in to make the film. While shopping the script, Landers and Roberts had bandied about a number of actors' names to play the lead, including Henry Fonda, Walter Matthau, and Lee Marvin. However, any question about who would be cast died when Winner was hired. Since Winner had just made two films with stone-faced tough guy Charles Bronson (*Chato's Land* and *The Mechanic* [both 1972]) and was working on a third (*The Stone Killer* [1973]) at the time, there was little doubt that Bronson would play the vigilante protagonist. Winner later told author Paul Talbot, "I said to Charlie, 'This is a wonderful script.' He said, 'I'd like to do it.' I said, 'The film?' He said, 'No, shoot muggers.'" Bronson then signed on to star in the film. Bronson's agent would try to talk him out of making *Death Wish*, but the actor was insistent.

"The Winner and Bronson marriage was made in heaven," assistant director Ralph Singleton says. "Winner's relationship with Bronson was great. You did not take one of them on without taking them both on. And Bronson, if you gave him the space, which we did, was fine. He hit his marks, said his lines. He was never a problem on set. He was a real pro. He knew why he was there. And Michael would do anything for him."

1974: Murder Is Down, But NYC Has a *Death Wish* / 119

According to *Death Wish* expert Talbot, the reason for the actor and director's collaborative partnership was simple: "Winner knew that if he had Bronson plus an appropriate script and a modest budget, the resulting movie was guaranteed to make a profit. Bronson didn't like to spend more than eight hours per day on a movie set, and he knew Winner never shot numerous takes or extraneous footage. They were the perfect director/star team for efficient action pictures in the 1970s."

With Winner and Bronson attached, the producers still had difficulty getting a studio to make the film. Eventually Dino De Laurentiis (*La Strada* [1954]), a friend and former collaborator of Winner's, attached himself to the project. Despite Paramount Pictures having passed on the film twice, De Laurentiis convinced them to reverse their decision. *Death Wish* would be made with a $3 million budget and a forty-day shooting schedule.

The film went into production in February 1974, and Winner's frequent collaborator Gerald Wilson took another pass at the script, changing the protagonist's last name and toughening him up. Interestingly, Bronson attempted to convince De Laurentiis to move the film to Los Angeles, but the producer refused. *Death Wish* had New York City in its DNA, and De Laurentiis knew better than to change that. Aside from a couple of scenes that take place in Tucson, Arizona, and Pasadena, California, the film would be shot on location all over NYC.

Paul Kersey's (Bronson) apartment was shot at 33 Riverside Drive at West 75th Street on the West Side of Manhattan. He busts a cap in his first mugger at the nearby Riverside Park. The office where Kersey works is located at 2 Park Avenue at 32nd Street in Murray Hill. When he obtains two rolls of quarters to put inside a sock to pummel bad guys, he gets the coins from the Central Savings Bank at 2100 Broadway. Kersey shoots his last three muggers (in this film anyway) north of Grant's Tomb, west of the Riverside Drive split. Other locations that appear in the film are the now-closed D'Agostino Supermarket on the corner of West 75th Street and Broadway in Manhattan, the Grand Central Terminal (pretending to be the Chicago Union Station), and the Brooklyn Bridge. When Winner and company needed a cemetery to shoot the funeral scene in, Ralph Singleton told them about the Jamaica Avenue cemetery location he'd secured for *Come Back Charleston Blue* (1972), so Cypress Hills Cemetery was used for *Death Wish* too.

Of the director, Singleton recalls, "Michael Winner could be an absolute son of a bitch. Tough guy. He was the writer/producer/director. And that's the most powerful person in the world. You don't mess with someone who's in that position. The situation with Winner was, he didn't demand loyalty from the department heads, but he got loyalty. They were very solid around him. He ran a very tough ship. It was good to see it, but he really wasn't the easiest person to be around. He was reasonable as long as you didn't try to screw him up. You never hustled him. If you didn't know, just say you didn't know. Don't try to fake him out. He was too smart for that." The assistant director adds, "I went to Winner when I worked with him again on *The Sentinel* in 1978. *Death Wish* was, of course, the biggest hit he'd ever had. I said to Winner, 'I looked at your career, Michael.' He was a real prick, but I liked him. I said, 'You did all these beautiful films in the early part of your career. Very sweet. Very adept character-driven pieces. And now you're doing *Chato's Land* and *Death Wish*. Why?' And he said, 'Because those weren't making any money.' And that was his drive. He didn't want to make art. He wanted to make successful commercial pictures."

Of the film's star, Singleton recalls, "Bronson could be difficult, and when he didn't memorize his lines, which did happen, he would garble his lines and then blame it on the sound mixer. And Jimmy Sabat, who was one of the best sound mixers in the business at the time, hated taking the heat for that."

Death Wish was released on July 24, 1974, a mere five months after shooting had begun. Many critics, as well as novelist Garfield, climbed onto their soapboxes to speak out against the film's violence. Actor Stuart Margolin later recalled an incident with *Shock Cinema*'s Anthony Petkovich: "When *Death Wish* was released, I thought, 'Oh, this is gonna be a big hit,' and I went to a theater over at UCLA, in Westwood, where they had kind of a premiere. And after the movie, there was a man on the phone saying [angrily], 'I want this movie taken out of every theater in America!' And it was Charles Champlin, the *LA Times* critic.

Guys like Champlin thought it was a very dangerous movie regarding vigilantism and stuff like that." Despite its naysayers, *Death Wish* became a smash hit—especially in New York City. The film resonated with the NYC audiences who were fed up with the violence and crime infesting the streets. As a result, *Death Wish* broke NYC theater house records.

"The movie had an added subtext for the New Yorkers who recognized the actual locations where the on-screen muggers lurked," Talbot says. "Audience members who had been victims of crime themselves screamed and applauded with delight as Bronson responded on-screen the way they wished they could have in real life. Producer Bobby Roberts and novelist Brian Garfield both told me that when they attended screenings, the audience stood up and cheered every time Bronson shot a mugger."

Death Wish, a cult favorite today, spawned four sequels and a number of rip-offs. Garfield wrote a sequel novel titled *Death Sentence*, which was adapted to film by director James Wan in 2007. *Death Wish* was remade by Eli Roth into an inferior film starring Bruce Willis in 2018. Garfield, Winner, and Bronson are all dead and buried, but it appears that nothing can stop the *Death Wish* train from rolling along.

The Education of Sonny Carson

Producer Irwin Yablans had only one credit (*Badge 373* [1973]) to his name before making *The Education of Sonny Carson*. Taking note of the fact that blaxploitation films were making big money, Yablans wanted to make something more positive and set his sights on making a movie about growing up in the ghetto in the 1950s. He was then introduced to Robert "Sonny" Carson, an outspoken civil rights activist who had just penned a memoir. Carson had been a promising honors student who joined a street gang. This led Carson down a dark path, and at the age of sixteen he became the youngest person ever incarcerated in the Sing Sing Correctional Facility.

Yablans optioned Carson's book (agreeing to split profits 50/50) and hired a screenwriter named Frank Hudson to help him fashion a treatment. After they were finished, Yablans presented it to his brother, Paramount Pictures president Frank Yablans, and got a greenlight to make the picture with a $1 million budget. The production quickly hit a snag, however, when Carson was indicted for murder (and was soon after convicted of kidnapping). Yablans forked over $50,000 for bail, and Carson was released so he could work as technical advisor on the film.

Yablans hired a white director named Michael Campus, who had just made another "black" film called *The Mack* (1973). "There were some people when I was making *The Mack*, and even more so with *Sonny Carson*, who said, 'What qualifies you to tell this story? Why isn't there an African American director doing this?'" Campus said. "I think you have to look at my childhood. I was born on the Upper West Side. I was the product of parents who were very left wing, parents who utterly believed in equality long before it was fashionable to do so. And the search for equality, for the expression of humanity became my mantra—the driving force in my life."

Rony Clanton, who portrayed Sonny Carson in the film, believes Campus' ability to portray black life so accurately comes from his being a true artist. "Mike is an artist, you know?" Clanton says. "He just wants to tell the truth. There's no other way but to tell the truth when you do the work. And when you have the right people around you as artists, you just tell the truth. Some of it is great, some of it is not as great. But as long as it's truthful and honest . . . Then the people who are playing in it, they just tell their truth."

White or no, Campus proved himself to be the perfect director for the film, not simply because of his artistry and passion for the project, but because he'd already learned ways to maneuver around the difficulties of shooting a film in gang-controlled urban areas on *The Mack*. On that film, which he'd shot in Oakland, Campus had hired Bobby Seale and the Black Panthers to protect the production. On *The Education of Sonny Carson*, Yablans and Campus would be shooting a film about street gangs in Brooklyn, where the turf was divvied up by four major gangs. Campus, through Carson, negotiated with them. "Nobody did nothing because Sonny Carson was involved,"

Clanton recalls. "He was very well-respected. Nobody messed with Sonny."

Another factor was Yablans and Campus' decision to cast the film (outside of a few primary roles) with real-life gang members. Nearly two thousand gang members were interviewed as potential actors. In the end, "several hundred" were cast. "They were all gang members," Clanton says of his costars. "There were guys that were the presidents of the major gangs in Harlem. I remember coming on the set and some of the gang members saying, 'Don't worry about a thing. We got you protected.' And they pulled out their pieces and showed them to me."

"Kato," the supreme president of the Tomahawks street gang, was initially cast but was arrested and charged with murder prior to shooting. He was then replaced in the film by "Champ," who became the new Tomahawks leader in Kato's absence. "I'm really enjoying it," Champ told *New York Times* reporter Paul L. Montgomery. "Only thing is, seems like as soon as we started the film, the cops started busting us."

Rony Clanton's casting as Sonny Carson is an interesting story. "I was making my rounds in New York City as an actor, slipping photographs and resumes under different casting directors' doors," Clanton explains. "As my day was dwindling down, I went to a telephone booth and picked up the phone. I said, 'Dear heavenly father, please send me a vehicle that'll put my work out there into the world and let everybody see your work through me. In Jesus Christ's name, amen.' And I hung up the telephone." A couple of weeks later, Clanton was called to audition. "Sonny Carson was there when I auditioned," Clanton recalls. "He was part of the audition process. On the first day of auditions, he came out and said, 'Listen, man, you're gonna play me in this movie. Don't worry about a thing.' That was before I was cast. Sonny was hands-on on this movie. No matter what was going on around me, final call, he said, 'You're gonna be in that movie.'" Clanton, a trained method actor, believes Carson recognized something in him that caused him to select him. "Sonny saw my rhythms. I grew up on the Lower East Side. I grew up in the projects. I grew up around gangs, you know? I knew that whole situation. I wasn't a gang member, but I was there. I saw all of those things, like people shooting up and people with their guns killing somebody."

In the middle of the shoot, Yablans told the *New York Times* that the filmmakers were "trying to show what the black experience was like without resorting to the usual *Super Fly* [1972] crime and sex stuff. There are no pushers, no mayhem." While Yablans' description sounds nice, it's not entirely accurate since *The Education of Sonny Carson* is a film about street gangs and gang violence. It also has a protagonist who is imprisoned for robbing and assaulting someone. The underlying theme of the film, however, is a positive one. Campus told interviewer Wilson Morales in 2002, "It's the story of the descent of this young person and his redemption as he finds a way out, which is really what happened. Sonny emerges from prison and, as we know, became a civic leader in Brooklyn. His message is very clear: save yourself, and once you've done that, save others."

While Campus' film is rough around the edges, it does a superb job of conveying the hopelessness and despair the young gang members feel. In one scene, a cop tells Sonny that his "kind" should be locked in cages from the day they're born. To this, the young Carson replies matter-of-factly, "We already are." In another scene, Sonny and his friends fantasize about living lives where they can do strange and exotic things. While fantasies of flying an airplane to the sun or commandeering a ship through the streets of Brooklyn aren't realistic, they capture the boys' innocent naivety and longing to escape the world they're confined to. However, when one of the boys dreams of becoming a pimp, the dreamlike quality of the moment is shattered, and the boys (and the audience) are immediately snapped back to the boys' reality.

When *The Education of Sonny Carson* was released on July 17, 1974, it received largely positive reviews, with critics commenting on the film's less-than-polished presentation but agreeing that it was a touching film with merit.

When one reflects on the film, two scenes stand out as being the most effective. The first depicts Sonny's father (Paul Benjamin) visiting him in Sing Sing. Carson tearfully begs his father to raise his head and look at him, but the older man can't bear to see his son behind bars. In this scene, Rony Clanton is so extraordinarily effective that the viewer feels like a voyeur observing something private. "In that scene in the jail, Mike [Campus] didn't want me to cry," Clanton says. "He said, 'Don't cry, Rony.' But me coming from my truth, and working with Paul Benjamin, that's what came out of that moment."

The other truly memorable and affecting scene is one where Sonny is brutalized by police officers in the station house basement. "It was a terrible beating that lasted about thirty minutes," Campus says. "On film, it lasts about one minute. When I first screened the film out here in California, somebody in the audience jumped up and said, 'How could you do that? How could you subject us to that?' It felt like it lasted forever. It didn't last forever—it lasted a minute. Sonny later said to the audience, 'If you had lived through what I lived through—if you had been subjected to that full thirty minutes that I went through—the theater would have been empty.'"

The Education of Sonny Carson wasn't screened in many theaters, so it didn't have a chance to make the splash it should have. "I thought that film would really put my career out there in a big way, but you know, things happen the way they happen for us artists," Clanton reflects. "But I've always wondered why that movie didn't take off like it should have. Sometimes you've got so much truth out there that maybe it's best to keep it uncovered."

The Education of Sonny Carson is woefully under-seen and underappreciated. While it came close to falling into obscurity, it's been rediscovered and embraced by the hip-hop community with artists such as Wu-Tang Clan, Ghostface Killah, AZ, Common, Mobb Deep, and Lauryn Hill sampling its dialogue in their songs.

The Gambler

James Toback, a City College lecturer and the author of a strangely self-centered biography of football star Jim Brown, set out to write a "blatantly autobiographical" (Toback's words) novel about his struggles with a gambling addiction. Gene Rudolf, who later worked as production designer on Toback's film *Fingers* (1977), says, "*The Gambler* is pretty much Jimmy Toback's story. He said, 'You never know you're a gambler until you have to hand someone two shopping bags full of cash in the backseat of a Cadillac!' Jimmy could not pass a pay phone on the street without trying to make a call and place a bet. So, *The Gambler* was very much the Jimmy Toback story." Because he was influenced by Fyodor Dostoevsky, Toback named the novel *The Gambler*, lifting its title from the Russian author's 1867 novel of the same title. (The piece was also influenced by the novels of Norman Mailer.) However, Toback eventually recognized his story was better suited to a screenplay than a novel, so he switched mediums.

Toback completed the first draft of his script in 1972. When this draft of the script was completed, he approached a young actor named Robert De Niro through a mutual friend. De Niro loved the script and agreed to play the lead role. Toback then hooked up with agent Mike Medavoy, who optioned the script and vowed to get the picture made.

When Medavoy told Toback that he needed a big-name actor attached as lead and suggested Robert Redford, the screenwriter was insistent that De Niro play the lead. To this, Medavoy said, "Then you need a star director." Medavoy suggested Karel Reisz, but the screenwriter wasn't familiar with his work. Medavoy explained to him that Reisz, along with filmmakers John Schlesinger, Tony Richardson, Lindsay Anderson, and Jack Clayton, was a part of the "British New Wave." True to his word, Medavoy persuaded Reisz, who'd never made an American film and hadn't directed a movie since 1968's *Isadora*, to make the movie. With Reisz attached, Medavoy secured a deal with Paramount in less than a week. At that point, the studio assigned producers Irwin Winkler and Robert Chartoff to oversee the production.

When Toback told Reisz that De Niro *had* to play the lead role, Reisz agreed to have dinner with the actor to size him up. After the dinner, Reisz called Toback and told him the actor was "too common." He went on to tell Toback, "I want to make the movie you want me to make, but not with him." When De Niro learned that Reisz wouldn't even allow him to audition, he suggested that Toback threaten to quit. By this time, however, the screenwriter understood that this was a battle he could not win. Eventually, Reisz cast another young actor, James Caan, who was in demand after having just been nominated for an Oscar for his turn in *The Godfather* (1972). "Caan became a great Axel Freed," Toback later wrote in *Vanity Fair*, "although obviously different from the character Robert De Niro would have created."

Having read Toback's book about Jim Brown, Reisz saw abundant possibilities for making the film more powerful. As such, he urged the screenwriter to dig deeper and lean further into the autobiographical aspects of the story. Reisz and Toback then worked together on the script for more than a year, fleshing it out and developing the story. While Reisz was not a screenwriter and didn't ask for a writing credit, he had a reputation for working closely with his writers to make the films the very best they could be.

The Gambler was shot on location in New York City. However, as Matthew Asprey Gear, the author and film journalist who performed the 2021 commentary for the film, observes, "The New York that we see in *The Gambler* is nowhere near as horrifyingly gritty as we see in [Toback's next film, 1978's] *Fingers*." Taking this a step further, it's safe to say that, although the film's storyline focuses on the dark underbelly of the city, *The Gambler* is visually different (and cleaner) than most of the other NYC crime films of the Seventies, which almost all seemed hell-bent on accentuating the lowest, seediest aspects of the city.

Humorously, when editor Roger Spottiswoode called Sue Kingsley to hire her to work on the film as his assistant editor, she'd never heard of James Caan, so she thought he said "James Coburn." As a result, Kingsley walked around for the next month believing she would be working with Coburn. Spottiswoode, Kingsley, and Jim Rivera were editing the film in London while it was being shot, so they were able to complete their first cut about a month after shooting commenced. Reisz then traveled to London and assisted editing for another year.

The film was released in the United States on December 4, 1974. The film's box office was middling, and critics were divided. Charles Champlin of the *Los Angeles Times* praised *The Gambler*, calling it "a cool, hard, perfectly cut gem of a movie, as brilliant and mysteriously deep as a fine diamond. At its center is an hypnotically absorbing performance, at once charming and dismaying, by James Caan, who must certainly have an Academy Award nomination for it." Roger Ebert of the *Chicago Sun-Times* gave the film four stars (of a possible four), writing that it "begins as a portrait of Axel Freed's personality, develops into the story of his world, and then pays off as a thriller. We become so absolutely contained by Axel's problems and dangers that they seem like our own." However, the *New York Times'* Vincent Canby wasn't having any of it, writing, "The movie follows Axel's downward path with such care that you keep thinking there must be some illuminating purpose, but there isn't. . . . Mr. Reisz and Mr. Toback reportedly worked a couple of years putting the screenplay into this shape, which is lifeless."

Sadly, awards season wasn't friendly to the film, which received only one nomination (and zero wins)—a Golden Globe nom—for Caan's performance. *The Gambler* was later remade in 2014 with Rupert Wyatt directing Mark Wahlberg in the lead role.

The Godfather Part II

Can you catch lightning in a bottle twice? Paramount Pictures hoped so when they green-lit this sequel to Francis Ford Coppola's massively successful film *The Godfather* (1972). With dollar signs in their eyes, the studio was excited about the prospect of a sequel. Coppola, however, was not. He joked that he would make a sequel only if he could make something akin to *Abbott and Costello Meet the Godfather*. Coppola wanted to make (what he saw as being) more ambitious films like *The Conversation* (1974), which he made through his own Zoetrope Studios.

Coppola suggested that Martin Scorsese, hot off a minor success with *Mean Streets* (1993), direct the picture with Coppola as producer. But Robert Evans, Paramount's head of production, who had also produced *The Godfather*, swore (for some reason) that Scorsese would never direct a film for Paramount. Additionally, Paramount CEO Charles Bludhorn was determined to have a sequel directed by Coppola. Paramount also had ideas for the film's story. These included storylines in which the new Godfather was killed or imprisoned. Coppola hated these ideas, and that hatred, along with a desire to maintain the purity of his characters, was part of the reason he eventually agreed to come back. When he finally agreed to take on the project, he did so with three conditions. The first was that the studio would have absolutely no say over the screenplay, direction, or casting. The second, perhaps most important condition to Coppola, was that Robert Evans could not be involved in any way. Evans had done everything in his power to hamstring Coppola and make the experience of making the first film a nightmare for him. (This included attempts to block Coppola's casting choices and threatening to fire him, even going so far as to have a backup director on set who could replace him at any moment.) This time, producer Albert S. Ruddy would also be absent. Coppola had nothing against Ruddy (as far as I know), but both Evans and Ruddy had attempted to take credit for much of *The Godfather*'s successes. (This is key.) Coppola's third condition for returning was that the film had to be titled *The Godfather Part II*. Coppola insisted it could be nothing else. Interestingly, Bludhorn had no problems with the first two conditions but balked at this. According to Coppola, Bludhorn believed audiences would think it was just the second half of the film they had already seen. Eventually, Bludhorn stepped aside and allowed Coppola to have his way, making *The Godfather Part II* the first American sequel with a sequence number in its title.

Coppola's primary interest in finally choosing to return to the Corleone family was the opportunity for him to show Michael's self-destruction and the immense pain and doubt that had come from his decisions, and him trying to live with that. The ever-ambitious Coppola decided that he wanted to depict two storylines simultaneously: the rise of Vito Corleone in the early 1900s and the transition of the family and its eventual decline under the leadership of son Michael after World War II. The screenwriter/director had already been toying with the idea of showing storylines in different time frames following a father and his son, but in this context he saw that idea made sense. By the time Coppola came on board, the studio had already commissioned Mario Puzo, the creator of *The Godfather*, to write a first draft. Although Puzo received credit as a co-writer, most of what would appear in *The Godfather Part II* was written by Coppola (or lifted from Puzo's novel and then rewritten by Coppola).

Casting the role of the young Vito Corleone would be key. Obviously, Marlon Brando, who had played the role in the first film, was way too old to return for these scenes. (Interestingly, Brando had agreed to return for a cameo in the birthday reunion scene but was ultimately a no-show. Since the scene was written with the character included, Coppola was forced to rewrite the scene so Vito's presence is implied but not shown.) Coppola wound up auditioning and casting thirty-year-old Robert De Niro, an actor he'd cast in a small role in the original film who ended up leaving to do a different film. While De Niro didn't look like Brando, there was something about his demeanor and the way he composed himself that made Coppola believe he was right for the part.

Pacino introduced Coppola to his mentor, Actor's Studio teacher Lee Strasberg, as a possibility to essay the Meyer Lansky–inspired role of Hyman Roth. Strasberg landed the role. Another inspired casting choice was *A Hatful of Rain* playwright Michael V. Gasso to play wiseguy Frankie Pentangeli. One of the aspects of making *The Godfather Part II* that intrigued Coppola was the opportunity to show that, as the Corleones have gained stature and respectability, the types of enemies they faced were changing; while there were still vengeful mobsters plotting their demise, now there were also scheming politicians. The primary character Coppola would use to portray this was Senator Pat Geary. For the role of Geary, Coppola and his casting directors hired G. D. Spradlin, who had worked mostly in television. According to Coppola, the actor rewrote all of his

1974: Murder Is Down, But NYC Has a *Death Wish* / 131

lines, primarily in an attempt to make his part bigger. The director loved Spradlin's contributions and used most of the lines in the film.

Going with the "if it ain't broke, don't fix it" line of thought, Coppola brought back many collaborators from the first film. Aside from Brando, pretty much all of the original cast returned. Also returning was cinematographer Gordon Willis, editors Barry Malkin and Peter Zinner, production designer Dean Tavoularis, and composer Nino Rota. Also, Coppola promoted casting director Fred Roos to the role of producer. Coppola would later say that he and Gordon Willis worked well together on *The Godfather Part II*, whereas they'd had some minor difficulties on the original film. Having collaborated on one of the greatest films ever made, the two creatives had likely gained respect for each other.

The shoot began on October 23, 1973, at Lake Tahoe. While a significant portion of the film was shot in New York City, other locations included Sicily, Las Vegas, Los Angeles, Cuba, and, again, Lake Tahoe. As for the NYC locations, most of the De Niro/Vito scenes were shot on East 6th Street with the Manhattan area dressed as early 1900s Little Italy. Most film buffs will remember the scenes that take place at Ellis Island (in which Vito becomes Vito *Corleone*). However, they might be shocked to learn that the Ellis Island interior scenes were actually filmed in Italy. The shoot lasted 104 days and wrapped in May 1974, coming in on a budget of $13 million.

With the film scheduled to be released in mid-December, the editing process was a fairly quick one. When the film screened two weeks before its release, the screening was a disaster. Coppola then returned to the editing bay, cutting and moving around scenes. Editor Walter Murch would later explain the primary change; the earlier version had gone back and forth between the past and present-day scenes more frequently, confusing the audience, so in the final release cut, the film alternated roughly half as many times. As the film headed into release, no one involved knew what to expect. Coppola and his team were too close to the project to see it objectively.

The film was released on December 18, 1974, and Coppola was finally able to relax; the critics loved *The Godfather Part II*. The film would be another huge success, earning $47.96 million at the box office. While this was less than a fifth of what the first film had made, it was still a hit, and there was no doubt that this was a *good* picture. *The Godfather Part II* received an impressive ten Academy Award nominations. (This was one less nomination than the first film had received.) Coppola took home three Oscars for Best Picture (with producers Roos and Gray Frederickson), Best Screenplay (with Puzo), and Best Director. Half the cast was recognized, with Al Pacino, De Niro, Talia Shire, Lee Strasberg, and Michael V. Gazzo all receiving nominations. De Niro was the only actor to win.

The Godfather Part II is frequently cited as *the* greatest sequel ever made, and some cineastes even argue that it's even better than the first film. With *The Godfather Part II* having been made without the participation of either Robert Evans or Albert Ruddy, it's safe to say that the true creative force behind *The Godfather* was Coppola (and, to a lesser extent, Puzo).

The Super Cops

In the wake of *The French Connection* (1971), studio execs were on the lookout for stories about real-life cops with extraordinary stories. So, when journalist Peter Maas penned a book about NYPD whistleblower Frank Serpico, the film rights were quickly snatched up. During this period, L. H. Whittemore wrote a book called *The Super Cops: The True Story of the Cops Called Batman and Robin* about a couple of unorthodox NYPD officers named David Greenberg and Robert Hantz. MGM optioned the film rights and immediately moved forward with a *Super Cops* biopic. Unlike *The French Connection* and *Serpico* (1973), however, *The Super Cops* would (for some odd reason) be a comedy.

With producer William Belasco leading the charge, a team was assembled to make the film. The script was written by Lorenzo Semple Jr., the screenwriter responsible for *The Parallax View* (1974) and *Three Days of the Condor* (1975). Gordon Parks, who was still hot from the successive (and successful) pictures *Shaft* (1971) and *Shaft's Big Score* (1972), was brought in to helm the film. The *Super Cops* team would also include Richard Kratina, the cinematographer who had lensed *Love Story* (1970) and *Born to Win* (1971).

Perhaps the most significant additions to the team were the actors who would play the titular characters. Ron Leibman, an NYC actor who'd come to Hollywood by way of the Actors Studio and had previously appeared in *Where's Poppa?* (1970), *The Hot Rock* (1972), and *Slaughterhouse Five* (1972), was cast to play David Greenberg. Although Michael Landon had expressed interest in playing Hantz, the filmmakers cast David Selby, an actor who had made a name for himself playing werewolf Quinton Collins on the television series *Dark Shadows* (1968–1971). To learn more about their characters, Leibman and Selby spent time with the real Greenberg and Hantz. Among the things the cops taught them were how police officers covered their partners, how they pursued suspects, the proper ways to search all of the rooms in an apartment, and how to forcibly remove suspects from their cars and frisk them.

"At first, when I read the script, I didn't even know David Greenberg existed," Leibman told the *New York Post*. "When I found out, I wasn't sure I wanted to meet him because I didn't want my portrayal influenced. . . . But as it turned out, we don't interfere with each other. I'm playing my own fantasy and using my own experience. It just happens that knowing Dave has [shown me] that a cop can be more intelligent, more in touch, and more caring than I had thought." The two men became friends and developed a friendship. Just as Leibman had nice things to say about Greenberg, Greenberg said equally nice things about the actor; Greenberg told *New York Times* reporter Phyllis Funke that Liebman was "just like me. He's just as crazy if not crazier." Greenberg went on to say, "I wish I could play a cop as well as he does."

Before the shoot began, black Muslims approached Belasco and offered to protect the cast and crew as they filmed in Bedford-Stuyvesant, which was one of the most dangerous neighborhoods in New York. The Muslims would also provide food on the set. "I had a huge black bodyguard named something like 36X," Leibman explained. "He wouldn't talk to me, wasn't friendly, but he did his job. About six months after we finished shooting the movie, I see the guy's picture in the paper and he was arrested for murder. I give a lot of credit to the cops and our protectors. The food wasn't very good, though."

Before filming, Gordon Parks explained his intent for the film to the *New York Times*, stating that his goal was to capture the "stark reality" of the cops' story. Filming began near the Brooklyn Bridge. The two leads, Leibman and Selby, became friendly and carpooled to the shoot each day. They also performed their own stunts, including a scene atop a wrecking ball. One early problem the technical advisors had to address was the actors' inauthentic diction and vocabulary. "It made everyone in Bedford-Stuyvesant sound as if they possessed doctorates in English," Greenberg said. While shooting in Bed-Stuy, the crew encountered hostile locals who sometimes refused to move out of the way. Not wanting to engage with them, Parks opted to simply film the scenes with the intruders in the shots.

"Do you know what I really remember about making *Super Cops*?" Selby says. "Gordon Parks. He was the best. He was wonderful. He hadn't directed much at that time, but he was the best. He stood by his actors, and he helped us however he could. He was our leader, our commander." Filming locations included old warehouses and the interiors of actual police stations. Although the entire film was scheduled to be shot in New York, the studio changed the plan midway through the shoot. "We were having trouble in New York," Selby recalls. "We got behind and I guess we were over budget, and they felt they needed to do something different. So, one of the producers came to the set one day and told us we were shutting down and they were moving us to LA." The remaining scenes would be shot at the MGM lot.

While working in Los Angeles, Liebman and Hantz also recorded ADR (Automated Dialogue Replacement) for scenes with poor sound. As the actors recorded their lines, Parks was upstairs in a meeting with the producer. "He came back down to the room where we were working," Selby says. "I asked him,

'How'd it go?' And he said, 'It went fine.' I can't remember exactly what he said, but I recall him saying, 'I hit him!' I said, 'What?!' He said, 'I socked him! I reached across the table and took a swing at him.' That was Gordon taking up for us."

The Super Cops was released on March 20, 1974, only four months after *Serpico* (1973) had been released. Neither critics nor moviegoers (or, in this case, movie-not-goers) were enthusiastic about the cop comedy. Despite the film's lackluster reception, Red Circle Comics released a one-off *Super Cops* comic book. Additionally, a half-hour pilot for a proposed television series starring Steven Keats and Alan Feinstein aired on CBS.

Unfortunately, the real-life "super cops," David Greenberg and Robert Hantz, would prove to be less than super; Hantz would be demoted and leave the department in disgrace after being busted for pot in 1975. Greenberg would go to jail in 1978 for mail fraud and obstruction of justice and then again a decade later for overstating the burglary losses of a business he owned and for more mail fraud. In 2012, a book by former Knapp Commission counsel Michael F. Armstrong revealed that Greenberg and Hantz had been investigated by the Brooklyn DA for the murder of two drug dealers. Armstrong also alleged that the duo robbed, shook down, and assaulted a number of suspects.

The Taking of Pelham One Two Three

The Taking of Pelham One Two Three first existed as a novel by John Godey (a pen name for author Morton Freedgood) published by Putnam in 1973. The story about criminals taking control of a subway car for ransom sparked enough interest that the film rights were snatched up and the paperback rights were purchased by Dell for $450,000 prior to the book's publication.

When the film's producers initially approached the New York Transit Authority about shooting the film in their tunnel and using one of their trains, the Transit Authority refused. This came at the height of skyjacking (the International Civil Aviation Organization reported in 1970 that there were an astounding 118 incidents of "unlawful seizure of an airplane" between January 1969 and the end of June 1970). Aware of this, the Transit Authority worried that the film might inspire a new subway-train-hijacking trend. While the studio continued trying to convince the city to let them make the film there, a number of other cities with subway systems were considered as backup locations. However, the New York Transit Authority eventually gave in.

There was a period in which the filmmakers negotiated with the city on exactly where they could shoot. Art director Gene Rudolf recalls, "We shut down at the start of the film while we were talking about where it was going to be made. Because the construction crew was already on it, they just came in and played cards in the morning and then went out to lunch and took the rest of the day off for at least four weeks." In the end, the city allowed the filmmakers to shoot in the Court Street Station for the sum of $250,000.

However, the Transit Authority had one stipulation: the filmmakers could not show any graffiti on the trains. This was laughable because the New York City subways were covered in graffiti at the time. They believed showing the graffiti would glorify it. Wanting to make a film that was gritty and realistic, producers Gabriel Katzka and Edgar J. Scherick begged that they be allowed to show the subway cars as they really were, but the Transit Authority would not relent.

Peter Stone was tapped to write the script. Joseph Sargent, a veteran filmmaker who had made the Burt Reynolds vehicle *White Lightning* (1973) the year before, was hired to direct. Recognizing how important having the right actors would be for a picture that takes place mostly inside a single enclosed space, the producers assembled an impressive cast featuring Walter Matthau, Robert Shaw, Martin Balsam, and Hector Elizondo.

Matthau's son, Charles, who directed his father in three films, believes the film's casting is a key reason why *The Taking of Pelham One Two Three* works as well as it does. "I think my dad was the perfect foil for Robert Shaw, who was a scary, larger-than-life villain," he says. "My dad was just sort of a regular guy who figures it all out through his determination and street smarts. I think that's why the original works so much better than the remake. Because when you see Denzel Washington playing the detective, you sort of expect him to come out on top; whereas the character my dad played was really more of an everyman. I think that was just better casting. It's a matter of getting the right actors for the parts, and I think the casting was spot-on."

Because the film shot six weeks aboveground (for the Matthau scenes) and six weeks underground, Rudolf says, "It was kind of like making two movies. You've got the aboveground movie, and then you've got the underground movie." Rudolf was tasked with constructing a giant Transit Authority office. "That was the biggest interior stage set I built until *Raging Bull* [1980]," he says. "It was really big. That set was 106 feet long, and God knows how many feet wide. And only eight feet high because it was full ceiling. And every ceiling piece in there was hinged so it could be lit from the top if we had to set the lights above it. I told Joe Sargent, 'This is the world's biggest phone booth!' He said, 'What do you mean?' 'After Matthau picks up the telephone, he's anchored to it; he can't go anyplace else.' So I had to make this set so that it looked interesting from every angle. It had to be able to be photographed from every bloody angle."

Some of the actors found director Sargent, who had worked primarily in television, difficult to work with because his methods were different from what they were accustomed to. Robert Shaw was the primary dissenter, and he challenged the director constantly throughout the shoot. Adding to the difficulties, the crew had to wear surgical masks whenever the trains moved because of the ridiculous amount of dust that filled the tunnel.

According to Gene Rudolf, Sargent and producer Edgar Scherick got into an explosive argument one day during lunch. The argument, about the film's schedule, resulted in one man hurling salad dressing at the other. Although Rudolf won't say who threw the salad dressing, he recalls being a victim of collateral damage when some of the dressing got on him. "I had clothes on that smelled like vinegar for the rest of the day," he laments. With all these problems, it's not surprising that Sargent would later call this the most difficult shoot of his career.

Most agree that the film succeeded in capturing the authentic flavor of early 1970s New York City. In the 2016 documentary *12 Minutes with Mr. Grey*, Hector Elizondo observed, "New York was on its knees for quite a few reasons. Fiscally, it was in great, great distress. The petty crime and the quality of life was almost demoralizing. It was before they had decided to—they meaning the New York police—to shift their focus from the big crime problems they were dealing with to the street quality of life issues, the broken windows issues they called it. It was just before that turn. So New York was in trouble. Also, there was graffiti smeared . . . it was just a symptom of what New York was going through. Everything was graffiti'd. Nothing was sacred. No space was sacred. It was a canvas for the graffiti artists. That's what they called themselves, and some were quite exceptional. My son, as a matter of fact, was in the periphery of that circle. So, that was New York then. It was gritty. It was tough. It was crime-ridden. And the movie reflected that."

In capturing the feel of the city, the filmmakers shot in a variety of NYC locations. Most of the film was shot in the Court Street Station, located between Joralemon and Montague Streets in Brooklyn. Gracie Mansion, located in Carl Schurz Park at East End Avenue and 88th Street in the Yorkville neighborhood of Manhattan, makes an appearance in the film. Since Gracie Mansion is the real-life residence of the New York City mayor, it appears as the home of the film's fictitious mayor (played by Lee Wallace). The scene where the ransom money is counted out was shot at the Federal Reserve Bank of New York, located at 33 Liberty Street in Little Italy. Wave Hill, a Riverdale, Bronx mansion stood in for the interiors of Gracie Mansion.

When the film was released on October 2, 1974 (following a screening at the San Sebastian Film Festival in August), it opened to generally positive reviews. New York City critics, understandably, paid close attention to the film's depiction of their city. *New York Times* critic Nora Sayre raved, "Throughout there's a skillful balance between the vulnerability of New Yorkers and the drastic, provocative sense of comedy that thrives all over our sidewalks. And the hijacking seems like a perfectly probable event for this town. (Perhaps the only element of fantasy is the implication that the city's departments could function so smoothly together.) Meanwhile, the movie adds up to a fine piece of reporting—and it's the only action picture I've seen this year that has a rousing plot." Because of the high number of 1974 films that depicted the city negatively, Vincent Canby, also of the *Times*, observed, "New York is a mess, say these films. It's run by fools. Its citizens are at the mercy of its criminals who, as often as not, are protected by an unholy alliance of civil libertarians and crooked cops. The air is foul. The traffic impossible. Services are diminishing and the morale is such that ordering a cup of coffee in a diner can turn into a request for a fat lip." However, "compared to the general run of New York City films," *The Taking of Pelham One Two Three* "is practically a tonic, a good-humored, often witty suspense melodrama in which the representatives of the law and decency triumph without bending the rules."

Despite good reviews, the film tanked, earning less than its $3.8 million budget at the box office. One of the film's producers later said that the film was actually a big hit in the few cities in the world that had subways, while being a flop everywhere else.

The Taking of Pelham One Two Three has gained stature over the years and is considered a classic in the genre. It has been remade twice (1998 and 2009). "I have been constantly amazed ever since that so many people have come up and said how much they liked the movie and how wonderful it is, and etcetera, etcetera, etcetera," Sargent explained in a Television Academy Foundation interview. "Because we just thought we were doing another caper movie . . . with hostages, with ransom money. And we were doing something a little bit more than that. You know, we were making certain comments about society, but we also had humor built into it."

Three the Hard Way

In 1973, when *Three the Hard Way* was produced, blaxploitation films were all the rage at the box office. It didn't take a rocket scientist to understand that making one of these movies with three of the biggest stars in the genre *should* be like printing money. So Harry Bernsen (Corbin's dad), a producer with only two minor production credits to his name at the time, and footballer-turned-movie-star Fred Williamson set out to make just such a film. The project, *Three the Hard Way*, was at first supposed to star Williamson, Williamson's former NFL colleague Jim Brown, and Richard Roundtree. However, Roundtree backed out of the project because he wanted to get away from "black films." This didn't sit well with Williamson; as late as 2011, Williamson was still fuming. That was when he commented on Roundtree's decision (indirectly) to Dutch journalist Roel Haanen: "Look at Richard Roundtree. He was doing *Shaft* and he should be doing *Shaft 226* by now. Instead, he's just a guy looking for a job. His agents told him, 'The world knows who you are now. You are Richard Roundtree, the actor. You don't have to take black parts anymore.' Hey! Wrong! You're black! You are who you are because the audience loves you. And your audience is always right. If they want to see you as Shaft, you play Shaft! No, what does he do? *Robinson Crusoe*! Playing Man Friday next to Michael Caine. Sitting in the sand with a stick. Where's your leather jacket? Where's your gun? Walking down the beach in raggedy-ass clothes. Guy lost his whole audience, because he threw away his image." After Roundtree's departure, Jim Kelly, a black martial artist with several films to his credit, including the Bruce Lee actioner *Enter the Dragon* (1973), was enlisted to fill the void.

Williamson discussed the idea behind the casting concept on the *Action Reloaded* podcast: "Jim Kelly came along when we decided to do a film, because Jim had done a couple films, so he was a marketable commodity, along with Jim Brown. They were marketable black actors at that time. So I figured the three of us together would make a very unique trio on the screen. And it worked out good, you know. Jim did his thing in *Three the Hard Way*, and Jim [Brown] did his one-liner grunt beat-up people thing. And I did my romantic kind of thing. So it was a great union between three different kinds of personalities."

Having had success with *Super Fly* (1972), Gordon Parks Jr. was tapped to direct. Screenwriter Eric Bercovici and Jerrold L. Ludwig, scribes with primarily television credits, wrote the script. The film's plot is ridiculous; our heroes must join forces to stop white supremacists who have a plan to poison black people (with a poison that affects *only* black people) via the water systems in several US cities. Now, most exploitation action movies in general (not just blaxploitation films) are constructed around silly plots. Could the plot of *Three the Hard Way* actually happen? Probably not. The storyline is nonsensical, primarily due to the unlikeliness that there could be a man-made toxin that kills only black people. Most viewers are smart enough to recognize upfront that exploitation movies usually have dumb plots. Who would be stupid enough to analyze and question such a plot? Enter talk show host Geraldo Rivera, who, on a 1974 episode of *Good Night America*, challenged Fred Williamson about the unlikeliness of someone administering a drug through the water system. (Again, that's not even the silliest aspect of the plot.) Visibly annoyed, Williamson gave him an equally cockeyed response: "Do you think it could not possibly happen? . . . I've been to some parties on the West Coast where there was an incident like that at a party at a big apartment house where somebody put some LSD in the punch, right? A couple of people got freaked out [and] they had to go to the hospital. They did get wiped out on LSD and they had . . . They're taking treatment for this LSD that was put in the punch. So, it's all practical, man. I'm not saying I agree with the script, you know? But I'm dealing with the practicality of it. It is possible. It's not totally impossible. A thing like that could happen." So, there you go. Case dismissed.

If the plot sounds silly, the ease with which Williamson, Brown, and Kelly dispatch the baddies is equally laughable. *Boston Phoenix* critic Mike Baron described this beautifully in his July 2, 1974, review: "Together and separately, the trio track down all of Feather's red-beret wearing neo-fascists and kill them with the difficulty one might experience spreading cheesewhiz on stale bread. Never, in the history of the cinema, has an army been so easily overcome. These three hard guys make Richard Burton and Clint Eastwood look like girl scouts." The body count is also incredibly high, as the three leads are responsible for the on-screen killing of *a lot* of bad guys. Jim Brown leads the way with fifty-five killings. Williamson comes in second, taking out forty-eight white supremacists. Kelly, relying more on martial arts than anything else, falls behind the others with a mere twelve Nazi scalps. Still, not bad for a day's work.

When the movie was released on June 26, 1974, no one was waiting with any anticipation except the critics, who had their knives out and ready. Having been made with a $1.8 million budget and earning a mere $1.2 million at the box office, *Three the Hard Way* was a financial flop. And to say that the critics were hard on the film would be an understatement. Interestingly, some of the harshest criticism came from the New York critics. Vincent Canby of the *New York Times* seemed personally offended by (what he viewed as) the poor quality of the film, which he called a "hideously inane black exploitation movie that glories in reverse racism." He went on to write, "The most startling thing about the film is that it was directed by Gordon Parks Jr., who seemed to know what he was doing when he made *Super Fly* (1972) and *Thomasine and Bushrod* (1974). *Three the Hard Way* is badly written, staged, and edited. It is also terribly acted by the stars as well as Jay Robinson, who plays the rich white fanatic with all the force of a man who should wear paperweights in his shoes." The *Village Voice*'s George Morris took the criticism a step further, writing, "The total incredibility of the plot is matched every step of the way by mindless motivation, inconsistent characterization, and the kind of direction that may generously be described as disinterested. The action sequences have a numbing sameness and are completely ruined by Parks' insistence on inserting slow motion and freeze frames right into the middle of chases and fights. The reverse racism that is inherent in the implications of the script never become as disturbing as it might have, because the entire film exists on a plane of unreality to which moral responsibility is alien."

Williamson, Brown, and Kelly would team up again the following year for *Take a Hard Ride* (1975), in which they essentially played the same characters, in a Western setting. In 1982, the three stars would unite for a third time in *One Down, Two to Go*, an unofficial *Three the Hard Way* sequel written, produced, and directed by Williamson.

Despite the film's lack of box-office success, *Three the Hard Way* has had a giant impact on popular culture. The films *I'm Gonna Git You, Sucka!* (1989), *Undercover Brother* (2002), and *Black Dynamite* (2009) all lift ideas from the film or directly parody it. The movie has also impacted hip-hop music with groups that include The Beastie Boys, Rodney-O and Joe Cooley, Jermaine Dupri, and Bahamadia naming songs after it. Additionally, at least two hip-hop groups have gone by the name Three the Hard Way.

Promotional artwork for the film Klute, 1971. *Source*: Warner Bros./Photofest © Warner Bros.

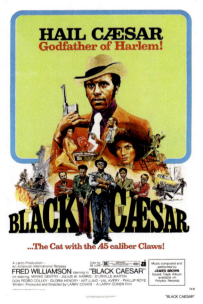

Promotional artwork for the film Black Caesar, 1973. *Source*: American International Pictures / Photofest © American International Pictures

Photograph of Frank Serpico. *Source*: Panthera

Still of actor Peter Boyle from the film *Crazy Joe*, 1974. *Source*: Columbia Pictures/Photofest © Columbia Pictures

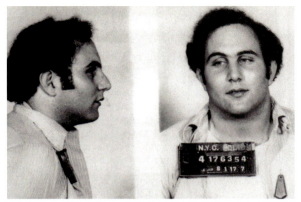

Photograph of David Berkowitz, aka The Son of Sam. *Source*: Everett Collection

Exterior of a peep show theater on 42nd Street. *Source*: Universal Images Group North America

Still of actors Charles Bronson and John Herzfeld in *Death Wish*, 1974. *Source*: Paramount Pictures/Photofest © Paramount Pictures

42nd Street between 7th and 8th Avenues, circa 1972. *Source*: Everett Collection

Abandoned burned-out tenement in the South Bronx in 1977. *Source*: Alain Le Garsmeur

Times Square in the 1970s. *Source*: Photograph by R. Krubner

Promotional artwork for the film *The French Connection*, **1971.** *Source*: 20th Century Fox/Photofest © 20th Century Fox

Photograph of New York City mayor John V. Lindsay receives a director's chair in 1971. *Source*: Photofest

Robert Shaw in *The Taking of Pelham One Two Three*, 1974. *Source*: RGR Collection

Promotional artwork for *The Panic in Needle Park*, 1971. *Source*: 20th Century Fox/Photofest © 20th Century Fox

New York City subway car covered in graffiti. *Source*: Everett Collection

Still of actor Richard Roundtree from *Shaft*, 1971. *Source*: MGM/Photofest © MGM

Promotional artwork for *Superfly*, 1972. *Source*: Warner Bros./Photofest © Warner Bros.

Still of actor Robert De Niro in *Taxi Driver*, 1976. *Source*: Columbia Pictures/Photofest © Columbia Pictures

Still of The Gang in *The Warriors*, 1979. *Source*: Paramount Pictures/Photofest © Paramount Pictures

Promotional artwork for *Across 110th Street*, 1972. *Source*: United Artists/Photofest © United Artists

1975

A Dog Day Afternoon *in Fear City*

The Seventies were a rough decade for the City That Never Sleeps, but 1975 was a particularly hard year. The entire country was struggling through a recession, but somehow things were worse in NYC. The city's unemployment rate in 1975 was a staggering 12 percent, which was high compared to the already high 8.5 percent unemployment rate the rest of the country was experiencing. But the citizens of the city weren't the only ones facing challenging economic times; NYC itself was nearly broke and on the verge of bankruptcy. Experts had seen the crisis coming for a long time, and yet, somehow, no one really believed things would or could become so dire. And yet here they were.

New York City had taken out sizable loans to stay afloat. Eventually, in spring that year, the banks cut them off. As a result, the city was forced to make difficult cuts to its payroll and general spending to slow the financial bleeding. This led to massive cuts from both the city's police and fire departments. Transit fares were increased, and tuition was imposed for the first time at city college. When Mayor Abraham Beame approached US president Gerald Ford with his figurative hat in hand to ask for a federal bailout, Ford denied him. Although the headline of the next day's issue of the *New York Daily News* famously announced "FORD TO CITY: DROP DEAD," it's now clear that the president never actually said those words. But the result was the same—New York City did not receive a bailout. Henry J. Stern, a former NYC parks commissioner and city councilman, would later assess, "Ford was good for New York, because he made us clean up our act." With help from New York governor Hugh L. Carey, who led the charge with a sizable rescue package, the city eventually got back on track.

In June 1975, as a reaction to Mayor Beame's cuts to the city's workforce, the police and firefighters' unions combined forces in an effort to scare away would-be tourists and frighten New Yorkers into speaking out. The unions' joint efforts led to the creation and distribution of a pamphlet with an image of the grim reaper on the front. It read, "WELCOME TO FEAR CITY: A SURVIVAL GUIDE FOR VISITORS TO THE CITY OF NEW YORK." The flyer informed the reader that "incidence [sic] of violence in New York City is shockingly high, and is getting worse every day." Then, after sharing some scary statistics showing that robberies, aggravated assault, larceny, and burglary were increasing, it told readers that "to 'solve' his budget problems, Mayor Beame is going to discharge substantial numbers of firefighters and law enforcement officers of all kinds." The foreboding pamphlet warned readers to "stay away from New York City if you possibly can." The warning ended with a line of sarcastic encouragement, saying simply, "Good luck." When Mayor Beame received news of the pamphlet, he was understandably irate. He tried to stop the distribution of the flyer, but the damage had already been done.

While the creation and distribution of the pamphlet could be seen as being a somewhat traitorous action, its claims that crime was on the rise were accurate. In 1975, homicide, which had dipped the previous year, rose again. Where there had been 1,554 murders in 1974, there were now 1,690.

In 1975, the first of the six (discovered) victims of the so-called "Bag Murders" were discovered. These men, which would be discovered over the next two years, had been dismembered before being placed inside garbage bags and unceremoniously dumped into the Hudson River. The victims, who were all found semi-dressed in leather, were believed to be homosexual men who had been partying in Greenwich Village "leather bars" before they were murdered. Gerald Walker's 1970 novel *Cruising*, and later William Friedkin's 1980 film adaptation of the same title, were inspired by the murders.

1975: A *Dog Day Afternoon* in Fear City / 147

In April, a Chinese-American engineer living in Brooklyn named Peter Yew was detained, stripped, and beaten by cops after he attempted to stop police officers from assaulting a fifteen-year-old. Yew was hospitalized after the encounter. The NYPD would later claim that he had assaulted an officer and had pending felony charges against him. This incident led to two massive gatherings (of thousands) of Chinese-Americans protesting police violence. The charges against Yew were ultimately dropped and the commanding officer of the Fifth Precinct police station was reassigned to a different post.

That year there were two significant bombings in New York City. The first took place on January 24, 1975, at the Fraunces Tavern restaurant at 54 Pearl Street at the corner of Broad Street in Lower Manhattan. The bombing took the lives of four people and injured another fifty. Although the Puerto Rican paramilitary organization Fuerzas Armadas de Liberación Nacional Puertorriqueña (Armed Forces of Puerto Rican National Liberation) claimed credit for the bombing, no arrests were ever made. The second bombing took place on December 29, 1975, at LaGuardia Airport. A bomb was left in the TWA baggage claim terminal. The explosion killed eleven people and injured seventy-four others. Although the terrorists were never identified and no arrests were ever made, it has been suggested that the act was carried out by either anti-Yugoslavian Croatians or members of Yugoslavia's State Security Administration.

We will be looking at only three films in this section. They are *Dog Day Afternoon*, *Report to the Commissioner*, and *Three Days of the Condor*. That year, Steven Spielberg's *Jaws*—the movie, like the shark it's about—devoured everything in sight. 1975 was the year of *Jaws*. Looking beyond that film, which is considered the first summer blockbuster, both *Dog Day Afternoon* and *Three Days of the Condor* held their own. *Dog Day Afternoon* was the fourth highest-grossing film of the year, and *Three Days of the Condor* was the sixth. While *Report to the Commissioner* failed to make much of a dent in terms of box office, it's a significant entry here because it's emblematic of the NYC crime pictures of the decade.

Dog Day Afternoon

On August 22, 1972, a twenty-seven-year-old Vietnam vet named John Wojtowicz and an accomplice named Salvatore Naturile attempted to rob the Chase Manhattan Bank at 450 Avenue P in Gravesend, Brooklyn. The two men botched the robbery and wound up holding seven bank employees hostage for fourteen hours. In the end, Naturile was killed by FBI agents, and Wojtowicz was sentenced to twenty years in Lewisburg Federal Penitentiary. The robbery became well known in New York City after WNYW (Channel 5) aired a live feed of the standoff for four straight hours. The incident gained even more notoriety when the *Los Angeles Times* reported that Wojtowicz had robbed the bank so he could pay for his male wife's (his word) gender reassignment surgery. (A side note: Wojtowicz and his wife Elizabeth Eden's marriage is believed to have been the first gay drag wedding ceremony in New York City.)

After reading a story about the robbery in a *Time* magazine article titled "The Boys in the Bank," producers Martin Bregman and Martin Elfand convinced Warner Bros. to purchase the film rights to the article. The selling point was that the article, written by P. F. Kluge and Thomas Moore, mentioned that Wojtowicz bore a strong resemblance to "Al Pacino or Dustin Hoffman." The two producers commissioned Frank Pierson, a scribe whose impressive credits included *Cat Ballou* (1965), *Cool Hand Luke* (1967), and *The Anderson Tapes* (1971), to write the script, which was then titled *The Boys in the Bank*. Bregman and Elfand hired Sidney Lumet to direct. Lumet approached Pacino, whom he'd worked with on *Serpico* (1973), to play the lead. Fresh off of *The Godfather Part II* (1974), Pacino, exhausted and needing a break, passed. Lumet persisted, eventually convincing the actor to come on board.

Pacino assisted Lumet and casting directors Don Phillips and Michael Chinich by suggesting several stage actors he'd worked with. Despite the fact that the real-life Naturile had been an eighteen-year-old that Pierson's screenplay described as having boyish good looks, Pacino wanted his good friend and *Godfather* (1973) costar, thirty-nine-year-old John Cazale, to play the role. Lumet initially thought Pacino was nuts and Cazale was completely wrong for the part. Then, when Cazale auditioned, Lumet changed his mind and cast him after he'd read a mere two lines. Pacino would later tell *Vulture*'s David Edelstein about his relationship with Cazale, saying, "We wanted to work with each other so much they had to separate us like when you're in school and you have a couple of clowns." Additionally, Penelope Allen, with whom Pacino had worked on *Scarecrow* (1973), was cast, as well as Judith Malina, with whom he'd worked at The Living Theater.

Before shooting, Lumet staged a three-week rehearsal. He started the rehearsal by addressing the cast, explaining what his intention with the film was. Lumet later recalled his speech to documentarian Nancy Buirski: "This is the only time I've got to talk about what's going to happen with this movie. On a Saturday night, at Loew's Pitkin, which was the fancy movie house in the Brownsville section of Brooklyn, I don't want a voice coming down from the balcony [saying], '*Hey, you fags!*' If that happens, we've done a lousy movie. And we've got to reach, on a fundamental level, into anybody watching this movie, to make them aware of the humanity of these two men."

Lumet set out to make the film appear so real that audiences would forget they were watching a movie. As such, he insisted that no part of the film be shot on the Warner Bros. lot. The film's story primarily took place in three locations: the bank, the street outside the bank, and the barber shop across the street from the bank. So Lumet selected and then acquired the use of a single block in the Windsor Terrace section of Brooklyn. His crew transformed an empty warehouse (located at Prospect Park West and 17th Street) into the Chase Manhattan Bank Wojtowicz and Naturile had attempted to rob. Lumet was not a director who allowed his actors to improvise, but *Dog Day Afternoon* would be the exception; on this film, he allowed some improvisation (while sticking to the structure of the screenplay), believing it made the dialogue feel more naturalistic and in-the-moment. (One highly effective instance of this improvisation is when Sonny asks Sal what country he would like to visit, and Sal says, "Montana.")

"[E]verything had to feel accidental—no planning, no color control," Lumet wrote in *Making Movies*. "I told the art director and the costume designer *not* to consult with each other. I wanted no relationship between the sets and the costumes. Whatever happened happened." Additionally, actors and extras were allowed to wear their own clothing rather than be outfitted for costumes. According to Lumet, the actors were paid an additional two dollars a day to wear their own clothing.

The crowd surrounding the bank would be comprised of three hundred extras and five hundred people from the neighborhood. Lumet coached these extras about who their "characters" were and why they would be observing the standoff. "One of the reasons I prefer working in New York is that real actors work as extras," Lumet later wrote. "They are members of the Screen Actors Guild, and many appear regularly on and off Broadway."

Interestingly, the film's most quoted line(s) where Sonny repeatedly yells "Attica!" at the police officers was also improvised. Pacino takes no credit for the line. Instead, he says he was trying to think of something to yell, and assistant director Burtt Harris whispered to him that he should say "Attica." Pacino thought the line sounded good, so he said it. And the rest is history. Pacino's repeated scream of the prison name has become so iconic that the American Film Institute eventually listed it at number eighty-six on their 2005 list of the all-time top movie quotes.

Lumet chose to film Pacino calling both Wojtowicz's male and female wives back-to-back, in a single take. The idea was that Pacino would get more and more worked up as the scene progressed. Since the full scene lasted fourteen minutes and the film reel lasted only twelve, Lumet had his director of photography, Victor J. Kemper, set up two cameras side by side. When the film ran out in one camera, the other picked up where the first had left off. This worked and Pacino's performance in the scene is nothing short of magnificent.

Lumet decided that *Dog Day Afternoon* would have no score. After all, he reasoned, music playing over a scene would break the illusion of reality. (Lumet had previously planned to do this on *Serpico* but wound up adding a scant fourteen minutes of music to appease producer Dino De Laurentiis and keep him from inserting his own score.)

Dog Day Afternoon would be released in New York City on September 25, 1975, and then nationwide the following month. The reviews were almost unanimously positive. The *New York Times*' Vincent Canby called *Dog Day Afternoon* a "gaudy street-carnival of a movie" and "Sidney Lumet's most accurate, most flamboyant New York movie." Roger Ebert of the *Chicago Sun-Times* saw the film as a reflection of American society at the time it was made: "The movie has a quirky, irreverent sense of humor, and we get some sense of the times we live in when the bank starts getting obscene phone calls—and the giggling tellers breathe heavily into the receiver." Stanley Kauffmann of the *New Republic* was one of the few critics who disliked the film. Kauffmann called the film "unsatisfying." It is, however, difficult to put much stock into the review as Kauffmann also dismissed Pacino's acting in the two *Godfather* films (in this same review), remarking about (what he considered to be) the actor's inability to "radiate quiet power" in them.

Dog Day Afternoon would be a huge success. It had cost $1.8 million to make, so the $55 million it earned at the box office was substantial. In addition to the critical and box-office successes, *Dog Day Afternoon* would receive five Academy Award nominations. These were: Best Picture, Best Director, Best Original Screenplay, Best Actor, and Best Supporting Actor (Chris Sarandon). In the end, Pierson would take home the film's only Oscar.

Report to the Commissioner

Report to the Commissioner may be the most "1970s New York City crime movie" ever made. It's dirty, gritty, and grimy. It's such a gritty film that its rats probably have fleas.

The movie, directed by Milton Katselas, feels about as authentic as a motion picture can feel. A great deal of the movie was shot on the streets of Manhattan (although streets in Los Angeles occasionally double for New York). There are panhandlers and prostitutes on street corners, pedestrians eating hot dogs from street vendors, there are piles of garbage in the street, there are strip clubs, bars, and liquor stores galore, and the cops are, of course, corrupt.

Interiors were shot on a Warner Bros. soundstage, but even those look and feel dirty. Set decorator John A. Kuri recalls, "Milton wanted to do the picture with the same kind of grittiness that *Serpico* [1973] had. He was looking for as much authenticity and grit as possible. To accomplish that, he wanted me to get a sense of Manhattan and its grittiness. He wanted me to *experience* Manhattan. Milton was a Manhattanite, and he knew a lot of people. So I was introduced to a detective there, and he arranged to take me out with him five nights in a row. He would meet me at the hotel at four-thirty or five in the afternoon, and then I was with him all night until sunrise. He took me to every underground club. I experienced things in Manhattan that Manhattanites never even see. This was at the very beginning of the cocaine world, and I was seeing a life that was alien to anything I knew coming out of Los Angeles. It was really an eye-opener. He arranged to take me to the Tombs [a Manhattan detention complex]. He took me to the prison psychiatric ward at Bellevue. He showed me everything I needed to see so I could replicate these things in Hollywood."

Kuri credits movie magic by cinematographer Mario Tosi for much of the gritty atmosphere in the interior scenes. "Mario was brilliant with lighting and camera. Almost every interior scene that we shot, he would smoke up the rooms. And you don't see that. You don't see it the way the naked eye would standing onstage, but what it would do to the film stock, to the emulsions, it would create a texture in the air that really gives it a very believable sense that you're capturing the actual moment. I will never forget how brilliant he was with lighting. He would use hardly any lights whatsoever. And he made everything look absolutely natural."

The interior of the police station looks filthy, and all the cops look disheveled. With the exception of actress Susan Blakely, no one in the film looks *pretty*. Sure, Richard Gere's pimp and Tony King's drug dealer are well dressed, but they're more greasy-slick than pretty. This is not a pretty movie in any way. *Report to the Commissioner* doesn't even look like a movie; it looks like documentary footage.

If there is anything in the film that seems less than authentic, it's Gere's devil-may-care white pimp, Billy. Because, as Harvey Keitel would learn a year later when he scoured New York City for a white pimp to study and emulate for his role as a pimp in *Taxi Driver* (1976), there were zero white pimps in NYC. So why did Milton Katselas, in a film that (otherwise) strives damned hard for authenticity, cast a white actor to play the role? Screenwriter Paul Schrader and director Martin Scorsese have conceded that the decision to cast Keitel as the pimp Travis Bickle murders in *Taxi Driver* was a compromise in an effort to avoid riots and [even more] claims that the film was racist. But why was it done in *Report to the Commissioner*? No one seems to know.

Times Square, described by Yaphet Kotto's veteran cop as a "jungle filled with animals," plays a prominent role in the film. Downtown Manhattan businesses of yesteryear including Orange Julius, Burger in the Park, the Flagg Bros. shoe store, Howard Johnson's, Swissair, and the Canadian Club appear in the film. The Central Fish Market and the Eighth Avenue Port Authority Bus Terminal also show up. Saks Fifth Avenue's Manhattan flagship store appears on screen multiple times, but it gets better treatment than those other businesses; a large chunk of the film's final third takes place inside the store (although this interior was actually a John A. Kuri–designed re-creation shot on a Hollywood soundstage). The sequence in question is a gloriously claustrophobic Mexican standoff between an undercover cop and a heroin dealer inside the Saks elevator. This phenomenal and extremely well-acted (by both Moriarty and Tony King) sequence alone is worth the price of admission. It's a shame that *Report to the Commissioner* hasn't gained a greater cult following, because the elevator standoff is one of the most intense sequences ever captured on celluloid.

A key scene in which Moriarty's and Blakely's characters meet for the first time takes place inside an underground 42nd Street club. While the club looks completely authentic, it's actually another Kuri re-creation. These scenes were actually filmed inside the heavily disguised ground floor lobby of a condemned hotel in downtown LA.

Report to the Commissioner was based on the 1972 novel by James Mills, who also authored *The Panic in Needle Park*. The *New York Times* bestselling book was adapted by screenwriters Abby Mann (*Judgment at Nuremberg* [1961]) and Ernest Tidyman, who wrote or co-wrote both the novel and film versions of *Shaft* (1971) and is also credited with co-writing the script for *The French Connection* (1971). The top-tier cast, which includes Michael Moriarty, Yaphet Kotto, Susan Blakely, Hector Elizondo, and Tony King, is fantastic from top to bottom. (Richard Gere and Bob Balaban also make their screen debuts.) There isn't a single weak link. Moriarty's performance is particularly noteworthy.

Despite his excellent performance in the film, Moriarty believes *Report to the Commissioner* damaged his career. In the early 1970s, the actor's stock was on the rise, but then in the middle of the decade, it slowed down. In 2002, Moriarty told *Shock Cinema*'s Harvey Chartrand, "Attempting a role because you identified with a character's inner-nightmare but, for which, under the Hollywood rules, you were too old and too unattractive and unsexy, is a fairly good explanation for my personal failure in it. Being hailed in Manhattan as the 'new Brando' was no help either. It simply made the critics sharpen their knives."

The reviews for the film, which the *New York Times'* Nora Sayre described as "an awkward mating of *Serpico* and *Watergate*," weren't particularly kind. A number of critics reprimanded the film for moralizing. David Rosenbaum of the *Boston Phoenix* wrote, "Like the Hindenburg, *Report to the Commissioner* is too big, full of gas, and probably the last of its breed."

Three Days of the Condor

Three Days of the Condor started out as a novel by James Grady titled *Six Days of the Condor*, and the idea for that novel came when the author was told a story about the poet Allen Ginsberg. The story Grady heard was that Ginsberg, having lost a close friend to heroin, had traveled to Vietnam to investigate rumors that the Central Intelligence Agency (CIA) was responsible for smuggling heroin into the United States. That story led to a short part of Grady's novel (that did not appear in the film adaptation) about rogue CIA agents transporting heroin.

Grady was living in Missoula, Montana, when he finished his espionage novel in 1973. He was poor and was living in what he describes as a "reconverted garage shed" at the time he submitted the novel to the publisher W.W. Norton and Company. Unbeknownst to Grady, who hadn't really expected to be published, W.W. Norton was conducting a unique experiment; the publisher selected three unpublished manuscripts from their slush pile and hired the William Morris Agency to shop them to Hollywood filmmakers. W.W. Norton editor-in-chief Starling Lawrence telephoned the young novelist to offer him a publication deal with a $1,000 advance. Before the phone call was finished, Starling said, "We think there's a movie in it." Extremely skeptical about this, Grady says he put his hand over the phone's receiver so Starling couldn't hear him snicker. After all, Grady explains, "Nobody gets their first book made into a movie." A few days later, Grady says he was attempting to assemble a shower made of "parts I'd found on the curb" and duct tape when Starling called a second time. Grady had strips of the gray tape hanging from his arms when he answered. This time, Starling said, "We just sold your book to the movies. Your share is $81,000." The producer who optioned the rights to the book was Dino De Laurentiis, who had produced Federico Fellini's *La Strada* (1954) and *Barbarella* (1968) and was fresh off of *Serpico* (1973). According to De Laurentiis, he knew the novel would be a movie after reading only four pages. The producer then hired Sydney Pollack to direct.

In the beginning, the film was to be something completely different. Screenwriter Lorenzo Semple Jr. wrote the first draft as an action spy film. "The first draft was full of heroes jumping out of airplanes," Grady recalls. "It was like the spy movies they make now, where it's all action." But this changed when Pollack's frequent collaborator Robert Redford was cast as the lead. One of multiple changes Redford requested was that the script be crafted into something more substantive. At that point, a second screenwriter, David Rayfiel, was hired to reshape the project. Redford also wanted another huge change made; Grady's original novel took place in Washington, D.C., but Redford wanted the location moved. "Redford and [Dustin] Hoffman were getting prepared to star in *All the President's Men* [1976] right after that," Grady recalls. "Robert Redford essentially said to Paramount, 'I love this Condor story. I'd love to do it. But I don't want to move my family from New York to Washington D.C. for essentially a year of me just working when they're never going to see me.' So they said, 'Robert, where do you want to shoot it?' And he said, 'New York.'

"And in some ways, that was a really artistically brilliant decision because it then made what was, at the time, the 'strangeness' of the CIA operations even more . . . It defined it more clearly. The idea that the CIA had an office in New York, which they did, was mind-blowing to most of the audience. They kept the production in New York City, in part for Redford, in part for money, and in part because I think they all just had a sense that, by making this a New York film, they were making this a film about America."

At the time the film was being made, Watergate, multiple stories about the CIA, and Vietnam were all over the news. Recognizing that this was an incredibly timely film, De Laurentiis had screenwriters Semple and Rayfiel incorporate new things regularly. "Every other day, the papers would break with some new relevant story," Grady recalls. "Wait! Nixon's guys did this! The CIA did this. . . ! The poor screenwriters had to keep rewriting to keep up with the news. So, the fiction they were making seemed as real as what you were reading in your morning newspaper."

The film's plot is simple: when low-level CIA researcher Joe Turner (Redford) manages to survive a massacre that leaves everyone else in his office dead, he must go into hiding. When he reaches out to his CIA contacts, he's double-crossed. This Hitchcockian storyline leaves Turner alone and hunted in New York City, unable to trust anyone.

Almost all of the film was shot in New York City, but there are a couple of exceptions. There was some brief "stolen" (shot without a permit) footage of CIA headquarters in Langley, Virginia, that nearly got the second-unit crew arrested. "The CIA has a sense of humor up to a point," second assistant director Ralph S. Singleton jokes. There were also three exterior shots of actor Max von Sydow (filmed on the actor's forty-fourth birthday) in Washington, D.C. (One at National Airport, one on the Memorial Bridge, and one at the Lincoln Memorial.) These three scenes were filmed in a single day and cost the production $125,000.

Most of the New York footage was shot in Manhattan. The CIA office where Turner (code name "Condor") works under the guise of "The American Literary Historical Society" was a former girl's school located at 55 East 77th Street at Madison Avenue. When Turner goes out the backdoor and through a lot to pick up lunch (as his comrades are being gunned down back in the office), he goes to the Lexington Candy Shop Luncheonette at 1226 Lexington Avenue on the corner of East 83rd Street. As the frightened CIA employee attempts to lay low and blend in, he walks around inside the Guggenheim Museum at 1071 Fifth Avenue.

In one scene, Turner checks on his friend and coworker, Heidegger, and finds him dead inside his apartment. The apartment where this was shot is located at 20 West 71st Street near Central Park West. Turner later visits his own apartment, located at 485 West 22nd Street on Tenth Avenue. When CIA controller Higgins (Cliff Robertson) instructs Turner to meet him in an alleyway, the alleyway appearing in the scene runs behind the historic Ansonia Building (a former hotel turned into a condominium building) located at 2109 Broadway, between 73rd and 74th Streets. The interior of Higgins' office, which is supposed to be in Washington, D.C., was filmed inside the World Trade Center. It may be the only film ever shot inside the World Trade Center, and the location was secured because of the relationship Ralph Singleton had established with the powers that be after previously filming scenes from *Godspell* (1973) on the building's roof. A scene in which a helicopter takes off from a CIA office was actually filmed at Hofstra University in Long Island.

The store where Turner kidnaps Kathy (Faye Dunaway) was a real clothing store located on Broadway at 76th Street. After driving across the Brooklyn Bridge, Kathy takes Turner to her basement apartment, located at 9 Cranberry Street, Brooklyn Heights. Turner says goodbye to Kathy at the Hoboken Railway Station.

Prior to shooting, the entire film was to be shot on location. This, however, had to be reconsidered when it came time to film. The interior of Kathy's Brooklyn Heights apartment proved to be too low for cinematographer Owen Roizman's camera, resulting in the construction of the film's single set. "We were supposed to start the first week of the movie at her apartment," Singleton recalls. "Owen looked at me and said, 'Ralph, it won't work.' I said, 'Okay.' The only way to make it happen was to build the interior of her apartment. That was a set on a soundstage. So we shuffled the schedule and moved those scenes to the end."

Three Days of the Condor was released on September 24, 1975, to generally favorable reviews. With a budget just under $8 million, the film was a smash hit and turned an impressive profit, raking in more than $41 million at the box office. Editor Don Guidice was nominated for the Academy Award for Best Editing, losing to Verna Fields for *Jaws* (1975).

The film is a popular culture staple and has been referenced on television shows and films as varied as *Seinfeld* (1997) and *Out of Sight* (1998). Author Grady has since penned several more novels about the ongoing adventures of "Condor," and a television series named *Condor* (based on the original novel) ran for two seasons.

1976

Travis Bickle Meets the Son of Sam

The crime rate in New York City rose to six times that of the national average in 1976. According to the *New York Times*, other major cities also experienced crime rates that were greater than the national average that year, but most were less than that of NYC. Felonies in 1976 were up a staggering 13.2 percent from the previous year. The total of 658,147 reported serious crimes equals an average of 1,803 per day. Taking this a step further, that equaled out to about seventy-five per hour. The number of total reported felonies was the most the city had experienced in a year since the NYPD had begun compiling these statistics forty-five years earlier. Additionally, the number of felony crimes rose in each of the five boroughs.

Violent crimes against people in the city increased by an overall 1.5 percent, with murder (1,620), rape (3,400), and assault (42,948) all declining. The declines weren't substantial, but the NYPD felt they were a step in the right direction. Having lost about six thousand officers the previous year because of cutbacks, the police chose to focus more on major crimes, paying less attention to misdemeanors. Because of this, felony arrests increased by 9.2 percent from the previous year, while misdemeanor arrests decreased by 3.3 percent. Property crimes, which includes burglary, larceny-theft, and motor vehicle theft, increased by 16.7 percent from 1975.

NYPD analysis of murders committed in 1976 found that half of all murder victims had prior arrest records. Almost the same amount of the victims were found to have detectable levels of alcohol and/or narcotics in their blood at the time of the murder.

On June 29, 1976, David Berkowitz, aka "the Son of Sam," aka "the .44 Caliber Killer," shot his first victims. Teenagers Jody Valenti and Donna Lauria were sitting inside Lauria's parked Oldsmobile in the Pelham Bay area in the Bronx when Berkowitz approached them, firing three shots into the car. Lauria was killed, and Valenti, shot in the thigh, lived. On October 3, Carl Denaro and Rosemary Keenan were shot at while sitting inside a parked car in a residential area of Flushing, Queens. Denaro was shot in the head, and Keenan was unscathed. Both victims lived. On November 27, Donna DeMasi and Joanne Lomino were attacked while driving to Lomino's home in Floral Park, Queens. They were approached by a pistol-wielding Berkowitz, who shot them both. DeMasi was shot in the neck, and Lomino was shot in the back and was paralyzed.

While his identity was still unknown, Berkowitz committed these first of eight shootings that year. Between October 1976 and July 31, 1977, he would wreak havoc on the New York City streets, and his terrifying deeds would sell lots of newspapers. *Daily News* editor Sam Roberts would later recall of Berkowitz's killing spree, "It had everything going for it as a tabloid perfect storm. It was an ongoing, unfolding crime story that New Yorkers were genuinely terrified about."

Another story that received a lot of attention that year was the police shooting of a fifteen-year-old boy named Randolph Evans. On Thanksgiving Day, NYPD officer Robert Torsney responded to a call saying that there was a man with a gun in the Cypress Hill housing projects. After Torsney confronted a group of teenagers, he shot one of them, Randolph Evans, point-blank in the head. Rather than checking on the young man he'd just shot, Evans instead returned to his partner waiting for him in their squad car and reloaded his pistol. The officer was charged with second-degree murder. When the case went to trial, Torsney was found not guilty by reason of insanity.

Not unrelated, that same year a section of the New York Civil Rights Law known as law 5-a was established. The purpose of this law was to protect police officers from being investigated by outside parties. The law ensured that "personal records [of police officers] were confidential and not subject to inspection or review." The excuse given for the establishment of this law was that it would protect cops who served as witnesses for the prosecution in trials. But the truth was, whether or not it was the law's intended purpose, 5-a resulted in an overall lack of police accountability. Critics have said that the law helped preserve institutional racism. Decades later, in 2020, the problematic law was repealed.

On September 8, 1976, a race riot took place at Washington Square Park in Greenwich Village. That day, a mob of twenty or so white men showed up at the park wielding pipes, baseball bats, and chains. Trying to send a message to the minorities moving into their neighborhood, they started beating every person of color they encountered. As a result, one man was killed and another suffered a fractured skull and lost an eye. Three of the attackers were later found guilty of manslaughter, and another three were found guilty of lesser charges.

In this section, we'll look at just two NYC crime films from 1976. These are *Marathon Man* and *Taxi Driver*, both of which are iconic. In fact, *Taxi Driver* may well be the definitive gritty 1970s' NYC crime picture. It's as gritty a picture as any ever made, and it helped cement (at least for the next couple of decades) the city's reputation for being a dirty, filthy, murderous cesspool overrun with crime.

Marathon Man

William Goldman, the acclaimed screenwriter and author, was living in the Upper East Side of Manhattan in the early 1970s. He had the seed of an idea for his eighth novel; he imagined the notoriously evil Nazi doctor Josef Mengele, still alive and hiding somewhere, coming to New York City to receive medical care. Goldman liked the idea of Mengele bumping around in NYC, but he didn't want to write about a medically frail character. After changing courses, he wrote the novel *Marathon*

Man, about a Nazi dentist (patterned after Mengele) named Dr. Christian Szell, torturing the innocent, unknowing brother ("Babe" Levy) of a double-crossing spy ("Doc" Levy) in search of stolen diamonds taken from Jewish prisoners in Auschwitz. When the book was completed in 1973, Goldman's agent, Evarts Ziegler, secured a $2 million three-book publishing deal (that would include *Marathon Man*, *Magic*, and *Tinseltown*) with Delacorte Press. Producer Sidney Beckerman, who had previously produced such films as *Kelly's Heroes* (1970) and *Joe Kidd* (1972), read the galleys and saw the potential for a great film. Beckerman then convinced Paramount Pictures head of production Robert Evans to option *Marathon Man* for $450,000. (That figure included payment for Goldman to write the screenplay.)

The producers discussed candidates for director. They approached John Schlesinger, who'd made the Best Picture winner *Midnight Cowboy* (1969). Schlesinger signed on and called his *Midnight Cowboy* star Dustin Hoffman. Hoffman told him he wasn't familiar with the book, so Schlesinger sent it to him. Hoffman read it, liked it, and signed on to play Babe, the protagonist.

When the book had still been in galley form, David Brown, who had produced the hit films *The Sting* (1973) and *Jaws* (1975), showed the book to actor Roy Scheider. The actor stayed up half the night and read the entire book in a single sitting. Brown asked Scheider for his opinion on the novel. Scheider told him he'd enjoyed the book and believed it had tremendous potential. However, Doc, the character he liked most, died midway through the book. Later, when the film was being cast, Scheider was approached to try out for that role. Scheider accepted primarily because he'd loved a scene in the novel where his character kills a couple of spies. When it eventually came time to shoot the scene, Scheider and Schlesinger disagreed about how they should approach the fight. When they took their disagreement to the producers, Beckerman and Evans agreed with Scheider's take. Scheider and an undisclosed martial artist wound up choreographing the fight. But later, in an early screening in San Francisco, an audience member stood up and yelled objections during the scene regarding the film's violence. As a result, Paramount became nervous and cut the scene from the film.

While searching for an actress to play Elsa, the female lead, Schlesinger, Evans, and Beckerman decided to meet with a Swiss actress they had seen in the French film *And Now My Love* (1974). Her name was Marthe Keller. Unbeknownst to the filmmakers, Keller didn't speak English. However, she tried out anyway, still not telling them this key detail. Keller learned her lines phonetically and delivered them perfectly without understanding what she was saying, and she landed the role.

The fourth important role—perhaps the *most* important role—was that of the Nazi dentist, Szell. The filmmakers reached out to Laurence Olivier, one of the greatest stage actors of all time. Olivier's film career had been less qualitative than his career in theater. Because of this, the actor wanted very badly to prove what he was capable of if given the right role. So, he agreed to play the part. There was just one problem—one *huge* problem—Olivier was frail and dying. Because of this, he was deemed impossible to insure. But Evans begged the insurance company to allow the filmmakers six weeks with the actor. (In truth, it was believed that the actor had only six weeks to live. However, Olivier would live another thirteen years.) The insurance company relented and allowed Olivier to be cast.

Hoffman studied his role meticulously. He also worked to get into shape. Each day he ran several miles and jumped rope for an hour at a time. As a result, he lost fifteen pounds for the role. Hoffman eventually balked at a scene in which he was supposed to kill the doctor. Hoffman said he felt it was wrong for his character, a Jew, to murder the Nazi because that would make the two characters essentially the same. At this point, Goldman had written three drafts of the script. *Chinatown* (1974) scribe Robert Towne was then brought in to rewrite the ending in a way that would satisfy Hoffman.

Although Olivier and Hoffman's acting styles were dramatically different, the older actor had just as much of a need and desire to understand his character and his motivations. Olivier's key scene in the film finds his character slowly extracting the protagonist's teeth as a means of torture. But Olivier wasn't sure how his character might approach such torture. And then, just before it was time to film the scene, Olivier observed something that made him understand his character's mentality in the scene. According to both Evans and Hoffman, Olivier said he sat and watched a gardener cutting roses (at either his or Evans' home, depending on who's telling the story). As he watched, Olivier took note of how delicately the man cut each rose. Olivier then concluded that Dr. Szell would pull each of Babe's teeth with that sort of care and respect for his craft.

The film shoot lasted from October 1975 to February 1976 and shot in a variety of locations around New York City (and a few others in Paris, France, and Los Angeles). Robert Evans would later say that beyond Hoffman, Scheider, Keller, and Olivier, there was a fifth equally important star involved with the film. "That's the city of New York," he explained in the 1976 documentary *The Magic of Hollywood . . . is the Magic of People*. "Some of the most dramatic sequences in the film were shot right in the Big Apple itself. . . . As a filmmaker, I think New York is just incredible."

Some of the key NYC locations included: Columbia University (between 116th and 120th Streets in Morningside Heights), where Babe studies; Babe runs each day on the jogging path surrounding the reservoir in Central Park between 86th and 96th Streets; Szell's brother is killed on East 91st Street outside the Carnegie Mansion at 22 East 91st Street; Elsa's apartment, which is supposed to be at 94th Street in the film, was actually shot on the corner of 76th Street and Lexington Avenue on the West Side; Babe and Elsa sit together on a bench by Bow Bridge; Szell freaks out in the Diamond District on 47th Street between Fifth and Sixth Avenues. One of the most famous scenes in the film is the scene in which William Devane chases Babe in his car. This scene took nine days to film and was shot on the Brooklyn Bridge before Babe jumps down onto the road to Federal Plaza.

As a humorous aside, Gene Rudolf, who worked as an uncredited art director on the picture, says of Hoffman's running scene beneath the Brooklyn Bridge, "Someplace in the reservoir that becomes a lake in Central Park is a .45 caliber automatic. After Dusty had shot and was tired of running, he just took it and threw that damn thing right over the fence!"

Marathon Man was released on October 8, 1976, and was both a critical and box-office success. There was a lot of discussion regarding the violence in the dentistry scene. *New Republic* critic Stanley Kauffmann responded to this discussion, writing, "While people said the violence in *Marathon Man* was excessive, I was surprised; I had wriggled through that dental torture, but it hadn't seemed a pinnacle in a year during which I had seen two penises cut off and another nailed to a board—in films from France and Japan." *Marathon Man* received a single Academy Award nomination for Laurence Olivier (Best Supporting Actor).

Goldman published a sequel novel in 1986 titled *Brothers*. Dr. Szell was later listed at number thirty-four on the American Film Institute's "100 Years . . . 100 Heroes and Villains" list. *Time* magazine also named Szell on their list of the twenty-five greatest movie villains. *Marathon Man* was listed on the AFI's "100 Years . . . 100 Thrills" list. The line "Is it safe?" was ranked at number seventy on their "100 Years . . . 100 Movie Quotes" list. The dental torture scene ranked at number sixty-six on Bravo's "100 Scariest Movie Moments" list.

Taxi Driver

In the summer of 1972, Paul Schrader was living in his car. Things were not going well for him. He'd lost his teaching position at the American Film Institute, his wife had left him, and he'd been trying for some time to sell his first script, *Pipeline*. Little did Schrader know there were bigger and better things just over the horizon. Of this bleakest of bleak periods, Schrader would later write in *Schrader on Schrader*, "I was enamored of guns. I was very suicidal, I was drinking heavily, I was obsessed with pornography the way a lonely person is." Drawing on all of this, a new screenplay would emerge. The script, written in a total of ten days (the first draft took seven, the rewrite three), was about "self-imposed loneliness." Schrader would later tell Marc Maron that the script was therapeutic, a way to battle feelings of "anger, loneliness, and incel-ness." The script was inspired by the diaries of attempted assassin Arthur Bremer,

Jean-Paul Sartre's existential novel *Nausea*, and John Ford's *The Searchers* (1956).

As soon as Schrader finished the script, about a lonely Vietnam vet who mans a cab, driving through the streets at night in search of an excuse to act out violently, he went to work shopping it. When he mentioned the screenplay to Brian De Palma during a game of chess, De Palma asked to read it. The director reported back that he loved the writing but didn't feel the project was a good fit for him. Wanting to help Schrader sell the script, De Palma showed it to his neighbor, producer Michael Phillips. Phillips then showed it to his partner, Julia Phillips (his wife). The producers agreed to make the film, although Julia would later admit in her memoir, *You'll Never Eat Lunch in This Town Again*, "I had found nothing really attractive about *Taxi Driver* when I first read it, except for its sociology. Travis was a nut case, a valid nut case but a nut case. I thought Schrader was, too."

The producers began their search for a director. Among the directors considered were John Milius, Irvin Kershner, Lamont Johnson, and Robert Mulligan. They also considered actors who might play the lead character, Travis Bickle. As strange as it may seem, singer Neil Diamond's name was briefly bandied about as a potential Bickle. Jeff Bridges was also considered. Of course, the film would ultimately find its director in Martin Scorsese. Once again, it was De Palma who saved the day when he showed Scorsese the script for *Taxi Driver*. Scorsese instantly connected with the material. "I know this guy Travis," Scorsese would later tell the *New York Times'* Guy Flatley. "I've had the feelings that he has, and those feelings have to be explored, taken out and examined. I know the feeling of rejection that Travis feels, of not being able to make relationships survive. I know the killing feeling, the feeling of really being angry."

Neither Schrader nor the Phillipses saw Scorsese as a legitimate contender to make the film. At the time, his only directing credit was the Roger Corman–produced exploitation film *Boxcar Bertha* (1972). But Scorsese wouldn't take no for an answer. Acting slightly Bickle-like, Scorsese made a point to show up at every party Schrader and/or the Phillipses attended, reminding them each time about his interest in the project. He also told them about the film he was editing called *Mean Streets* (1973). When *Mean Streets* was finished, Scorsese's agent convinced Schrader and the Phillipses to screen the film. An hour and fifty-two minutes later, the *Taxi Driver* team had changed their minds. In fact, the film had such an effect on them that they wanted Scorsese and *Mean Streets* actor Robert De Niro to reteam for their project. De Niro read the script and was startled to find similarities to a script he was writing about a political assassin. The actor liked the writing, found he could relate to it, and scrapped his own script. He signed on to the project.

Now that *Taxi Driver* had a director and lead actor attached, the Phillipses still faced the uphill battle of selling this bleak, depressing film to a studio. The duo had door after door shut in their faces, each studio telling them the project wasn't commercial enough. Warner Bros. chieftain John Calley expressed interest, but he couldn't decide whether or not to pull the trigger on a deal. He eventually agreed to make the film, but only with the caveat that they make it on a $750,000 budget. All of the creative parties were still interested in making *Taxi Driver* but were now working on other films. Believing the film couldn't be made for less than a million dollars, Warner Bros. got nervous and pulled the plug. After De Niro won an Oscar for his role in *The Godfather Part II* (1974), David Begelman at Columbia Pictures agreed to make the film for $1.5 million. Because of their passion for the material, Scorsese, De Niro, and Schrader all signed on to make the film for less money than they were now making on other projects. The director filled out the cast with Cybill Shepherd, Jodie Foster, Harvey Keitel, and Albert Brooks.

Because Travis Bickle was obviously racist, Scorsese and Schrader were concerned that the film itself would be seen as being racist. It was for this reason that Sport, the pimp Travis guns down—a black character in Schrader's script—became a white character in the film. The thinking was that a film perceived as being racist would incite violence in theaters. While Columbia Pictures was still afraid the film would draw ire from uncomfortable black audiences, there was no backlash aside from a few angry op-ed pieces.

While scouting locations, Scorsese witnessed an act of random violence that further convinced him the film he was making was valid. "The ballet had just let out and a number of women were crossing to catch a bus," Scorsese said in a 1977 issue of *Penthouse*. "Suddenly a big guy walked over to a very old lady and punched her in the mouth, and a young lady began screaming and crying. The guy just walked away. Senseless violence. Yet if you got into that guy's head—who knows?" In another instance of real-life violence, an actual murder took place just around the corner while the crew was filming the scene where Travis shoots a robber in a bodega.

Much of the reason for *Taxi Driver*'s authentic feel was Scorsese's superb location choices. Many nighttime scenes featuring Times Square at its seediest appear in the film. "We were on the streets of Manhattan down on 42nd Street, Eighth Avenue for two weeks of night shooting," second assistant director Ralph Singleton explains. "We shot from dusk until dawn. The funny thing that happened to us there was, we would get there at dusk. When we first started getting set up, we'd see the johns and the prostitutes wandering the streets, and they were afraid of us because we were a movie company and they didn't want all this exposure. After about four or five days, it was kind of like [that cartoon with] the sheepdog and the fox where they punch in and go to work, and then they punch out after they've chased each other all day. We would get there at dusk to set up, and we'd see the johns and the prostitutes, and we were waving to each other. They were going to their job, we were going to ours. They'd finish at sun up, we'd finish at sun up."

In a scene in which Travis is asked by presidential candidate Charles Palantine (Leonard Harris) what bothers him most, the cabbie goes on a long rant that pretty much sums up the state of New York City—particularly Times Square—at the time the film was made: "[Y]ou should clean up this city here, because this city here is like an open sewer, you know. It's full of filth and scum. Sometimes I can hardly take it. Whatever, whoever becomes president should just really clean it up. You know what I mean? Sometimes I go out and I smell it, I get headaches it's so bad, you know. They just never go away, you know. It's like . . .

I think the president should just clean up this whole mess here. You should just flush it right down the fucking toilet."

There are a lot of NYC locations in the film. For instance, the cab office where Travis works was located at 57th Street and Eleventh Avenue. The adult film theater where he takes Betsy on their date was the Lyric Theatre, located at 214 West 43rd Street. At night, Travis and the other cabbies drink coffee and talk shit at the now long-gone Belmore Cafeteria on Park Avenue South. The doorway where Sport hangs out was located at 204 East 13th Street in East Village. The dilapidated hotel where Iris meets her johns was located just down the street at 226 East 13th Street (again in East Village). Travis purchases his guns at 87 Columbia Heights in Brooklyn. When Travis shoots the aforementioned bodega robber, he does this at 546 Columbia Avenue on the Upper West Side. At Senator Palantine's rally, the politician speaks in front of the statue commemorating the victims of the USS *Maine* disaster.

Of one prominent location Ralph Singleton recalls, "Since we didn't have any money, we realized we couldn't build any sets. So we found this condemned building on Columbus Avenue. Columbus Avenue is like boutique city now, but it sure wasn't in 1975. It was drug city. There were a lot of needles in that area at that time. A lot of drugs going on. A lot of heroin. We found this building, and the art director went in and built a set. And this condemned building became Travis Bickle's apartment."

Following a long shoot—technically only twenty-five days, but the hours were so long that much of the crew turned to cocaine—and multiple recuts, *Taxi Driver* opened on February 8, 1976. "When the movie came out," Singleton recalls, "most of us believed it was going to be so dark that no one's gonna go see this picture." Critics were divided on the film. Despite this, the film earned more than $25 million at the box office. In May 1976, *Taxi Driver* won the Palme d'Or at Cannes. However, the joyous moment was slightly marred by a statement clearly aimed at the film (scolding filmmakers making violent films) that was read at the festival by jury president Tennessee Williams. The film received many accolades, including a Best Picture nomination (one of four noms the film received) at the 1977 Academy Awards.

Today *Taxi Driver* is universally recognized as a classic. Some film academics believe it to be the finest film of Scorsese's long and fabled career, although that's highly subjective. The line "You talkin' to me?" has become iconic, and the American Film Institute ranked it as the tenth greatest movie line on their 2005 "100 Years . . . 100 Movie Quotes" list.

1977

The Night the Lights Went Out on Cherry Street

A lot was happening in NYC in 1977. It was the year that the city caught disco fever and Studio 54 opened its doors in Midtown Manhattan. Tension between Yankees manager Billy Martin and slugger Reggie Jackson somehow overshadowed a one hundred–win season in which the Bronx Bombers became World Series champions for the twenty-first time. A state representative and former city councilman named Ed Koch was elected as the city's 105th mayor.

But there was also a lot of crime. 1977 is the year that everybody talks about in regards to crime; the one year of the decade that gets the most ink. And while plenty of interesting things happened that year, most of the attention comes due to the events of a single night. On July 13, 1977, three separate lightning strikes led to a twenty-five-hour loss of electricity that left eight million New Yorkers in the dark. With the city already terrified by constant updates about the "Son of Sam" murders, affected by both severe economic downturn and the start of a nine-day heat wave, New Yorkers went crazy. Crime soared during the night, leading to 3,776 arrests. There were more than 1,000 fires reported. Rampant looting took place, and more than $300 million worth of property was damaged or destroyed. Surprisingly, there was only one murder. Strangely enough, that night—a night the *New York Post* dubbed "Twenty-Four Hours of Terror"—is credited with kicking the still-new hip-hop genre into overdrive; at a time when the DJ was the center of the genre, hundreds of would-be DJs broke into music stores and stole the equipment they needed to work in music.

Serial killer David Berkowitz, the "Son of Sam," continued his shooting rampage well into 1977. He shot another nine victims, killing five. On April 17, 1977, Berkowitz left a handwritten note behind at a crime scene, calling himself the "Son of Sam" and promising that there were more shootings to come. On May 30, *Daily News* columnist Jimmy Breslin received a second handwritten missive from Berkowitz. In the letter, the killer told Breslin that "Sam" was a "thirsty lad" who wouldn't allow him to stop killing "until he [got] his fill of blood." Berkowitz once again signed the letter as the Son of Sam. On August 10, twenty-three-year-old Yonkers native Berkowitz was arrested after police discovered a rifle, ammunition, and crime scene maps in the backseat of his car. Berkowitz would plead guilty to the murders. He also claimed to have set an astounding 1,500 fires around the city. Berkowitz told police that the Sam whom he believed had been commanding him to kill was (he believed) an evil spirit speaking through his neighbor's barking black Lab. (He eventually admitted that he'd concocted the dog story.)

In 1977, New York City experienced 1,557 murders, which was a decline from the previous year. This was the second straight year the number of murders had decreased. Violent crimes also decreased by 9.1 percent, with 121,916 reported, as opposed to the 134,153 the year before.

While an exact number of subway crimes reported in 1977 isn't available, it's believed that there were more than two hundred subway crimes committed per week. These staggering statistics led to the NYPD instituting an operation they called "Subway Sweep." This operation led to the arrest of more than two hundred potential felons. However, the sting proved to be ineffective as the majority of these arrests failed to yield convictions.

The frightening statistics regarding subway crime (and possibly too many viewings of *Death Wish* [1974]) led to the establishment of an unarmed vigilante group calling themselves the "Magnificent 13." The group, organized by a Bronx McDonalds' assistant manager named Curtis Sliwa, eventually became known as the "Guardian Angels." Mayor Koch would have a public love/hate relationship with Sliwa and his group. Early on, Koch was opposed to them. But later, he praised them for their efforts in helping to combat crime. *Washington Post* journalist Joyce Wadler equated the Guardian Angels to a street gang and poked fun at Sliwa, identifying him as "the only gang leader in the country with a publicist." Sliwa later admitted he'd exaggerated the exploits of the Guardian Angels. He would also admit to concocting a story about him being kidnapped by off-duty cops. In 2021, Sliwa would make an unsuccessful bid for New York City mayor.

While fires were a problem throughout the decade, there is one incident from 1977 that would help to define the city during the decade. On October 12, the Yankees were hosting the Los Angeles Dodgers for game two of the World Series. The game itself didn't offer much for New Yorkers to enjoy or discuss—the Dodgers beat the Yanks six to one—but a raging fire near the stadium made both headlines and history. The network camera panned over to the fire decimating a nearby school. As the story goes, legendary broadcaster Howard Cosell then uttered the immortal words, "There it is, ladies and gentlemen, the Bronx is burning." Interestingly, although that line would become seared in the collective mind of New Yorkers, it's a myth; Cosell never actually said it. With the Bronx losing more than 97 percent of its buildings to fire and abandonment between the years of 1970 and 1980, and with 13,752 recorded arsons, fires were an everyday occurrence. "The smell is one thing I remember," retired firefighter Tom Henderson later told the *New York Post*. "That smell of burning—it was always there, through the whole borough almost."

While a lot of things occurred in New York City in 1977, the year saw the release of very few crime films shot there. The only film we'll discuss here is a television film called *Contract on Cherry Street*, starring Frank Sinatra.

Contract on Cherry Street

In the 1970s, made for television films were still fairly new. While there was still a stigma to working on episodic television, talented actors and directors sometimes slummed, making NBC original "Movies of the Week." In the 1970s, Frank Sinatra was now in his sixties and, as such, made an effort to move away from the swinging "Rat Pack" films he'd made with buddies Dean Martin, Sammy Davis Jr., Peter Lawford, and Joey Bishop. He now sought to make serious detective films and cop dramas. The crooner had originally been cast to play Detective Harry Callahan in *Dirty Harry* (1971) but had backed out, citing health problems. (Picture what *that* film would have looked like. I think it's safe to say it would have been very different from the Clint Eastwood movie that exists today.)

Sinatra later made the television cop film *Contract on Cherry Street*, which was adapted from Philip Rosenberg's novel of the same title. The story/legend about how he came to make the film is an interesting one. Assistant director Ralph Singleton explains, "This is the story, and I believe this to be true. Frank Sinatra's mom read the book and said to her boy, 'I want you to do this.' Frank did not want to do this movie. It was an NBC Movie of the Week as I recall. It wasn't a feature. And he agreed to do it. The irony of all this is that his mom was going from Palm Beach to Vegas to see a show. Through the various contacts that Sinatra had, they had arranged a private airplane out of the Palm Springs airport. The plane crashed and his mother was killed. This was about three or four months before he started the movie. And because of his mother wanting him to do the movie, he did it for her."

This was Sinatra's first film role in seven years. It would also be the second to last starring role of his career. Martin Balsam, Verna Bloom, Harry Guardino, and Henry Silva were cast in supporting roles. *French Connection* (1971) alums Sonny Grosso and Randy Jurgensen also make appearances. Rosenberg's novel was adapted by two-time Academy Award–winner Edward Anhalt. (Anhalt had won Oscars for *Panic in the Streets* [1951] and *Beckett* [1965]. He'd also been nominated a third time for *The Sniper* [1953].) *Contract on Cherry Street* would also feature a score by Jerry Goldsmith, who would ultimately receive an astounding eighteen career Academy Award nominations (resulting in a single win).

The director, William A. Graham, had been working in television since the 1950s, and his credits include episodes of such iconic series as *Route 66*, *The Virginian*, *Dr. Kildare*, *The Fugitive*, and *Batman*. His film credits were mostly television films, but he had directed the Elvis Presley vehicle *Change of Habit* (1969). Graham's reputation was that of a director with questionable organizational skills and a man who didn't always know what was happening with lighting and other technical aspects of production. While "good enough" might have been good enough for Elvis, it didn't fly with Old Blue Eyes. As such, the atmosphere during the shoot was tense. Sensing weakness in the director, Sinatra made it clear to everyone that he didn't want to be there. While shooting a fairly elaborate scene, Sinatra decided he was finished for the day and called *"Cut!"* before walking off the set. With filming already behind schedule, Graham and company needed to finish shooting the scene. "I looked at the whole crew," Ralph Singleton recalls. "I've got 150 people there, and the director. I said, 'What the hell are we gonna do now?' So we bring his double in, and his stunt guy in, and we shoot the rest of the sequence without Sinatra. I'm pretty sure we went into night, because at night you can cheat a lot. What you light is what you see. But it was pretty funny, because what do you do? Go home? You can't go home."

The entire film was shot in New York City. The shoot corresponded with the infamous two-day blackout that took place on July 13 and 14 of 1977. During the blackout, the sixty-one-year-old Sinatra was forced to walk down twenty floors from his penthouse to shoot a scene. The walk garnered him hard-earned applause from the actors and crew members on set. In 2018, costar Robert Davi told *Fox News* reporter Elizabeth Zwirz that Sinatra demanded that he drink Jack Daniels with him after hours. When Davi told him he didn't drink, Sinatra forced the issue, saying, "You don't drink, you're fired."

After a problematic shoot that Sinatra was happy to put in his rearview mirror, *Contract on Cherry Street* aired on Saturday, November 19, 1977, on NBC. Sinatra appeared on the cover of

TV Guide that week to promote the film. The telefilm was met with predominantly favorable reviews. After the film received a nomination for Best TV Feature/Miniseries at the 1978 Edgar Allan Poe Awards, a theatrical release was briefly considered but ultimately scrapped.

1978
Donnie Brasco and the Biggest Heist in US History

The biggest New York City crime story of the year took place on December 11, 1978, when a group of mobsters allegedly led by Lucchese crime family associate Jimmy Burke pulled off the largest (at the time) successful cash heist in US history. The robbery, which took place at John F. Kennedy International Airport, netted the wiseguys an estimated $5.8 million. (That amount would be the equivalent of about $27 million today.) The cash and jewels were stolen as they were being transferred through the German airline Lufthansa. Only one man, Louis Werner, an airport employee who helped the robbers, was arrested. However, many of the robbers later turned up dead, allegedly murdered by Burke in an effort to evade prison. The Lufthansa heist would be reenacted in Martin Scorsese's now-classic film *Goodfellas* (1990). The story would also serve as the basis for the lesser-known television films *The Ten Million Dollar Getaway* (1991) and *The Big Heist* (2001).

In other mob-related news, the Federal Bureau of Investigations kicked off an operation with the enigmatic code name "Sun-Apple." In the operation, which was initially planned to last six months, an undercover agent named Joseph D. Pistone would infiltrate the Bonanno crime family. In doing so, Pistone assumed the identity of a jewel thief named Donnie Brasco. Pistone would prove to be so successful that the operation was extended for another two years. In that time, Pistone managed not only to infiltrate the Bonanno family, but also to compromise the Colombo family. Pistone's brave and tireless undercover work ultimately led to more than two hundred indictments and more than one hundred convictions of mobsters. As a result of Pistone's successful infiltration, the Mafia put out a $500,000 contract on him. That contract was later withdrawn. Pistone would eventually lean on his fame to author a handful of books, executive-produce films, and even host a podcast. His story would become the basis for the film *Donnie Brasco* (1997) and the short-lived TV series *Falcone*.

In 1978, Paul Castellano, the boss of the Gambino crime family, brokered a partnership between the Gambino family and the Irish-American gang known as the Westies. There were also bullets flying, per usual, and some mob-related murders. Genovese hit man and Teamsters official Salvatore Briguglio was gunned down in Little Italy before he could testify in a murder case. Lucchese family associate and pimp Michael DiCarlo was tortured and killed by the Gambino family's infamous Roy DeMeo crew. His body has never been found. But not every notable New York Mafia-related death was a violent one; former Colombo family boss Joe Colombo, who had been shot and left paralyzed six years before, died peacefully in his home.

By 1978, the career of the influential English punk band The Sex Pistols was in full swing. However, the band's meteoric rise would come crashing down on October 12 in one of the most dramatic ways possible. Bassist Sid Vicious' twenty-year-old American girlfriend, Nancy Spungen, was found dead in the bathroom of the couple's room at the Chelsea Hotel (222 West 23rd Street in Manhattan). Spungen had been stabbed to death. The couple (allegedly) had a history of domestic abuse, so it appeared to be a no-brainer; Vicious was charged with second-degree murder. He claimed that he was innocent but, being a junkie, offered multiple conflicting accounts of the night of Spungen's death. Vicious would never make it to trial because he died of an overdose the following February.

David Berkowitz, the self-proclaimed "Son of Sam" who'd been involved in eight shootings and two stabbings and had killed six New Yorkers, went to trial. The killer pretended to be insane but was found competent. He was sentenced to six consecutive life sentences. When it was speculated that Berkowitz might try to sell his story for a book and/or film, the New York State Legislature enacted new statutes, which have been dubbed "the Son of Sam laws," preventing criminals from profiting from their crimes.

On June 14, Samuel Miller, a Caribbean immigrant, was visited by two NYPD officers delivering a summons because he'd allegedly left debris on a construction site where he and his brothers were building a wedding hall. An argument ensued after it was learned that Miller's driver's license had been suspended. Miller insisted that he'd paid his fines, and the cops called for backup. Miller attempted to run, and approximately a dozen more police officers arrived on the scene. Miller's brothers, Arthur and Joseph, also showed up. Because Arthur Miller, a thirty-year-old respected businessman and community leader in Crown Heights, had a pistol tucked into his waistband, he was swarmed and beaten by sixteen officers brandishing nightsticks. When he struggled to break free, a police officer attempted to choke him into submission. Miller gasped that he could not breathe, but the officer refused to relent, even when foam started to come out of his mouth. Witnesses later said they saw Miller's feet sticking out of the window of a police cruiser as it drove away. Predictably, no officer was suspended, fired, or tried for murder.

The year 1978 was another slow year for the release of crime films shot in New York City. As a result, this chapter, like the last, focuses on a single film, James Toback's gangster picture *Fingers*.

Fingers

James Toback broke into Hollywood when he sold his semi-autobiographical screenplay, *The Gambler*, to Paramount Pictures in 1972. After the script was made into a film directed by Karel Reisz, George Barry, owner and CEO of Fabergé, convinced Toback to write a script based on the life of Victoria Woodhull. The film was to star Faye Dunaway, but the project fell apart. Barry then told Toback that he would finance a movie for him to direct if he could write something he could shoot for less than a million dollars. Seeing this as a challenge, Toback sat down and wrote a new screenplay titled *Fingers* in just four days. Although the script was about a Mafia debt collector with aspirations of becoming a concert pianist, Toback still managed to incorporate elements of his own life into it.

Barry read the script, approved it, and Toback began casting. During this time, he met Harvey Keitel at the Beverly Hills Hotel and offered him the lead role. Despite the fact that they had never met before, the would-be director asked the actor to accept the role without even reading the script, telling him he "should feel lucky" to work with him. Naturally, Keitel insisted on reading the script before committing. Keitel read *Fingers* that night and agreed to be in the film the following day. *Fingers* would give Keitel his first leading role since *Mean Streets* five years before. But more importantly, Keitel saw an opportunity to improve on his craft by delving deeply into both the role and his own soul to produce something genuine. "I told Jimmy [Toback] immediately that I didn't want to come near this film unless we did it as completely and as honestly as we could," Keitel later told author Marshall Fine. "I wanted it to be a total commitment. No lies. Because so many of us go through an identity crisis because of that need to be loved. We're not taught to seek our own place in the world."

Toback also asked Jim Brown to be in *Fingers*, offering him a role as a prizefighter that was darker and more challenging than anything Brown had previously done. Because the two were friends, Brown accepted the part without hesitation. Toback also offered a role to Mia Farrow's sister, Tisa, who was driving a cab and working as a waitress in a bar at the time. He convinced her to quit both jobs and appear in his film. Toback ultimately assembled a cast that included Keitel, Farrow, Brown, Danny Aiello, Michael Gazzo, and Michael Chapman. Everything was in place, and Toback was ready to make the film.

But then, out of the blue, Barry told him (by way of an intermediate) that he had decided not to make the film. Instead, he'd decided to pay off everyone involved and walk away. Toback would later tell Nicholas Jarecki, "I think [Barry] really wanted to get out of it because he was listening to a lot of people around him who said, 'Toback doesn't know what he's doing; he's never made a movie before. You can't make a movie for $1 million, it's gonna be chaotic. He's not a director, and look at the behavior in this movie; look at what these people are doing. You're gonna give a first-time director who has never even made a short free rein to do this? We're Fabergé, this is a perfume company, what the hell are you thinking?'"

Toback flew into a rage. Not the kind of person to take this news sitting down, Toback went to Barry's office to confront him. But then something odd happened; when Toback walked into Barry's office, he encountered Cary Grant there, waiting for George Steinbrenner to pick him up to take him to a Yankees game. When Toback saw Grant, his angry demeanor fell away, and he confessed to the legendary actor that he felt overwhelmed to be in the same room with him. Grant downplayed this in his normal, nonchalant Cary Grant way. Toback then went about trying to convince Barry to move forward with the film. After Toback made his pitch, Barry turned to Grant and asked him if he should make *Fingers*. Grant just shrugged, likely disinterested in all of this, and said, "Sure, why not?" Toback would later credit Cary Grant as being one of the primary reasons the film ended up being made.

Filming on *Fingers* began one week later. It would be a nineteen-day shoot. The first thing Toback shot was a tracking shot of a homeless woman in a doorway near the 59th Street bridge. That afternoon, they shot a scene in which a little girl does cartwheels while Keitel is being arrested. On *Fingers*, Barry allowed first-time director Toback to make the film as he saw fit, with no interference whatsoever. The director allowed his actors to improvise while sticking close to the script's original intent, doing what he would later refer to as "controlled experimentation."

Because the role demanded that Keitel play the piano, and because he didn't know anything about the piano, he began taking lessons before going abroad to make *The Duellists* (1978), which he was making before *Fingers*. Keitel insisted that he have a piano in his hotel room, so he could sit and practice after each day's shooting. While Keitel's own music wouldn't actually be used in *Fingers*, he would do a fine enough job pretending that no one would suspect it wasn't really him playing.

Fingers would be released theatrically on March 2, 1978, to mostly negative reviews. For instance, Vincent Canby of the *New York Times* panned the film with great vitriol: "*Fingers* is to the films of Martin Scorsese and Paul Schrader—films that *Fingers* seems to ape—what that long list of failed 'youth pictures' was to *Easy Rider* [1969]. A spin-off. Mr. Scorsese and Mr. Schrader, even when their films are less than great, are original talents. Their obsessions with religion, sex, violence, guilt, and the general quality of American life are matched by their knowledge of cinema. They know what the cinema can and cannot do. Mr. Toback's obsession is much simpler. He wants very much to make a movie. Any movie. He wants to see his name in lights. But it's as if he hadn't spent much time thinking about what kind of movie he'd like to make or even much about how movies are made, that is, what makes them different from the literary models he evokes, much like an aggressively talkative but none too sensitive comp-lit student." Janet Maslin, another *New York Times* writer, also took a swipe: "Mr. Toback, having created a character whose intrinsic charm plus fifty cents would only barely get him onto the subway, seems incapable of putting his hero in any kind of dramatic perspective, and he is apparently unwilling to explore him in terms more intimate than those of an introductory psychology course."

New Yorker critic Pauline Kael wrote a more positive review. Having already been taken to task by Toback, who was now a close friend, for her criticisms of *The Gambler*, Kael once again drew the filmmaker's ire. Kael's review was far more praising than the other reviews *Fingers* received, but Toback was nevertheless outraged by Kael writing, "Normality doesn't interest Toback. He's playing the literary adolescent's game of wanting to go crazy so he can watch his own reaction." Believing she was accusing him of being a phony "crazy" person, he angrily scolded her, saying (according to Brian Kellow's biography of Kael), "You refer to a literary adolescent's way of playing crazy. I went clinically insane for eight days under LSD, at nineteen, as you well know. It was the seminal event of my life. And you, who have never experienced insanity, don't know what the fuck you're talking about. And for you to deliberately throw in a line like that is embarrassing and lightweight and not worthy of you." In *National Review*, critic John Simon would later accuse Kael of "shoddy journalism," giving *Fingers* a positive review merely because of her friendship with Toback. This caused Toback to respond in typical Toback fashion: "John Simon actually wrote and implied that I was fucking Pauline Kael—that's why she wrote what she did about the movie—and then said it at UCLA at a big gathering they had. And they asked me about it on a big TV interview after that and I said, 'I have fucked Pauline Kael the same number of times I've fucked John Simon.'"

Fingers is a film that has all but fallen through the cracks. It's fairly difficult to find. While it's far from the best NYC gangster movie, it's a fascinating watch. It was later remade in France as *The Beat That My Heart Skipped* (2005).

1979
The Wanderers *and* The Warriors *Run the Streets*

As one would expect from a city with a (then-) population of seven million people, there was a lot going on in New York City in 1979. But then, there's always a lot going on in NYC. Yankees fans mourned the death of their thirty-two-year-old starting catcher and team captain, Thurman Munson, who was tragically killed in an aircraft accident. The noted off-Broadway theater company known as the New York Theatre Workshop was established. Future US vice presidential candidate Geraldine Ferraro became a US representative for NYC's Ninth Congressional District, and future President Ronald Reagan announced his presidential candidacy at the New York Hilton (234 West 42nd Street) on November 13, 1979.

That year, New York City set a personal record (at the time) for homicides, topping 1,700 for the first time. The number of homicides had increased by 15 percent from the year before. The previous record for NYC homicides had been 1,691, set in 1972. The city averaged roughly 4.75 murders per day in 1979. This increase in homicides was the biggest jump the city had seen since 1971, when NYC suffered through 1,466 homicides as opposed to the 1,146 the year before. But why had the murder rate jumped so spectacularly in 1979? Police weren't entirely sure, but they attributed some of it to an increase in murders committed during robberies.

On May 25, 1979, six-year-old Etan Patz walked down the street from his 113 Prince Street apartment in Lower Manhattan to await the school bus at his neighborhood bus stop. Somehow, during the course of that walk, Patz disappeared. The boy's teacher noticed that he was missing from class but never thought to tell anyone. When Patz didn't come home after school that day, his mother became alarmed and contacted the police. The NYPD engaged in a massive search effort, utilizing approximately one hundred police officers, as well as a team of dogs. Flyers displaying a photograph of the young boy on them became a staple around the borough, and his photo was displayed on screens in Times Square. Patz became one of the first children to appear as a missing child on milk cartons. Sadly, police were unable to find the boy. Four years later, President Reagan proclaimed May 25, the day Patz had gone missing, National Missing Children's Day. Twenty-three years later, a suspect named Pedro Hernandez confessed to abducting and murdering Patz. After two trials, the first of which ended in a mistrial, Hernandez would be sentenced to twenty-five-years-to-life.

In the summer of 1979, $600,000 was stolen from the headquarters of the New York Transit Authority. Mayor Ed Koch had declared a war on subway crime, but that only meant the curtailing of obvious crimes such as assault, rape, and murder. To give you an idea how prevalent subway crime was in 1979, the *New York Times* reported that there were 320 subway robberies in the month of January alone. But again, that was the usual subway crime. What about the cash absconded from the Brooklyn-based Transit Authority headquarters? It's believed that a power outage allowed the robbers (the FBI concluded that there were likely three to six of them) to go unnoticed entering the money room through a shoddily patched-up hole in a wall between that room and the women's bathroom. The money was never found, nor was the case solved.

The big Mafia news of the year was the July 13 assassination of Bonanno crime family boss Carmine Galante. The mob boss and two of his associates were enjoying dinner at Joe & Mary's Italian Restaurant (on Knickerbocker Avenue in Brooklyn) when multiple gunmen, including Galante's own bodyguards, strolled in and gunned them down.

That same year, infamous Gambino family captain Roy DeMeo and his bloodthirsty crew killed *a lot* of people. Their known victims were: coke dealer and police informant Peter Waring, who was murdered and dismembered on February 7; Frederick Todaro, who was stabbed, dismembered, and dropped off at Brooklyn's Fountain Avenue Dump on February 19; Charles Padnick, William Serano, and two unidentified associates were shot and dismembered on March 17; on April 19, DeMeo mistook nineteen-year-old college student Dominick Ragucci for a hit man and chased him by car before shooting and killing him; DeMeo crew member Harvey Rosenberg was killed on May 11 after he'd ripped off a Colombian drug dealer; Gambino family members James Eppolito and James Eppolito Jr. were shot on October 1; used car dealers Ronald Falcaro and Khaled Daoud were killed, dismembered, and disposed of on October 12 for threatening to tell the cops about a car theft ring DeMeo operated.

Okay, so what was playing in theaters? We'll take a look at four films from 1979. These are *The Driller Killer, From Corleone to Brooklyn, The Wanderers,* and *The Warriors*. While *The Driller Killer*, and later, in 1980, *Maniac*, were poignant at the time of their release with the Son of Sam having frightened the city for the latter part of the decade, and the Torso Killer just on the cusp of being captured, the real story of 1979 were the releases of two street gang pictures, *The Wanderers* and *The Warriors*. Because these similarly titled films would stir up the media and various busybody concerned citizens groups, they stand as the most visible representations of the year in NYC crime cinema.

The Driller Killer

In 1978, Abel Ferrara had directed only one film—an adult picture called *9 Lives of a Wet Pussy* (1976). That film had proven that Ferrara could make a film, but after *9 Lives*, he decided he was through with adult films; he wanted to become a "proper" filmmaker. Inspired by the success of low-budget horror film *Texas Chainsaw Massacre* (1974), a project made for somewhere around $100,000 (accounts vary) that made more than $30 million, Ferrara decided to make a horror film. "I wasn't the John

Waters type," he later told author Nicholas Jarecki. "I figured that I could hustle up a *Driller Killer* more easily than I could a *Pink Flamingos* [1972]." In reality, he saw the movie he wanted to make as being more of a "twisted art movie," but he (correctly) believed he could more easily find funding if he pitched it as a straight horror film. Ferrara funded the $70,000 picture with money given to him by his mother and funds secured by *Debbie Does Dallas* (1978) producer Arthur Weisberg. (Interestingly, Weisberg left his name off the film, instead crediting his daughter, Rochelle Weisberg.)

Ferrara decided to shoot the film at, and in the neighborhood around, he and his roommate Douglas Anthony Metro's Fifth Avenue fifth-floor apartment. The director decided to cast himself in the lead role (using the pseudonym Jimmy Laine) because he didn't know how long the shoot might last, and he wanted to cast someone he knew he could count on to stay around for the duration of the shoot. His roommate, Metro, also plays a significant role in the film, Tony Coca-Cola. Ferrara would later say that *The Driller Killer* could be considered a documentary of the roommates' life at the time. Since the film's lead character, Reno, is supposed to be a painter, they used artwork painted by Metro. Additionally, Metro co-conceived the film, allowed Ferrara to make out with his girlfriend in the film, and co-wrote (with Ferrara) all the songs his band performs in the movie.

While Ferrara seems a little bit embarrassed by the somewhat amateur nature of the film today, he is proud of the fact that *The Driller Killer* captures nighttime NYC as it actually was. "The world [of the film] was the world we were living in—New York City, 1977, 1978," Ferrara would later say in the documentary *Laine and Abel: An Interview with the Driller Killer* (2016). Rather than using extras, Ferrara and cinematographer Ken Kelsch captured footage of real homeless men and passersby on the streets to give the film an authentic feel. The crew shot the entire film guerrilla style, without permits. The director laughingly recalls, much to the dismay of onlookers, wandering the streets of New York and getting onto the subway covered in blood and carrying a power drill. Another scene shot without permission features a man being stabbed to death in the middle of a busy street in broad daylight. Ferrara would later remark that he was surprised the actor wasn't shot or arrested since police would have had no way of knowing he was just acting.

The film started shooting in December 1977 and continued through most of 1978. *The Driller Killer* was shot on sixteen-millimeter film. At least in the beginning, filming was done on weekends only, and none of the actors were paid. Screenwriter Nicholas St. John, who would write many other Ferrara films, including *Ms. 45* (1981) and *King of New York* (1990), wrote the script as the shoot progressed, the idea (Ferrara's) being that they would discover the film organically as they proceeded. While writing about the schizophrenic lead character, St. John and Ferrara frequently referred to an academic book about schizophrenia.

Several musical scenes were shot at the famed and now-defunct nightclub Max's Kansas City (213 Park Avenue). Ferrara says it took two months of pleading with the club's owners before they gave him permission to film there. Then, when they were filming at Max's, Douglas Anthony Metro got trashed before performing and then refused to leave the stage, leading to Ferrara and his crew being asked to leave. Another memorable scene—the film's opening—was shot in a Catholic church on Mulberry Street in Little Italy, just around the corner from where Martin Scorsese grew up. Ferrara also used an abandoned loft situated between Fifth Avenue and Broadway as a set, shooting several scenes there.

The Driller Killer was released theatrically in approximately twenty theaters, including Portland, Seattle, and Kansas City on June 15, 1979. It immediately became a smash hit in terms of the money it made in proportion to its cost. Most reviews of the film were scathing. For instance, *Variety* panned, "The most stupid thing about the film is why, when he turns into a murderer with an electric drill, he doesn't go downstairs and eliminate the band, which could have improved the tone of the film by at least a thousand percent." The film would eventually be reassessed and grow in stature. One such reassessment appeared in Chas Balun's 1992 book *Connoisseur's Guide to the Contemporary Horror Film*: "An extremely knowledgeable group assembled this little-heralded, minor masterpiece, attaining a thoroughness, style, and pace that one rarely witnesses in today's genre offerings. A literate, cynical script that always keeps the film in bounds without its drifting into ridiculous excesses or inept parody. Nicely lit sets, fluid and imaginative camera work, and a steadfast lead performance by director Abel Ferrara makes *The Driller Killer* far more than just another forgettable exploitation hack-job."

Largely due to the film's graphic VHS artwork, *The Driller Killer* became one of the United Kingdom's "video nasties" and was banned until 1999. The film has developed a substantial cult following in the decades since its release.

From Corleone to Brooklyn

New York City wasn't the only place going through difficult times in the 1970s. Some four thousand miles away, Italy was in the midst of a period that would come to be known as the "Years of Lead." This period, which lasted from roughly 1968 to 1988 (depending on the source), was a time of social turmoil and political violence. During these years, there were countless incidents of kidnapping, bombings, assassination, and other acts of violence carried out by political extremists. During this time, there were also two large-scale wars between members of the Sicilian Mafia.

While this was undoubtedly a bleak period, there was at least one bright spot; a new cinematic sub-genre known as *"Poliziotteschi"* would emerge from this unrest. This movement would last from the late 1960s to approximately 1980 and would include more than one hundred films. These were violent crime pictures that were heavily influenced by crime and exploitation movies from the United States and, to a lesser extent, France. The plots and themes of many of these were lifted almost directly from such Hollywood pictures as *Dirty Harry* (1971), *The French Connection* (1971), *The Godfather* (1972), and *Death Wish* (1974). These Italian productions focused on subjects that included organized crime, heists, police procedurals, and vigilantism.

Although the stories were inspired by American films that took place in locales such as Los Angeles and New York City, the *Poliziotteschi* pictures primarily took place in Italian cities such as Naples and Rome. To make these films enticing to American audiences, they often featured a Hollywood actor. These included Charles Bronson, Telly Savalas, Woody Strode, Joseph Cotten, Jack Palance, Fred Williamson, and Oliver Reed, to name a few. Although the Italian mystery/horror sub-genre known as *"Giallo"* occurred concurrently with the *Poliziotteschi* movement, they were completely different kinds of film (although some films are difficult to categorize as they fit into both sub-genres).

During the run of the *Poliziotteschi* films, a number of actors and filmmakers rose to prominence because of their work in the sub-genre. Two of the most recognized were director Umberto Lenzi and actor Maurizio Merli. The two artists would join forces to make the film *From Corleone to Brooklyn*. Lenzi directed many of the finest *Poliziotteschi* films, and Merli has become the de facto face of the cycle. Lenzi and Merli had previously collaborated on the films *The Tough Ones* [aka *Rome, Armed to the Teeth*] (1976), *Violent Naples* (1976), and *The Cynic, the Rat and the Fist* (1977). *From Corleone to Brooklyn* would ultimately be the least popular of the four collaborations, but it is significant for our purposes because it was largely shot in Brooklyn.

Mike Malloy, director of the 2012 documentary *Eurocrime: The Italian Cop and Gangster Films That Ruled the 70s*, says, "In the 1960s, the Italian crime films were just ramping up to the popularity that would peak in the next decade. And because the Spaghetti Westerns were still selling well around the world, including the United States, I think that's why these early Eurocrime films tried to be as big and as international as they could during the 1960s. They often shot in locations like San Francisco and New York City, with some of the films shot in New York being *The Hired Killer* from 1966 and *Assassination* from 1967. By about 1973, the producers of Italian crime movies seemed resigned to the fact that these films wouldn't be as big as their previous Westerns, so it became a much more Italo-centric genre for a while.

"And by the end of the 1970s," Malloy explains, "the Italian crime genre was largely made on the cheap in Naples, and producers weren't even bothering to make English-language dubs for many of them. To differentiate themselves, the few well-funded Italian crime films at the time seemed intent on going in the opposite direction, going back to the model of trying to be international in scope. And so New York shoots were included for 1978 films like *The Squeeze* and *Little Italy* and for 1979 films like *From Corleone to Brooklyn* and *The Gang That Sold America*."

In addition to Merli, *From Corleone to Brooklyn* also featured Mario Merola, Biagio Pelligra, Venantino Venantini, and Laura Belli. Van Johnson, star of such noted films as *The Caine Mutiny* and *Brigadoon* (both 1954), filled the role of mandatory "past his expiration date" Hollywood veteran on the production. Cinematographer Guglielmo Mancori, who had previously worked with Lenzi on the films *Spasmo* (1974) and *Manhunt* (1975), lensed the picture.

The film's plot (from a script by Lenzi, Anselmo Manciori, and Vincenzo Mannino) tells the story of an Italian cop (Merli) transporting a witness from Corleone to the United States so he can testify against a mob boss hiding in New York City. On their journey to the United States, they, predictably, encounter a number of mobsters trying to stop them and silence the witness. In an effort to protect the cop and his witness, the police convince the newspapers to run a story falsely reporting that the witness has been killed. In the end, the witness actually gets shot and killed before he can testify. However, the police find a handwritten note in his pocket stating that the mob boss is indeed the killer. It's a ridiculous plot, but nonetheless entertaining. It should be noted that there are elements of the storyline—particularly the cop taking the witness to his ex-wife's home—that would later appear in the Martin Brest–directed *Midnight Run* (1988).

"It's a film I care a lot about," Lenzi would later tell an audience before a screening of the film. "I remember that we had a lot of help from the police in Palermo and also from the New York police. They lent us cars and offices, and in New York they asked us for eight dollars a day to give us everything [with the] policemen, including that, among other things, they were already dressed in uniforms. We walked around the offices of a police station while the policemen worked at their desks."

The film's NYC scenes were shot in February when it was extremely cold. When corresponding scenes were shot in Italy, the weather was warm. In order to provide a sense that the scenes were being shot in the winter, Lenzi instructed his actors to fill their mouths with ice and then spit it out just before each scene. According to Lenzi, the production had no extras for the NYC portion of the shoot. So when extras were needed for a scene in which a group of men beat up Merli's character, the director told his assistant to walk into a bar and recruit three or four men with the "ugliest" faces. When the assistant returned, his recruits were drunk. As a result of using drunks instead of real actors, these men actually punched Merli. Luckily, the actor wasn't hurt. Also of note, the Twin Towers are visible in the background during this scene.

In a 2013 review of *From Corleone to Brooklyn*, Brian Bankston of *Cool Ass Cinema* wrote: "Umberto Lenzi takes his bow in the Italian crime genre directing his last violent, yet surprisingly subtle entry before moving on to literal greener pastures with gory jungle adventures and bloody horror movies that would, sadly, become the staples of his long career. Lenzi is/was seemingly in love with New York City. So many of his movies have scenes shot there and this time, a good portion of this Italian-made potboiler is set on the streets of Manhattan and Times Square. This adds a great deal to the exploitation appeal of the picture; and with Lenzi's name attached, it's an instant sale."

The Wanderers

The story behind *The Wanderers* begins with a would-be writer named Richard Price, who lived in the Parkside Projects in the Bronx. Looking out his apartment's third-floor window, past the L trains that streaked by throughout the day, Price observed the gangs who roamed the neighborhood. The most prevalent gang in the area was a group who called themselves "The Wanderers." Inspired by the real-life gang members, Price penned a collection of stories about their imagined lives and exploits. During an MFA writing course at Columbia University, Price shared the first chapter of his work-in-progress to the class. According to Price, his instructor and all of his classmates *hated* it. Undeterred, he kept writing. When the twenty-three-year-old writer finished *The Wanderers*, he sold it for publication to Houghton Mifflin. Samuel Goldwyn Jr., the producer behind such films as *Cotton Comes to Harlem* (1970) and *Come Back, Charleston Blue* (1972), optioned the film rights.

When Price was hired to adapt his novel into screenplay form, the author struggled through two "failed" (Price's words) drafts. Somewhere during this time, director Philip Kaufman's son, Peter, read *The Wanderers* and suggested it to his father as something he should make. Kaufman agreed. His wife, Rose Kaufman, then wrote a script. After that, Philip and Rose wrote several more drafts. Their primary difficulty was figuring out how exactly they could adapt a group of short stories that take place over the course of many years into a storyline. Eventually they figured it out, and after two years, the Kaufmans finalized their script. Throughout the process, Italian producer Alberto Grimaldi, best known for *For a Few Dollars More* and *The Good, the Bad and the Ugly* [both 1967], tried in vain to find financing. As Grimaldi kept looking, Kaufman attempted to make a *Star Trek* motion picture that was ultimately aborted. He then helmed Donald Sutherland in a hit remake of *Invasion of the Body Snatchers* (1978). Kaufman finally pulled the reins from Grimaldi and found his own financing for *The Wanderers* through producer Martin Ransohoff.

Because of its modest budget (amount unknown), Kaufman decided to cast unknowns. Some of the actors he cast, such as Ken Wahl, who was working in a pizza parlor, had never done any acting. Wahl was brought in to read for a small part, but when Kaufman met him, he recognized immediately that Wahl had the looks and charisma to pull off a larger role, so he made him the lead. Another of the film's key performers, Tony Ganios, hadn't done any acting either. Ganios would later confess that he'd grown up seeing actors as being soft and had picked on them. Ganios only auditioned because his uncle, who intimidated him, demanded he do so. Kaufman also filled many small parts in the film with non-actors in the hopes of making the picture feel more authentic.

Dawn of the Dead (1978) star Ken Foree makes an appearance in the film as a rival gang member. Future Indiana Jones gal pal Karen Allen, future Oscar winner Olympia Dukakis, and future *Sopranos* regular Toni Kalem had all done *some* acting, but *The Wanderers* gave them their biggest roles to date.

Kalem auditioned eight times in three months. Overhearing Kaufman saying he wasn't sure if her breasts were large enough, Kalem wore a tube top and pushed her breasts up before her final audition, asking the director, *"Are these fuckin' big enough?!"* In addition to her strong will and outspoken nature, Kalem also brought a level of preparation to her role that was unmatched by her costars. Because Kalem, who is not Italian despite now having made a career of playing Italians, had no accent, she spent three months on Arthur Avenue studying the way Bronx Italian women spoke. She then met a woman named Linda whom she saw as being the living embodiment of her character, Despie. She then spent a number of days with this "real-life Despie," even staying at her house, to study her mannerisms. Additionally, Kalem would fill her purse with items that would be authentic to Despie, despite the fact that they would never be seen, to aid her in knowing and becoming the character.

For *The Wanderers*, which takes place in 1963, Kaufman wanted to capture the details and feel of the era but decided he would also strive to give the film a stylized look. In order to achieve this, he would make the exterior scenes brighter (depicting the characters' lives as being brighter) than the darker interior scenes (showing where the characters had come from). Kaufman would have his characters wear colorful clothing and then shoot scenes with dim lighting or overcast skies to make those colors "pop."

The film's soundtrack would feature one of the greatest assemblages of songs from the early 1960s. Richard Price played a major role in this. As "music advisor," Price bought hundreds of records featuring his favorite songs of the era. He would then make suggestions and work closely with Kaufman to determine which songs would be used and where in the film they would appear. Memorable songs used in the film include "The Times They Are a Changin'" by Bob Dylan, "Sherry" by The Four Seasons, "Tequila" by The Champs, "Stand by Me" by Ben E. King (in its first of many film appearances), "My Boyfriend's Back" by The Angels, "Runaround Sue" and, of course, "The Wanderer" by Dion.

Film started rolling on *The Wanderers* in September 1978, shooting entirely on location throughout the Bronx. Early in the shoot, a Puerto Rican motorcycle gang showed up during the filming of one of the "Baldies" scenes. After menacingly pushing their way through the crowd, they ran into statuesque, menacing-looking actor Erland van Lidth. Realizing the potential trouble they were in for if they started a ruckus or demanded money, the bikers backed down and left. Another instance of NYC craziness involves the scene in which the Wanderers meet with members of other gangs around a bonfire as an L Train speeds by overhead. According to Kaufman, the NYPD discovered a dead body in that same location not long after the scene was filmed.

"We had a great New York crew," Kaufman would later recall in a 2017 audio commentary. "They were always pushing you to get the shot, put it on a dolly, make some moves, light it in a special way. They believe in the artistry and the craftsmanship of the work they were doing."

Kaufman had a long-standing theory that a director and his cinematographer should be "best friends" throughout a shoot. The director of photography on this film, (future) two-time Oscar-nominee Michael Chapman, known for NYC crime classics *Taxi Driver* (1976) and *Fingers* (1978), was the cameraman on *The Wanderers*. This was Kaufman and Chapman's third collaboration, the two having already made *The White Dawn* (1974) and *Invasion of the Body Snatchers*. As such, the artists were simpatico and did their finest work of their four collaborations here. (Their fourth collaboration would be *Rising Sun* [1993].)

Interestingly, there are a number of cameos in the film. These include Richard Price and author John Califano as bowling hustlers the Galassos must teach a lesson. Burtt Harris, who was known in the industry as a production manager, plays a Marine recruiter. But the most interesting cameo is provided by Bob Dylan, who appears in a scene playing himself. What makes this appearance particularly interesting is that the Greenwich Village club he's seen playing in, Folk City, was an actual bar where Dylan had routinely performed in the early 1960s.

The Wanderers proved to be incredibly popular when it screened for a test audience. However, it was poorly marketed due to controversy (regarding violence in the film and also violence in theaters) surrounding the recent release of another "gang" picture, *The Warriors* (1979). So when the film was released on July 4, 1979, it earned an underwhelming $5 million in the United States. However, it would be a huge hit in Europe, earning another $18 million.

Reviews were largely positive. *New West* critic Stephen Farber raved, "*The Wanderers* is like *West Side Story* [1961] flavored with the comic grotesquerie and melancholy poetry of Fellini." Susan Morrison of *CineAction* magazine would later assess, "What Kaufman and his wife Rose have done is to take a prize-winning 1971 novel by Richard Price and turn it into an extremely intelligent and witty narrative that comments on its time period (early 1960s) and characters in a critical yet genuinely affectionate way, a feature all too often missing in the American cinema where characters and situations are so frequently stereotyped and predictable.... *The Wanderers* is an exceptional film."

Author Price would later recount three interesting interactions he had following the release of the film. The first (and most humorous) took place when Price attempted to impress a first date by taking her to the theater to see "his" movie. While Price and his date were in line to purchase tickets, a woman in the line was telling everyone who would listen how much she loved the movie and that she had already seen it five times. Price then asked her if she knew the film was based on a book. The woman said she'd tried to read the book but hadn't been able to finish it "because it sucked." Imagine Price's embarrassment at hearing this alongside his date!

The other two interactions were with real-life members of the gangs depicted in the book and film. The first took place at a Fordham Road screening, where a large, angry man cornered him, claiming to be the "real" Terror. The man believed the character was based on him, and he demanded to know why Price believed he had the right to write about him. Before the man could pummel the stuttering author, actor/stuntman Danny Aiello III stepped in and saved him. The second of these interactions involved a member of the real Wanderers. When the man wrote Price a letter, asking to meet him, Price obliged. They wound up having dinner, and the man revealed that he'd invited Price for the sole reason of attempting to convince him to write a sequel.

In the years following the film's release, it has developed a massive cult following. A "Wanderers Club" was established in Telluride, Colorado, and meets and screens the film multiple times a year. Although there is no sequel to *The Wanderers*, Tony Ganios later reprised his role as Perry in the oddly non-similar *Rising Sun*. (After fans pointed out that Ganios' *Rising Sun* character bore the same name and also chewed on a match like his *Wanderers* character, Ganios confirmed that it was the same character.) In 2017, a director's cut of *The Wanderers* restored six minutes of excised footage and was re-released theatrically.

The Warriors

Sol Yurick, a Bronx would-be author working as a "social investigator" for the Department of Welfare, wrote a first novel titled *Fertig* in the early 1960s. The only problem was, nearly every publisher in existence rejected it. Nevertheless, he had faith and continued shopping his book. (It would eventually be published in 1966.) During this time, he decided he should start another novel rather than sitting around waiting for it to sell. He'd been kicking around an idea for a novel that would update Xenophon's *The Anabasis* as a contemporary street gang story set in New York City. The novel would also be influenced by John Milton's *Paradise Lost* and *The Water Margin*. The story

Yurick envisioned would be something diametrically opposed to Jerome Robbins' popular play (and Robert Wise's 1961 film adaptation), *West Side Story*. Where that story felt phony and inauthentic, his would be gritty and realistic. After doing extensive research on gangs, he ultimately decided to base his characters on the gangs he saw in his neighborhood. Yurick sat down behind a typewriter and hammered out his novel, *The Warriors*, in a mere three weeks. This novel, unlike *Fertig*, quickly sold to Holt, Rinehart and Winston, who published it as a 199-page hardcover in 1965. The book would receive critical praise, but it would not be a big hit.

Lawrence Gordon, a film producer with two production credits, *The Point* (1971) and *Dillinger* (1973), was perusing a used bookstore one day. In doing so, he picked up a hardback copy of *The Warriors* that was missing its cover. Gordon liked the idea of the book (although he would later say he didn't care for the book itself), so he decided to pursue the film rights. When Gordon's offer came, Yurick was close to signing the book rights over to someone else, but he accepted Gordon's offer because he was in need of money. Gordon then began shopping the project with Walter Hill tentatively attached as director. After receiving several rejections, Gordon landed a production deal for *The Warriors* at Paramount. The studio suggested David Shaber, a screenwriter known at the time for working as an uncredited script doctor, to adapt the novel. Much to Yurick's chagrin, he was not involved with the screenwriting process in any way. Shaber wrote a single draft, which director Hill loathed and rewrote with input from Gordon.

Hill and Gordon were prepared to make a Western called *Last Gun*, but they lost financing for the project at the last minute. With Hill and Gordon now available and an open slot on the Paramount production schedule, the studio green-lit *The Warriors* in April 1978. The filmmakers immediately began auditioning. According to the film's pressbook, "newcomers were cast in the film in order to maintain the look and feel of real people caught in dangerous situations." As a gesture of goodwill to the real-life gangs operating in what producer Gordon called "shitty and gritty" areas of the city where they would be filming, the filmmakers auditioned gang members. At least one gang member would be cast in a speaking role. However, the gangs demanded more gang members be cast.

Hill originally planned to make the film a direct representation of contemporary New York City street gangs. As such, his cast would be comprised of black and Hispanic actors. However, this changed when Paramount Pictures balked at Hill's idea, insisting the cast be diverse (read: white) in the hopes that the film would be a bigger box-office draw. "I graduated in 1974 and there were tons of gangs in New York, but there was no such thing as an interracial gang," Dorsey Wright, the black actor who plays Warriors leader Cleon, told author Sean Egan. "You might find a gang that has maybe blacks and Puerto Ricans, but you would never find a gang that had whites, blacks, and Puerto Ricans. So when they did that in the film, it kind of threw me." This forced Hill to retool the script, setting it in an alternate reality New York. The reworking consisted primarily of making the gang characters wear bizarre, garish attire as well as including lots of white characters. Despite the fact that the clothing and white characters were intended to separate *The Warriors* from the realism of the city, the locations would accurately capture (and heighten to some degree) the gritty, grimy appearance of 1970s NYC. Every building shown in the film would be rundown, and most (as well as the subway) would be blanketed in graffiti. In Hill's world, even the automobiles would be covered with graffiti.

Having to dress 120 different gangs and give each their own distinct look, costume designer Bobbie Mannix went for an outlandish and fantastical look that was in keeping Hill's new comic book–style vision. Working closely with Hill, Mannix dressed the gangs in clothing such as baseball uniforms, denim overalls, Western and Native American garb, leather, and face paint.

Shooting began in June 26, 1978, with a budget of approximately $4 million. The earliest scenes to be shot were daytime scenes that took place at Coney Island. (When Hill decided to change the film so that it took place almost entirely at night,

1979: *The Wanderers* and *The Warriors* Run the Streets / 201

these scenes were scrapped and re-shot.) The *Warriors* shoot would ultimately include sixty dates of night shooting.

Hill and company would face the same problems with street gangs that were commonplace for New York City location shoots in the 1970s. Because *The Warriors* was a film about street gangs, the problems with the gangs were exacerbated. When a Hispanic gang went to Gordon and Hill and expressed their disdain for the movie being made on their turf, the filmmakers cast them as extras to smooth things over. This didn't set well with other gangs, and they threatened the crew. Because of this, the filmmakers were forced to hire extra protection. During the shoot, the film crew were occasionally showered with flying bottles, bricks, and urine from the rooftops surrounding them. During one lunch break in Harlem, thousands of dollars' worth of film equipment was destroyed by angry gang members. In order to keep this from happening again, Gordon was forced to pay one of the gangs $500 per night. The police sometimes told the filmmakers flat-out that they should do whatever the gangs asked, because they couldn't control them. This led to even more gang members being cast.

In addition to the filmmakers' dealings with the gangs, there were other indicators as to how rough the city was. One scene was interrupted by a police chase. Actor Joel Weiss recalls another scene being shut down because there was a real-life homicide nearby. Since the filmmakers would be shooting on the subway (at night), which had become a ridiculously dangerous place, they had to coordinate shooting with the NYPD and the Transit Authority to ensure protection. The NYPD warned against filming on the subway at night, but the filmmakers insisted. This would mark the first time a film crew was given unlimited access to shooting on subway trains across the city.

Since the entire storyline takes place in a single night, director of photography Andrew Laszlo, anticipating New York City summertime rains, suggested that the streets be kept wet throughout the shoot in order to avoid continuity problems. Hill agreed. This turned out to be a wise decision since that summer turned out to be the city's rainiest in several decades.

Filming the fight scenes proved to be dangerous. While filming one scene, actress Deborah Van Valkenburgh was accidentally struck in the head with a baseball bat. In another scene, a stuntman broke three ribs.

Actor Thomas Waites, whose character was supposed to be the lead, found himself at odds with Walter Hill. The two didn't see eye to eye, and Waites was constantly complaining and arguing during the shoot. Hill was not pleased with his performance, and Waites didn't seem to have very strong chemistry with his love interest, played by Van Valkenburgh. When the actor's agent refused to give the filmmakers an option on him, that was the final straw. In a strange move that somehow had little effect on the final film, Hill fired Waites, killed off his character by having a stunt double fall beneath a moving train, and restructured the plot to cover the character's absence.

When the rough cut of *The Warriors* was screened for the cast, crew, and studio execs, the studio *hated* it. Additionally, actress Pamela Poitier became enraged and screamed at the filmmakers when she learned that her scenes had been cut from the film. Making matters worse, an early preview screening in Long Beach went sideways, as the audience walked out and/or voiced genuine displeasure. Things looked bleak for *The Warriors* as it moved closer to its theatrical release.

Early promotional materials announced: "These are the armies of the night. They are 100,000 strong. They outnumber the cops five to one. They could run the city." Paramount Pictures immediately received backlash for the line, which many feared would cause an uprising, and the line was removed from promotional materials. When the film was released on February 9, 1979, opening in 670 theaters, it received mixed reviews but was famously championed by *New Yorker* film critic Pauline Kael, who wrote: "*The Warriors* is a real moviemaker's movie: it has in visual terms the kind of impact that 'Rock Around the Clock' did behind the titles of *Blackboard Jungle* (1955). *The Warriors* is like visual rock."

Unfortunately, the film also resonated with real-life NYC gang members, who showed up at screenings *en masse*, leading to altercations. Convinced *The Warriors* was a dangerous film inciting violence, a volunteer group calling themselves the Magnificent Thirteen called for the film to be withdrawn. Carl Smucker, a member of the group, told WABC reporter Sandy Pearl, "We've seen what it's done to people and read in the papers about the violence that's been inspired by this kind of movie, and we don't think children should be allowed to see this movie, let alone adults." Despite the fact that *The Warriors* had earned $16.4 million in six weeks of release, Paramount bowed to pressure and pulled the film from theaters.

The Warriors has since developed a massive cult following, and it's grown in stature. In 2003, the *New York Times* included it on their list of the "1,000 Best Movies Ever Made." *Entertainment Weekly* ranked it at number sixteen on their "Top 50 Greatest Cult Films" list and at number fourteen on their list of the "Twenty-Five Most Controversial Movies Ever." Action movies, a board game, and two separate video games based on the film have been released, and there is ongoing talk of a possible remake.

1980

The Last Batch of 1970s Crime Films

"Why the hell is 1980 in this book?" you're saying. "It's 1980, so clearly it's not a year in the 1970s." If you really are saying that, you're very astute. You must have graduated at the top of your class. But seriously, why *is* 1980 covered here?

The films released in 1980 were made in 1979, and they still *felt* like 1970s films. Not just in the crime genre, either. I implore you to look at Scorsese's *Raging Bull* (1980) and not see a 1970s film. The 1970s are in that film's DNA, through and through, just as it is with crime pictures like *Cruising* and *Gloria*. While the look and feel of movies didn't change right away, overall, the films of that decade were a different breed. Not every film, mind you—there are outliers, just as there are with anything, but by and large, they're different. In the 1980s, Hollywood had a change of heart and mind; where the 1970s had been about experimentation and pushing boundaries, in terms of both story and craft, the 1980s were a decade where the studios played it safe. While there are obviously some great films from that decade, just as there are with *every* decade, the majority of 1980s films felt like watered-down products made with the sole purpose of making money for the studio fat cats. That had always been Hollywood's primary goal, sure, but in the 1980s, it suddenly felt like the artists had packed up and left, leaving Hollywood to the stodgy old businessmen.

So, sadly, the six films we'll discuss here represent the end of an era. There were still a few notable and/or interesting NYC crime films made in the 1980s—*Ms .45* (1981), *Prince of the City* (1981), *Vigilante* (1982), *Once Upon a Time in America* (1984), and *Death Wish 3* (1985) come to mind—but overall, much like the 1970s itself, the kinds of films it had produced were a thing of the past.

The films we'll examine here are *Cruising*, *Dressed to Kill*, *The Exterminator*, *The First Deadly Sin*, *Gloria*, and *Maniac*. Because this book is about the 1970s, we won't spend time discussing the events of the city that took place outside the movie houses.

Cruising

At some point in the early 1970s, *French Connection* (1971) producer Phillip D'Antoni optioned *New York Times* journalist Gerald Walker's 1970 novel *Cruising*. The novel followed a straight cop working undercover as a homosexual man in the hopes of catching a serial killer preying on the gay community. The producer had tried to set up a studio deal but found no takers. After D'Antoni let the option expire, Jerry Weintraub, the producer of such films as *Nashville* (1975) and *Oh God!* (1977), optioned the novel. In search of a name director he could attach to the project, Weintraub set up a dinner with his friend William Friedkin. During the dinner, Weintraub gave Friedkin a copy of the book and told him about the project. (Since D'Antoni and Friedkin had collaborated on *The French Connection*, one wonders why D'Antoni hadn't already approached him.)

Friedkin didn't initially find the subject matter all that interesting. Additionally, he thought the material was dated since the gay club scene in New York City had changed since Walker had written the book. (According to the director, the clubs had largely given way to underground "S&M leather bars.") Shortly after his conversation with Weintraub, Friedkin read several articles about a string of mysterious murders that were connected to the city's leather bars. Gruesomely, the victims' bodies had turned up in pieces floating in the East River. This piqued his interest, and Friedkin agreed to make *Cruising* if he could change its storyline into a murder mystery about contemporary leather bars.

Weintraub agreed, and the director went to work spending time inside the clubs alongside his pal, ex-cop Sonny Grosso, who had been one of the subjects of *The French Connection*.

When he discovered that Randy Jurgensen, another ex-cop he'd worked with on *The French Connection*, had spent time undercover in the gay club scene (in search of men who posed as cops and attacked and robbed clubgoers), he began to pick his brain for information. He and Jurgensen then toured the clubs the cop had frequented, as well as other locations where he'd spent time while working undercover. Friedkin then worked details of Jurgensen's story into the script for *Cruising*. In the hopes of understanding the mentality of a killer, Friedkin also went to Riker's Island and interviewed a murderer.

Al Pacino's representatives reached out to Weintraub and Friedman, informing them the actor was interested in starring in their film. The filmmakers thought he was a good fit and cast him. In preparing for the film, Pacino also spent time in the leather bars and questioned Jurgensen about his experiences. Pacino would eventually take it upon himself to get his hair cut in a style that was popular in the gay community. However, the hair style would turn out looking strange on Pacino, so the entire production would have to be halted until his hair grew back.

Friedkin's crew on the film was largely made up of people he'd worked with previously on other projects and had felt comfortable working with. As he and casting director Louis DiGiaimo worked on casting the supporting roles, the director urged all of the actors to spend time in the leather bars to study the clubgoers and become acquainted with the milieu they would be working in. Wanting to film inside real clubs, Friedkin asked Matty "The Horse" Ianniello, a mobster who owned several of them, for permission to film inside. Ianniello agreed. The main club used in the film was The Mineshaft, which was located at 835 Washington Street at Little West 12th Street in Manhattan.

When the gay community learned that Friedkin was going to make the film, many of their most prominent representatives began speaking out in opposition. Trying to get in front of a potentially bad situation, the filmmakers urged members of the gay community to be a part of the film. Many did appear in the film, adding to the film's authenticity. However, a great deal of the gay community were angry, believing the film would depict negative stereotypes of gay people and cause further violence against them. This led to groups of protesters gathering anywhere Friedkin tried to film, screaming, chanting, and making noises in an effort to disrupt filming. (Because of this, the film would need heavy ADR work to fix scenes that had been shot with unusable sound.) Chants included "Stop the movie *Cruising*!" and "Hey! Hey! Ho! Ho! *Cruising*'s got to go!" The protesters also threw bottles and other items. At times, there were as many as three hundred NYPD officers present to protect the shoot.

Allan Miller, who plays the chief of police, shares a story about Friedkin's desire to make the film as realistic as possible. "I went down to the location where we were shooting," Miller recalls. "It was in a couple of rooms. One door was closed off and I could hear yelling on the other side of the door. A couple of other actors were waiting around to go in and do whatever they were going to do. Then, all of a sudden, the door flew open, and a big black guy wearing a gun belt and jockey shorts came bursting in. I thought, 'What the fuck is happening here? I thought this was supposed to be a cop movie.' I got curious and I asked if I could go in and watch. I was allowed in nicely. There was an actor with a knife in his hand doing that thing where you come down between the fingers [to simulate stabbing someone], and he's going up and down, up and down on a young guy who's scared shitless. All of a sudden—I couldn't help myself—I said, *'Excuse me! Stop! Is that a real knife?'* Everybody stopped, and nobody knew what to say. I came over and looked and I said, *'This is a real knife! You can't use that!'* Everybody's looking at me, and Friedkin's over there looking at me. I said, *'That's not allowed! You're not allowed to use a real weapon in a violent scene!'* Friedkin called someone over, maybe the AD, and he said, 'Get me a prop knife.' Everybody took a break. After that, I was persona non grata for having stopped Friedkin from using the real knife. I shot two scenes, but he never said another word to me."

Actress Karen Allen remembers seeing a different side of Friedkin during the shoot. "I knew that Billy Friedkin had a reputation for being tough, but he was fun," she told *Shock Cinema*'s Mark Burger. "He was very playful. *The Exorcist* [1973] had been re-released in the theaters while we were filming, and he kept trying to slip the paperback with the logo into the scenes in my apartment. The crew would have to tell him to stop, and he'd act innocent. *'Oh, did I do that?'*"

When Friedkin handed in his first cut of *Cruising*, the MPAA demanded copious cuts and changes in order for the film to avoid receiving an X rating. According to the director, the film went through fifty exchanges with the MPAA before it finally received an R rating. In order to obtain the rating, Friedkin and editor Bud S. Smith were forced to cut forty minutes from the original cut. For decades, fans would speculate about what those forty minutes of excised footage contained. At a 2013 Q&A at the Aero Theater in Santa Monica, California, Friedkin revealed that the cut footage "was just pure pornography that I shot because I could."

When *Cruising* was released on February 15, 1980, it was, as expected, lambasted by the gay community. Chuck Lee Morris, publisher of gay San Francisco newspaper *The Sentinel*, summed up the community's sentiment: "Every day in this city dozens of gay people are beaten up [and] come close to being murdered. This film not only exaggerates that, it is almost an incitement to go out and murder people." Friedkin insisted that he had no agenda when he made *Cruising* other than trying to make a good film. At a 2017 film festival in Strasbourg, France, Friedkin reiterated, "*Cruising* only interested me as an exotic background for a murder mystery. That's it. I had no political . . . and I have never on any film that I've made, had any sense of what the politics of those films are. Other people read things into them, but I don't approach cinema from a political position at all."

While Weintraub and Friedkin couldn't have been surprised by the gay community's reaction to the film, they probably didn't expect the across-the-board critical thrashing *Cruising* received. Remarks made by Gene Siskel and Roger Ebert on a 1980 episode of *Sneak Previews* are representative of the critical consensus. Siskel weighed in by stating "*Cruising* is a pretty bad movie" containing a "bad performance by Pacino." Ebert followed his partner with this assessment: "Major director with Friedkin, major actor with Pacino, and it's a major mess of a movie." The film received three Golden Raspberry Award nominations for Worst Screenplay, Worst Director, and Worst Film. The film's popularity has increased some over the years, becoming less reviled. (*Cruising*'s Rotten Tomatoes rating is sitting at an even fifty at the time of this writing.)

Actor and filmmaker James Franco has reportedly pursued the rights to remake *Cruising* on multiple occasions. In 2007, Franco was, according to Friedkin, making a film about the director's battle with the MPAA over the film's rating. However, the film has never emerged and no one has spoken about the concept (at least publicly) in the years since.

Dressed to Kill

After having spent a fair amount of time trying to secure the film rights to Gerald Walker's book *Cruising* and failing to do so, writer/director Brian De Palma decided he would channel his creative energy into making something original. The germ of the idea (about a male psychiatrist with a female persona who would kill women who aroused him) would come from De Palma seeing an interview with a transexual woman on *The Phil Donahue Show*. Since he was seeing a psychiatrist himself, the filmmaker based much of the doctor's attributes on his own doctor. Additionally, he showed the script to the psychiatrist and asked questions in an effort to accurately portray such a doctor. De Palma also integrated a number of autobiographical elements into the project. When the screenplay was completed, De Palma asked his *Obsession* (1976) producer, George Litto, to read the script, which was now titled *Dressed to Kill*. Litto asked for two hours to lock himself in a room and read the script. Litto liked the screenplay and called De Palma, jokingly threatening to murder him if he didn't allow him to produce the film.

Litto was friends with veteran producer and movie mogul Samuel Z. Arkoff. Knowing Arkoff was a fan of De Palma's work, Litto asked if he would be interested in financing the film. Arkoff agreed, giving Litto and De Palma $6 million and complete creative control.

Although the resulting film would be violent and bloody, the original screenplay for *Dressed to Kill* was even more gruesome. In fact, the script opened with a scene featuring the psychiatrist slicing off his penis. The violence led Liv Ullman to pass on the project when she was offered the primary female role. De Palma then offered the role to Jill Clayburgh, who declined due to scheduling conflicts. Ultimately, the role went to Angie Dickinson, who had just concluded a four-year run on the television series *Police Woman*, on which she'd been the lead. Dickinson would later tell filmmaker Laurent Bouzereau that she'd been concerned about the film's nudity and had almost passed herself. "My initial reaction when I read it was, *'Oh my God, I can't do this! I'm Police Woman!'*" However, De Palma convinced Dickinson to make the film with the agreement that a body double be used for the nude scenes.

Sean Connery was offered the psychiatrist role, but like Clayburgh, he was committed to other projects. In the end, Michael Caine was cast. It should be noted that the casting of Nancy Allen in the secondary role of Liz Blake came easily for De Palma since she was his wife at the time.

The shoot began in October 1979 (and would wrap the following January). De Palma and Litto planned to shoot the entire film in New York City. However, the scenes that take place inside the art museum threw a monkey wrench into the plan. After the filmmakers were unable to secure the Metropolitan Museum of Art, the Museum of Modern Art, or any of the other NYC museums they approached, they wound up shooting these scenes inside the Philadelphia Museum of Art. However, the Metropolitan Museum of Art was used for the exterior shots.

De Palma used a Wall Street hotel known for being a place where brokers took their mistresses and prostitutes for rendezvous for the location where the mysterious stranger takes Dickinson's character, Kate (and also where she's ultimately murdered). Then the interior of the room where the stranger and Kate meet was an apartment located just above De Palma's own apartment. In that scene, Dickinson's character finds a letter informing her mystery man that he's contracted syphilis. When he was writing the script, De Palma found inspiration for the scene from being present when an ex-girlfriend received a similar letter.

Dennis Franz, who plays a cop in the film, closely studied the actions and mannerisms of real NYPD officers for the role. He would later credit his role in the film as laying the groundwork for when he would go on to play cops on the television series *Hill Street Blues* and *NYPD Blue*.

When De Palma submitted *Dressed to Kill* to the Motion Picture Association of America, he was told that he would have to make substantial cuts in order to receive an R rating. This angered De Palma, who vented in the press, saying he felt his film was being penalized for being too effective. The cuts De Palma and editor Jerry Greenberg would be forced to make included nudity in the shower scene, violence in the elevator murder scene, and offensive language. In addition to these problems with the MPAA, *Dressed to Kill* would come under attack from feminist groups who believed it was misogynistic.

Dressed to Kill would premiere simultaneously in Los Angeles and New York City on July 25, 1980. It then opened in 591 theaters, earning more than $3 million in its first weekend. It would ultimately make $31.9 million in the United States, making it the twenty-first highest-grossing film of 1980.

Most of the critics were appreciative of the film, although many pointed to its stylistic similarities to Alfred Hitchcock's work. The *New York Times'* Vincent Canby called the film witty, romantic, and "very funny, which helps to defuse the effect of the graphically photographed violence. In addition, the film is, in its own inside-out way, peculiarly moral." Roger Ebert of the *Chicago Sun-Times* called the museum sequence "brilliant," adding "*Dressed to Kill* is an exercise in style, not narrative; it would rather look and feel like a thriller than make sense, but De Palma has so much fun with the conventions of the thriller that we forgive him and go along." Sheila Benson from the *Los Angeles*

Times wrote, "The brilliance of *Dressed to Kill* is apparent within seconds of its opening gliding shot; it is a sustained work of terror—elegant, sensual, erotic, bloody, a directorial tour de force."

"Everything worked," De Palma later said. "It worked in the script. It worked in the casting. It was like a charmed experience because everything always worked about it, right through the success of it. Of course, there was a bitter aftertaste of it—being chased around as a misogynist and a Hitchcock imitator, which is the way the press basically attacked it. But it was one of those moments where you had an idea and you followed it all the way through, and everything about it worked."

The Exterminator

Indie filmmaker James Glickenhaus broke into the film business by sinking $20,000 he'd inherited from a deceased relative into the 1975 horror film *The Astrologer*. Despite having gone to film school, he was fairly naive about moviemaking, so the film crashed and burned. Glickenhaus later assessed the film as being "nearly unwatchable," saying it had too much talking and little else. After his disappointing experience with *The Astrologer*, Glickenhaus met with exhibitors and foreign film distributors to find out what kinds of movies audiences liked and what kinds of movies sold internationally. He then determined that the key to getting international distribution was to make something that didn't need many subtitles or dubbing; not only did audiences not want movies with lots of dialogue and no action, but Glickenhaus learned that the nuances of the English language didn't translate properly. From US exhibitors, he learned basically the same thing—American audiences also wanted films with more action than dialogue. After that, Glickenhaus took the lessons he'd learned and applied them to his next film, *The Exterminator*.

This film would be a vigilante film in the *Death Wish* (1974) vein. Sticking to the "less talk, more action" rule he'd set for himself, Glickenhaus wrote a script with almost no dialogue. (While the finished film would have very little dialogue, his original screenplay contained even less.) As he went into production on *The Exterminator*, Glickenhaus planned to make the film for $850,000, which was more than forty times the budget he'd had for *The Astrologer*.

When Glickenhaus went to cast his lead, he decided he would cast someone very different from such action stars as Charles Bronson or Clint Eastwood; he wanted his lead to seem like an Everyman that audiences could relate to, making them feel like they could be him. So he decided to cast Joseph Bottoms, who'd just finished working on Disney's *The Black Hole* (1980), which was poised to be a huge hit. Glickenhaus knew that if that film became as big a hit as everyone anticipated it being, Bottoms would become an overnight superstar. That meant for him to get Bottoms in *The Exterminator*, he was going to have to make him an offer he couldn't refuse. It's unclear what Glickenhaus promised to pay the actor upfront, but Bottoms stood to make a large percentage of the film's profits. As the movie moved towards shooting, Glickenhaus felt confident his film would have a huge star as its lead. However, on the day Bottoms was to come in for his wardrobe fitting, he didn't show up. Then, later that day, the actor's agent telephoned Glickenhaus, telling him Bottoms was holding out for an additional $10,000. Since the film was to begin shooting in less than two weeks, the agent believed he had Glickenhaus over a barrel. This enraged Glickenhaus, who felt the actor and his agent were trying to screw him over, and he refused to negotiate any further. Instead, he recast the role, going with an actor named Robert Ginty whom he'd seen in *Coming Home* (1978). It should be noted that, not only did Bottoms' agent screw him out of *a lot* of money, but *The Black Hole* performed poorly and Bottoms never became a star. After missing out on *The Exterminator*, Bottoms exterminated his own film career and became a soap opera actor.

Stuntman-turned-bit-actor Steve James read for the part of the bartender. However, Glickenhaus liked James' reading so much that he rewrote the role of the Exterminator's sidekick, whom he'd originally written to be Puerto Rican, as a black man so James could play the part. Additionally, Glickenhaus cast Christopher George and Samantha Eggar in supporting roles. George, who had appeared on the 1960s TV series *Rat Patrol*, and Eggar, who had won a Golden Globe in 1965 for her turn in *The Collector*, were semi-famous, giving the cast a degree of credibility.

Glickenhaus also hired future nine-time Oscar-nominated and four-time Oscar-winning special makeup-effects whiz Stan Winston to work on *The Exterminator*. Winston would be responsible for such memorably vomit-inducing effects as a gory beheading and an even gorier scene featuring a character being ground up in a meat grinder. As Glickenhaus would explain in a 2012 *Flashback Files* interview, the inclusion of realistic violence in the film was important to him. "It was a time in which violence was on everybody's mind, because of the war in Vietnam. And television and film had sanitized violence for a long time. Someone points a gun, it goes bang and on the other side of the street some guy goes, 'Aaaaah,' and falls down. But violence is really unpleasant and I thought I had an obligation to portray it that way."

The film opens with scenes taking place in Vietnam. These sequences were filmed in Indian Dunes, California, which would later be the site of the infamous *Twilight Zone: The Movie* (1982) accident that left actor Vic Morrow and two children dead. (While filming *that* film's Vietnam scenes, a Bell UH-1 Iroquois helicopter crashed.) Glickenhaus and his crew had already shot most of the film by this time. These scenes wound up costing $400,000, driving the film's budget up. (The total budget of *The Exterminator* would eventually reach $2 million.)

For the Vietnam sequence, Glickenhaus scripted an elaborate stunt in which a character leaps from an exploding mountaintop. Stunt coordinator Kenny Endoso helped him plan the "Vietcong Fire Gag," but they needed a stuntman to make the actual jump. Because the stunt required the jumper to leap out twenty-one feet to reach the airbag, with an explosion behind him, with a sixty-foot drop below, and with more explosions below, most stuntmen considered the job too dangerous. So, the first five stuntmen Endoso approached turned it down. Endoso then approached Jack Gill, an up-and-coming stuntman who was working on television's *The Dukes of Hazzard*. Gill, who was young, maybe naive, maybe crazy, probably both, assessed the

216 / The Taking of New York City

situation and agreed to do the dangerous stunt for (his words) a "whopping $750." After accepting the job, Gill's mother pleaded with him not to do the stunt and even offered him twice what he was being paid *not to do it*. But Gill was stubborn and believed he could do it.

In order to make the jump, Gill decided he would use an "air ram," a projection device that was new at the time that most stuntmen were afraid to use because it had broken several stuntmen's legs. As Gill explains, "If you don't get off right, it will break your leg in half." In 1979, the protective gel that stuntmen use today when possibly coming into contact with fire did not exist. At that time, all Gill could do was soak his body in water. After the air ram misfired multiple times right before Gill did the actual jump, he asked the effects guy, "If this thing misfires, will the explosions still go off?" To this, the effects guy answered, "Yes, it's tied to my button. So you'll be sitting on top of the cliff stuck when thirteen gallons of gasoline go off." When the time for the jump came, Gill ran (carrying the character's M-16 in his hands) and hit the air ram, getting off of it perfectly. "I felt like I had been hit in the middle of my back—right in the middle of my back—with a flathead shovel," Gill says of the explosion behind him during the leap. Gill hit the airbag perfectly, without catching fire. As this was happening, crew members and onlookers on the ground were running in fear because the explosions on the side of the mountain were larger than expected, causing fire to rain down on them. But Gill's stunt went perfectly, and the scene looks great in the film.

"After I had done the rehearsals, I knew I could do it," Gill says. "And at the time, in 1979, $750 was a lot of money. And everyone made a big deal about it, and that got my name around the business pretty quickly since the other guys had turned it down. So, would I ever do it again? *Not in a million years!* I think that was a one-of-a-kind stunt that will never be performed again." Gill, who has since become one of the most in-demand stuntmen in the business, says that younger stuntmen still ask him how he managed to pull off that legendary stunt without the wires and fire gel stuntmen have today. Gill explains, "You make do with what you have at the time. Those were the best safety precautions we had at the time, so we did what we could with it."

When the film was finished, the MPAA ratings board would demand a number of cuts. Although the cuts would result in the trimming of a mere forty-seven seconds—mostly from the beheading sequence—the difference between the US release cut and the original director's cut is significant. (The original cut was released only in Japan.) The MPAA also balked at a scene that they believed showed a man's penis. "In one scene in the massage parlor, they maintained that behind Bob Ginty on the wall was a gay pinup showing a guy with a semi-erect penis," Glickenhaus told author John Gallagher. "We then freeze-framed the shot, blew it up, and in fact it was not a semi-erect penis. What they were referring to was his leg. Then we had this infamous day with them when they implied that we were implying that they didn't know what a penis looked like. As a compromise, we actually took some Vaseline, put it on the lens of the optical printer, and, if you look at the film, you'll see in the corner that there's a blurry dot where this photo was. It's totally absurd."

When *The Exterminator* screened at Cannes, Glickenhaus rented a larger theater than the other films were being screened in. Glickenhaus claims that a thousand people showed up to the six hundred–seat theater. This resulted in fights and yelling. Then, when the film started, someone stood to leave during a violent scene and fainted, causing people to believe he'd had a heart attack. Glickenhaus claims he paid the projectionist to lock the door and continue running the film as paramedics ran into the theater. *The Exterminator* became the talk of the festival and Glickenhaus sold distribution for the film around the world.

The little $2 million action film became a $5 million box-office sensation. Most reviewers waggled their fingers in judgment due to the film's violence. In *Punch* magazine, critic Dilys Powell refused to review it, writing, "I suppose I should mention also *The Exterminator*. . . . since I find the action (including a victim being put through a meat grinder) nauseating, I won't go on about it." Roger Ebert of the *Chicago Sun-Times* wrote, "*The Exterminator* is a sick example of the almost unbelievable descent into gruesome savagery in American movies. . . . It is essentially just a sadistic exercise in moronic violence, supported by a laughable plot." *Variety* dismissed the film as "an action film with little action. Contrived script instead opts for grotesque violence in a series of glum, distasteful scenes."

The First Deadly Sin

Having secured the rights to Lawrence Sanders' 1973 novel *The First Deadly Sin*, Columbia Pictures set about adapting it to film. They signed Roman Polanski to adapt and direct for $625,000 in January 1977. Polanski wasn't particularly keen to make a commercial thriller but signed on because, after the failure of his film *The Tenant* (1976), he needed a hit. The writer/director then went to New York to spend time at a Manhattan police station and [as instructed, per a Columbia memo] become "personally acquainted with arrests, booking procedure [and] interrogation." A retired cop named Sol Rizzo also gave him a tour of the police world, including the city morgue, where he observed an autopsy. Humorously, Polanski reportedly "stood casually eating an apple." Polanski initially hoped to cast Robert De Niro as the film's serial killer, but nothing came of his talks with the actor. Production was slated to begin in May 1977, but the film was shut down after Polanski was charged with the statutory rape of a thirteen-year-old girl. Columbia Pictures fired Polanski, who then fled the country, never to return (at least as of this writing), and *The First Deadly Sin* was erased from the studio's production schedule.

Two years later, producer Elliott Kastner sought to breathe new life into the dormant project. With Columbia now out of the picture, Filmways Pictures came on board to fund and distribute it. Polanski was replaced by Brian G. Hutton, a director Kastner had worked with on the films *Where Eagles Dare* (1968), *XY and Zee* (1972), and *Sol Madrid* (1972). Kastner's first casting choice for the film's lead was Marlon Brando, but Brando wasn't interested. The producer next looked to Frank Sinatra, whom he (and director Jack Smight) had attempted to land for the lead of the 1966 film *Harper*. The Chairman of the Board had turned down

Harper but now agreed to play the lead in *The First Deadly Sin* for a cool $4 million. Sinatra also came on as a producer. With that role, he was able to make personnel "suggestions," which led to the hiring of *Contract on Cherry Street* (1977) cinematographer Jack Priestley. Sinatra also brought on longtime collaborator Gordon Jenkins to score the film.

Interestingly, there were two non-cast members who momentarily moved into the spotlight for their supposed involvement with the production. Newspapers and gossip rags reported that rock star David Bowie had been approached to play the film's serial killer Daniel Blank. According to Bowie spokesmen, however, the rocker didn't care for the script and had passed on the film. This is curious since Kastner vehemently denied having approached Bowie. The other casting oddity was Johnny Carson sidekick Ed McMahon, who claimed he'd been cast to appear in the film as Sinatra's sidekick. This claim is even more questionable than Bowie's considering that the film features no such character and, furthermore, McMahon does not appear in the film *as any character*.

The cast also included Faye Dunaway, James Whitmore, David Dukes, Brenda Vaccaro, Martin Gabel, and an ill-fitting toupee worn by Sinatra. Joe Spinell (*Taxi Driver* [1976], *Maniac* [1980]) makes a brief but memorable appearance, playing one of his trademark sleazy characters; this time a money-hungry doorman. The film also featured the first appearance by future star Bruce Willis (in an uncredited role as a man in the diner). On the flip side of that, *The First Deadly Sin* would be Sinatra's final appearance as a leading man.

Filming began on March 10, 1980, and wrapped on May 20, 1980. The film was shot on location in Manhattan. Filming locations include Mt. Pleasant Baptist Church, located at 140–142 West 81st Street; the Mother Cabrini Medical Center, at 227 East 19th Street; the "Arms and Armor" galleries at the Metropolitan Museum of Art, at 405 Lexington Avenue; the Bayview Correctional Facility, at 550 West 20th Street; and 300 East 74th Street is the actual location where the serial killer's apartment scene was filmed.

While there have been many tales of notoriously bad behavior by Sinatra on various films, he seems to have been on his best behavior here. Faye Dunaway has repeatedly talked about how much of a gentleman he was to work with. Joe Spinell told *Psychotronic Video*'s Tom Rainone, "Everyone said how tough he was to work with and what not, but he was a complete professional." Spinell went on to report, "He sent my mother $1,000 worth of food, and then he gave me two tickets to see him at Carnegie Hall."

The novel had been a hit, but screenwriter Mann Rubin (whose credits were mostly TV shows) decided to change a great deal of its story in his adaptation. One thing from the book that's sorely missed is Daniel Blank's backstory; while it's understandable why this was cut in terms of running time and pacing, the backstory explained why Blank did the things he did. Perhaps the most significant alteration was the story's ending. In Sanders' novel, Daniel Blank goes away to a place called Devil's Needle in upstate New York, where he dies from dehydration. In the film, Sinatra's detective Delaney catches Blank, who states with confidence that he'll beat the rap for his crimes. When Blank attempts to call the police to report Delaney for breaking into his apartment, Delaney shoots him in the head. One unneeded change was the location of Blank's apartment. In the novel, the plush forty-one-story high-rise apartment building where Blank resides in on the Upper East Side, near the river. However, in the film the high-rise sits on West 83rd Street. However, there were no buildings of that kind on West 83rd Street, causing NYC audiences to shake their heads in disbelief.

The film premiered at a charity screening (for Mother Cabrini Medical Center, which was featured heavily in the film) at Loew's State Theater on October 23, 1980. Box-office receipts were poor, effectively ending any possibility for a franchise. Critical reviews were middling at best. Many reviewers, such as Roger Ebert of the *Chicago Sun-Times*, pointed at Sinatra's performance as being one of, if not *the*, finest in his long career. However, critics by and large hated the film. In *Films in Review*, Michael Buckley wrote, "*The First Deadly Sin*, by the way, is meant to be pride . . . [T]here can be very little pride connected with this film." *Time* magazine's Richard Corliss wrote, "Lawrence Sanders' novel could serve as the basis for a taut, lurid little *film noir*, but this adaptation is as plodding and routine as most police work." And then there's this humorous barb from John Roberts in Los Angeles Valley College's *Valley Star*: "*The First Deadly Sin* is deadly boring."

Gloria

The year was 1979. Having spent his own money to fund *The Killing of a Chinese Bookie* (1976) and *Opening Night* (1977), maverick director John Cassavetes needed to make money. After Cassavetes' wife, actress Gena Rowlands, remarked that he never made movies about children and that she wished he would, MGM exec David Begelman called him to ask if he had any desire to write a script for child actor Ricky Schroeder. If he did, Begelman promised he would purchase it. Remembering his wife's comment, Cassavetes said what the hell and wrote a screenplay about a gangster's moll risking her life to protect a young boy. The script was titled *One Winter Night*, and Cassavetes hammered it out in a mere two weeks. He then sent it to the MGM exec, who wanted the script but was perplexed by Cassavetes' decision to write the child character as a very un-Schroeder-like Puerto Rican boy. However, this proved irrelevant when Schroeder subsequently left MGM and signed with Disney.

Cassavetes' agent, Guy McElwaine, was a fan of the script and asked if he could shop it. Cassavetes agreed to sell it with two stipulations. One, he only wanted to sell it, not direct it. Two, he wanted Rowlands attached to play the lead. Shortly thereafter, McElwaine came back, informing Cassavetes that Columbia wanted to make the film with Rowlands, but only if Cassavetes agreed to direct. Cassavetes wasn't enthused about this prospect, primarily because he didn't want to make something so commercial. Plus, he hated the idea of directing a violent film. (In the end, he would ultimately decide the film was more about emotional violence than physical violence.) Despite his initial reluctance, Cassavetes wanted to make a film that he didn't have to mortgage his home to finance. Plus, his wife wanted him to do it. So Cassavetes signed on to direct. Now working with a major studio, Cassavetes would have to make concessions: he would be given only nine weeks to shoot the film as opposed to the open schedules he was accustomed to, the film would not be shot in chronological order the way he did on his independent projects, and he would not have final cut.

This part is a little bit murky in terms of the timeline: at some point before Rowlands was contracted to play the lead, Barbra Streisand was offered the role. (It's unclear whether it was MGM, Columbia, or Cassavetes who made this request, but it seems unlikely that it was Cassavetes since he'd previously told confidants he had no desire to work with her.) Perhaps still feeling stung by Cassavetes' refusal to direct *A Star Is Born* when she'd approached him a few years earlier, Streisand declined, saying she believed she was too young to play a maternal figure and that she worried such a role might hurt her image.

So Rowlands played the lead. She and Cassavetes were given a combined $1 million to make the film. (The film's total budget was $4 million.) Since Rowlands had *just* made back-to-back telefilms (*A Question of Love* and *Strangers: The Story of a Mother and Daughter* [both 1977]), Cassavetes moved principal photography back to late July. Cassavetes and producer Sam Shaw then went to work rewriting the script to make the film more personal and, in the process, less commercial. The shooting script would be the fifth draft, dated July 9, 1979. The film's title was also changed from *One Winter Night* to *One Summer Night*, since it would be filmed in summer. In addition to rewriting the script, the ever-busy Cassavetes also acted in a TV movie and wrote another screenplay in the two months of pre-production.

When Cassavetes held a casting call for the part of the young boy, Phil, more than three hundred children showed up. Instead of having the kids act, Cassavetes asked them questions about themselves. He ultimately offered the role to a six-year-old named John Adames. Before accepting the role, Adames asked the director how many new words he could learn while making the movie, to which Cassavetes said, "350 easy." The notion of learning 350 words excited Adames, so he took the role.

After another actor turned down the role of the mob accountant, Cassavetes' agent suggested another of his clients, Buck Henry, informing him that Henry was a fan of his work. Cassavetes offered Henry a different role, but the actor convinced him to let him play the accountant, despite the fact that the nebbish white man was an odd choice to play a mob employee with a Puerto Rican family living in a tenement. Frequent Cassavetes collaborator Seymour Cassel begged the director to give him the role, but Cassavetes refused, telling him the part was Henry's.

Tom Noonan, who plays one of the gangsters who kills the accountant, cockily told Cassavetes he would make the film only if the director came and watched him in a play he was doing at the time. Lawrence Tierney, whom Cassavetes had worked with on his television series *Johnny Staccato* and also the film *Too Late Blues* (1961), was cast as a bartender. Producer Sam Shaw's daughter appeared in a small role, and Cassavetes' buddy John Finnegan, who'd appeared in several of Cassavetes' films, was also given a role as a gangster. Cassavetes' personal assistant Richard Kaye was cast as another gangster. Val Avery, an actor who had appeared in many of Cassavetes' films, played yet another gangster. One interesting bit of casting was Basilio Franchina, a screenwriter who'd worked with directors Frederico Fellini and Vittorio DeSica, to play mob boss Tony Tanzini.

Since this would be a union film, Cassavetes worked without his usual crew. When he went looking for a cinematographer, Cassavetes hired Fred Schuler, a camera operator who'd worked on the NYC classics *Dog Day Afternoon* (1975), *Taxi Driver* (1976), and *Annie Hall* (1977). Schuler thought there was a mistake, so he informed Cassavetes that he was a camera operator, not a cinematographer. But Cassavetes wouldn't hear of it; Fred Schuler was getting a promotion.

The film began shooting on July 25, 1979, at Concord Plaza Hotel. The hotel, once a real-life mob hangout, was deserted and disheveled, but Cassavetes appreciated the location's grittiness. When the set designers attempted to clean graffiti off the walls, Cassavetes stopped them. An apartment building at 800

Riverside Drive at 158th Street provided three different locations: Gloria's sister's place, the hotel room where Phil waits for Gloria, and Tanzini's base of operations. Yankee Stadium, Penn Station, and Times Square also show up in the film. Of the locations, Cassavetes is quoted in Ray Carney's *Cassavetes on Cassavetes* as saying, "I love New York! I grew up there, and it seemed to me that all the pictures that are made about New York never concentrate on neighborhoods. And New York to me is comprised of a series of neighborhoods. But I didn't want people to say, 'Okay. Now we're here. Now we're on 58th Street.' It was very important not to make the scenery the center of attention, because, I don't know, I just feel that there should be more respect given to *life* than to the making of a film."

In an effort to achieve authenticity, Cassavetes and Shaw put a number of real-life gangsters and people off the street in the film. One of the actors, the gangster Gloria shoots on her way to the elevator, was allegedly a real hit man.

Cassavetes fired his editor, John McSweeney, during the first week of shooting because he believed he was a studio spy. The director argued every day with production manager Stephen Kesten about the budget and shooting schedule. Cassavetes and Kesten had several screaming matches on set, one of which almost brought them to blows. Cassavetes detested the crew, believing they were lazy and didn't care about the film. Cassavetes and Rowlands also got into on-set fights routinely because he pushed her harder than she would have liked (although she would later credit his pushing for her performance, which is arguably the best of her career). Rowlands fell victim to the heat one day and passed out on set. Refusing to be slowed down, Cassavetes continued filming despite having lost his lead. Interestingly, Rowlands remained in character when the cameras were off, treating her young costar, Adames, as coldly as her character does in the film.

Post-production began in late 1979, but the film wasn't released for nearly a year. The film, retitled again, this time as *Gloria*, debuted at the Venice Film Festival, where it tied with Louis Malle's *Atlantic City* (1980) for the prestigious Golden Lion Award. Additionally, Rowlands won the award for Best Actress and Julie Carmen took home the honors for Best Supporting Actress. *Gloria* was released on October 1, 1980, at the Manhattan Cinema I.

Richard Corliss of *Time* magazine wrote, "The movie's achievement is that it manages to be almost as effective as it is predictable. Its failure is in pretending to a naturalism it cannot maintain whenever movie actress and crew go slumming through the Big Apple and bystanders gawk into the lens, auditioning for stardom in some future Cassavetes film." David Ansen of *Newsweek* remarked, "[*Gloria* is] Cassavetes' loopy version of an action movie, laced with hard-bitten sentimentality and wild, poker-faced humor. You don't have to believe *Gloria* for a minute to enjoy it. *Gloria* is pure, unembarrassed jive—a hipster's lark of a movie." *Films in Review* critic Rob Edelman observed, "*Gloria* may be irritating in its inconsistencies, but it is nonetheless exciting, like free form jazz. Cassavetes, not afraid to take chances as a director, has chosen not to direct 'packages' and count his money. There is a special rawness to *Gloria*, that of a hungry novice."

Rowlands was nominated for a Best Actress Academy Award, but the Oscar ultimately went to Sissy Spacek for *Coal Miner's Daughter* (1980). In the passing years, *Gloria* fell into relative obscurity, although it was later given the standard inferior remake treatment in 1999, directed by Sidney Lumet and starring Sharon Stone.

In his book *American Dreaming: The Films of John Cassavetes and the American Experience*, Raymond Carney perfectly sums up the film: "Caught halfway between a Warner Bros. thriller and Disney fairy tale, *Gloria* will probably satisfy neither children nor adults, but it could never be confused with the work of any other director."

Maniac

William Lustig and actor Joe Spinell met during the shooting of *The Seven-Ups* (1973). Lustig was working as a production assistant (still a few years away from making his directorial debut with the adult film *The Violation of Claudia* [1977]), and Spinell had a small role. The two men quickly formed a bond over their mutual love of horror movies. Lustig started directing adult films, and Spinell was landing one supporting role after another (specializing in scumbag characters) in such noted films as *The Godfather Part II* (1974), *Taxi Driver* (1976), and *Rocky* (1976).

According to producer Andrew Garroni, the idea to go out and make a feature film came from their dissatisfaction with the movies that were out at the time. "Me, Bill, and Joe used to get together at Bill's apartment on West 57th Street," Garroni explains. "And we did what you do when you're young. Every Friday, we would go to the eleven o'clock screening at Times Square, and we'd watch whatever the hot movie was at the time. Then we'd go and order Chinese food and drink beer and criticize the movie. We'd talk about how we could have done it better. I think we just got tired of listening to each other."

"My goal was to make a horror film," Lustig says. "I really loved horror films, and I really wanted to make one. So Joe and I started developing some scripts. We had developed one script and decided it was out of our ability to raise the money [that was] required to make it. Then we wrote *Maniac*, but it was more conventional at that point; it was a detective chasing a serial killer in New York City." Spinell's friend Jason Miller of *The Exorcist* (1973) fame was originally cast to play the lead detective. When Miller eventually dropped out of the project, the script was rewritten and the detective character was cut out completely.

Lustig and Garroni worked on Italian filmmaker Dario Argento's film *Inferno* (1980), assisting with scenes shot in New York City, and the three became friendly. Lustig recalls, "I particularly got close to him because we used to sit in Central Park while we were shooting, off to the side, and talk about horror films and about all his movies. I was really the only person on the set who was a fan of Dario Argento's work and had seen all his movies. This was before he became really well-known." At some point during these conversations, Lustig told Argento about his desire to make a horror film. Argento expressed interest in helping, and he and his production partner Claudio

Simonetti agreed to co-finance the picture. (In the deal, Argento's wife would have appeared in the film and Argento's band, Goblin, would have performed the score.) Argento and Lustig would seem to have been a collaborative marriage made in heaven. However, it was not to be. "I kind of sensed that Dario was losing interest," Lustig says. "It kind of unraveled."

Lustig, Spinell, and Garroni were undaunted. Lustig says, "We were determined, Joe, myself, and Andy, and we said, 'Fuck it. Let's just [use] the money we have.'" Spinell pitched in the $6,000 he'd made from his appearance in *Cruising* (1979). Garroni pulled the entirety of his $12,000 savings out of his bank account. Lustig himself had $30,000. "You just get to a point where you can't wait around anymore," Lustig observes. "If you're going to make the movie, you just have to go do it." The three then went to work making the movie with their $48,000 budget.

Lustig was privy to an early screening of George Romero's *Dawn of the Dead* (1978) and was amazed by the gory effects done by (now legendary, but then up-and-coming) SFX whiz Tom Savini. Wanting those same kinds of expert effects in his serial killer film *Maniac*, Lustig, Spinell, and Garroni climbed into a car and drove to the *Friday the 13th* (1980) set in New Jersey where Savini was working. They managed to convince Savini to come and work on their film, but Lustig says it wasn't because of the quality of their script but because of issues in Savini's personal life. "Really what convinced him to do the movie was that he had just broken up with a girl in Pittsburgh and didn't want to go back home after the movie wrapped. So he asked if we'd put him up in an apartment in New York while we were on pre-production on *Maniac*. We said sure, we'd put him up in an apartment, and that was that. Tom came on board the movie."

The rest of the crew beyond Lustig, Spinell (who stars as the madman lead character), Garroni, and Savini was rounded out by crew members Lustig had worked with while making adult films. "We had a fairly small crew, by industry standards," Lustig says. "It was a really small crew, a small production."

While rumors abound about the crew shooting much of the film without permits, Lustig denies this. "People say that, but that's not entirely true. We did have permits for a lot of what we shot. We were just working under the radar." When Lustig and crew filed for these permits, they listed the film's title, which was always supposed to be *Maniac*, as the less-eyebrow-raising *On the Run* to avoid unwanted attention. While the crew had permits, the film's most famous FX scene (in which a man is shotgunned to death sitting next to his girlfriend in his car) had to be shot without a proper permit. Why? "There was no permit in existence that would allow you to fire a shotgun on city streets," Lustig says. "Yes, we had a permit to be there, but back then, they would not scrutinize us since we were not shooting downtown. By the highway, where we were shooting, we didn't need the police to block off the streets."

Savini himself appears as the man Spinell's madman shoots with the shotgun. At the time, Savini was planning on getting a nose job. He had a very realistic pre-made dummy head bearing his likeness. "We decided he would get the role and then blow up his own head that he would have no more use for in a few weeks." Savini's FX work is extremely convincing in the scene. (And in case you were wondering, Savini got the planned plastic surgery just after the shoot concluded.)

Many have praised *Maniac* for capturing the grittiness of 1970s New York City in a way few films did. Garroni agrees. "For its time, I think we did capture the grittiness of 42nd Street. It was a relatively dangerous place if you weren't careful. There are separate police units that work with the mayor's office for film and television. I remember those guys saying, 'Look, who knows what's going to happen?' It's 42nd Street and Times Square, right? So you always had to be careful." However, Garroni says the crew wasn't really afraid because "Bill had spent his formative high school years in Times Square at the grindhouse theaters watching exploitation movies."

"It wasn't too hard to capture the seedy side at that time because it was the real deal," Lustig says. "Times Square was dangerous and it was riddled with prostitution and drugs and all the rest of it. But I gotta tell you, I prefer that incarnation over what Times Square has now become. Today, it's Universal City. It's terrible. It's really awful what Times Square has become today. I avoid it like the plague. I hate tourists anyway. You know, they fuck up everything, and they managed to do it to Times Square." As for the film's generally gritty nature, the director believes its low budget was a factor. "We shot the movie on sixteen-millimeter and blew it up to thirty-five. So right off the bat, it's going to have an inherent gritty look. We didn't have any money to do any major lighting, so you're working on the edge of the film. Again, it's going to have an inherent gritty look to it."

Through deferments, a little stock market luck, and assistance from a British producer named Judd Hamilton, Lustig and company eventually raised the film's total budget to $350,000. While still a small budget, even then, it was significantly more than the $48,000 budget they'd started with.

Maniac premiered at the Cannes Film Festival. When the film was released theatrically, it stirred up controversy. Much of this came from a group calling themselves the National Organization of Women, and the charge was led by a woman who admitted that she'd never watched the film. Lustig even received death threats. "I understood that there was a backlash," Lustig recalls. "I understood what people were concerned about. There were a lot of those [slasher] movies at the time, and people had legitimate concerns." As the director is quick to point out, there was an upside to the controversy because it brought an enormous amount of attention to the small film.

In the decades that have followed the film's release, it has gained a cult following. There was a far less effective 2012 remake starring Elijah Wood. All one has to do is look at Spinell in the original to be creeped out. No matter how you slice it (pun intended), Frodo could never be half as frightening.

"I think the legacy of *Maniac* is Joe Spinell's performance," Lustig observes. "Joe was a brilliant character actor, which could be seen in the numerous films he was in. But this is really his only starring role in a movie that had some visibility. I really feel Joe was proud of the movie, and I'm very proud of the work that Joe did."

Selected Bibliography

Agan, Patrick, *Robert De Niro: The Man, the Myth and the Movies*, Robert Hale, 1993.
Alleman, Richard, *New York: The Movie Lover's Guide*, Penguin, 2005.
Balun, Chas, *Chas Balun's Connoisseur's Guide to the Contemporary Horror Film*, Fantasco Books, 1992.
Baron, Mike, "Phil D'Antoni in Hot Pursuit," *Boston Phoenix*, December 18, 1973.
Bart, Peter, *Infamous Players: A Tale of Movies, the Mob (and Sex)*, Weinstein Books, 2011.
Base, Ron, *If the Other Guy Isn't Jack Nicholson, I've Got the Part*, Contemporary Books, 1994.
Baxter, John, *De Niro: A Biography*, Grafton, 2002.
Bertram, Colin, "The Son of Sam: A Timeline of the Killings That Terrorized New York City," Biography, May 4, 2021.
Blauveldt, Christian, *Cinematic Cities: New York*, Running Press, 2019.
Blowen, Michael, "The Reel Gamble: Why Hollywood Has No Sure Bets for Box Office Winners," *Boston Globe*, November 20, 1980.
Bogdanovich, Peter, *Who the Devil Made It: Conversations with Legendary Film Directors*, Ballantine Books, 1997.
Breslin, Jimmy, *I Want to Thank My Brain for Remembering Me: A Memoir*, Little, Brown and Co., 1997.
Brode, Douglas, *The Films of Robert De Niro*, Citadel, 1998.
Buchman, Dian Dincin, "Al Pacino: An Actor Who Believes in Taking Chances," *Show*, 1971.
Buder, Leonard, "Half of 1976 Murder Victims Had Police Records," *New York Times*, August 28, 1977.
Burger, Mark, "Karen Allen," *Shock Cinema*, number 63, 2022.

Burger, Mark, "Richard Benjamin and Paula Prentiss," *Shock Cinema*, number 58, 2020.
Burnham, David, "1972 Crime Total in City Fell 18% As Violence Rose," *New York Times*, March 7, 1973.
Burnham, David, "A Wide Disparity Is Found in Crime Throughout City," *New York Times*, February 14, 1972.
Burrough, Bryan, "The Untold Story Behind New York's Most Brutal Cop Killings," *Politico*, April 21, 2015.
Carney, Raymond, *American Dreaming: The Films of John Cassavetes and the American Experience*, University of California Press, 1985.
Carney, Ray, *Cassavetes on Cassavetes*, Farrar, Straus and Giroux, 2001.
Chartrand, Harvey, "Interview with Michael Moriarty," *Shock Cinema*, issue 20, 2002.
"Crime Rate Up 11 Percent For Nation in 1970," New York Times, September 10, 1971.
D'Antoni, Philip, "The Seven-Ups," *Action*, September–October 1973.
Daugherty, Tracy, *The Last Love Song: A Biography of Joan Didion*, St. Martin's Press, 2015.
Donohue, Margo, *Filmed in Brooklyn*, The History Press, 2022.
Ebert, Roger, "Gordon Parks' Big Score," *Chicago Sun-Times*, July 2, 1972.
Ebert, Roger, *The Great Movies*, Broadway Books, 2002.
Egan, Sean, and Beck, Michael, *Can You Dig It: The Phenomenon of The Warriors*, Bear Manor Media, 2022.
Emery, Robert, *The Directors: Take One*, Allworth, 2002.
Evans, Robert, *The Kid Stays in the Picture*, Hyperion, 1994.
Fine, Marshall, *Accidental Genius: How John Cassavetes Invented American Independent Film*, Hyperion Books, 2005.
Fine, Marshall, *Harvey Keitel: The Art of Darkness*, Fromm, 1997.
Fleetwood, Blake, "The New Elite and an Urban Renaissance," *New York Times*, January 14, 1979.
Flood, Joe, "Why the Bronx Burned," *New York Post*, May 16, 2010.
Ford, Luke, *The Producers: Profiles in Frustration*, iUniverse, 2004.
Funke, Phyllis, "Daring Duo on Brooklyn Street," *New York Times*, June 3, 1973.
Gallagher, John, *Directors on Directing*, Praeger, 1989.
Gilvey, John Anthony, *Jerry Orbach, Prince of the City*, Applause, 2011.
Green, Robin, "Shooting the Gang That Couldn't," *Rolling Stone*, November 25, 1971.
Greenberg, Bob, *Henry Winkler as Fonzie of Happy Days*, Top Flight, 1976.

Selected Bibliography / 233

Grobel, Lawrence, *Al Pacino in Conversation with Lawrence Grobel*, Simon Spotlight Entertainment, 2008.
Hoberman, J., "Off the Hippies: '*Joe*' and the Chaotic Summer of '70," *New York Times*, July 30, 2000.
Hofler, Robert, *Money, Murder, and Dominick Dunne: A Life in Several Acts*, University of Wisconsin Press, 2017.
Janson, David, "Rizzo's First Year: Crime Off Slightly," *New York Times*, January 7, 1973.
Johnstone, Nick, *Abel Ferrara: The King of New York*, Omnibus, 1999.
Jones, Grace, *I'll Never Write My Memoirs*, Gallery Books, 2015.
Kael, Pauline, *500 Nights at the Movies*, Holt, Rinehart and Winston, 1982.
Kael, Pauline, *Reeling*, Little Brown, 1976.
Kellow, Brian, *Pauline Kael: A Life in the Dark*, Viking, 2011.
LaLiberty, Justin, "Born to Lose: Ivan Presser's Born to Win and NYC Loser Cinema," *Born to Win* DVD liner notes, 2022.
Latson, Jennifer, "Why the 1977 Blackout Was One of New York's Darkest Hours," *Time*, July 13, 2015.
Leaming, Barbara, *Roman Polanski: His Life and Films*, Hamish Hamilton, 1982.
Levy, Shawn, *De Niro: A Life*, Three Rivers Press, 2014.
Lumenick, Lou, "DVD Extra: Ron Leibman on *The Super Cops*," *New York Post*, October 13, 2011.
Lumet, Sidney, *Making Movies*, Alfred A. Knopf, 1995.
MacDougall, Fiona, "The Star of Needle Park," *Teen*, December 1971.
Malesevic, Dusica Sue, "Welcome to Fear City!" *Daily Mail*, December 25, 2018.
Martin, James, "British Director Peter Yates Finds His Action in America," *Chicago Tribune*, April 16, 1972.
Martinez, Gerald, *What It Is, What It Was: The Black Film Explosion of the '70s in Words and Pictures*, Hyperion Books, 1998.
McGilligan, Patrick, "The Worst Happens," *Sight and Sound*, Autumn 1990.
Meier, Andrew, "'The Only People They Hit Were Black': When a Race Riot Roiled New York," *New York Times*, December 12, 2022.
Montgomery, Paul L., "Gang Members Play Roles in Film on Sonny Carson," *New York Times*, October 12, 1973.
Moritz, Owen, "Looters Prey on the City During the Blackout," *Daily News*, July 15, 1977.
Murray, James P., *To Find an Image: Black Films from Uncle Tom to Super Fly*, Bobbs-Merrill, 1973.

234 / Selected Bibliography

Narvaez, Alfonso, "Young Lords Seize Lincoln Hospital Building," *New York Times*, July 15, 1970.

Neibuar, James, and Schneeberger, Gary, *Frank Sinatra on the Big Screen: The Singer as Actor and Filmmaker*, McFarland and Company, 2022.

Nette, Andrew, "Why 1973 Was the Year Sidney Lumet Took on Police Corruption," *Crime Reads*, March 23, 2023.

Nussbaum, Albert, "An Inside Look at Donald Westlake," *Take One*, January–February, 1974.

O'Brien, Daniel, *The Frank Sinatra Film Guide*, Batsford, 2014.

Petkovich, Anthony, "Chris Sarandon," *Shock Cinema*, number 51, 2016.

Petkovich, Anthony, "David Selby," *Shock Cinema*, number 63, 2022.

Petkovich, Anthony, "Stuart Margolin," *Shock Cinema*, number 50, 2015.

Phillips-Fein, Kim, "How the 1977 Blackout Unleashed New York's Tough-on-Crime Politics," *Washington Post*, July 13, 2017.

Phillips-Fein, Kim, "The Legacy of the 1970s Fiscal Crisis," *The Nation*, April 16, 2013.

Phillips, Gary D., *Godfather: The Intimate Francis Ford Coppola*, University Press of Kentucky, 2004.

Phillips, Julia, *You'll Never Eat Lunch in This Town Again*, Random House, 1991.

Powell, Larry, *The Films of John G. Avildsen*, McFarland and Company, 2013.

Raab, Selwyn, "Felonies in New York in 1976 Up 13.2%, Worst Rate on Record," *New York Times*, March 5, 1977.

Raab, Selwyn, "Sharp Rise Reported for Serious Crimes in All Five Boroughs," *New York Times*, April 10, 1977.

Rausch, Andrew J., *Fifty Filmmakers: Conversations with Directors from Roger Avary to Steven Zaillian*, McFarland and Company, 2008.

Rausch, Andrew J., *The Films of Martin Scorsese and Robert De Niro*, Scarecrow Press, 2010.

Rausch, Andrew J., *Gods of Grindhouse: Interviews with Exploitation Filmmakers*, Bear Manor Media, 2013.

Rausch, Andrew J., "*Maniac* Lives Again: An Interview with Director William Lustig," *Screem*, issue number 36, 2018.

"Report Says Police Corruption in 1971 Involved Well Over Half on the Force," *New York Times*, December 28, 1972.

Saito, Steve, "It Was Pornography: William Friedkin Closes the Book on the Missing 40 Minutes of *Cruising*," The Moveable Fest, May 13, 2013.

Samaha, Albert, "The Rise and Fall of Crime in New York City: A Timeline," *Village Voice*, August 7, 2014.

Selected Bibliography / 235

Sanders, James, *Scenes from the City: Filmmaking in New York 1966–2006*, Rizzoli International Publications, 2006.

Sandford, Christopher, *Polanski*, Century, 2007.

Santopietro, Tom, *The Godfather Effect: Changing Hollywood, America and Me*, St. Martin's Press, 2012.

Schickel, Richard, *Conversations with Scorsese*, Alfred A. Knopf, 2011.

Schneider, Steven Jay, *1001 Movies to See Before You Die*, Quintet Publishing Ltd., 2003.

Schoell, William, *The Films of Al Pacino*, Carol Publishing Group, 1995.

Schrader, Paul, and Jackson, Kevin, *Schrader on Schrader*, Faber and Faber, 1992.

Schwartz, Tony, "Year's 1,700 Homicides Break a Record," *New York Times*, December 26, 1979.

Segaloff, Nat, *Hurricane Billy: The Stormy Life and Films of Sidney Lumet*, William Morrow, 1990.

Severo, Richard, "Homicide Rate Rises 30% in First Part of 1971 Here," *New York Times*, March 28, 1971.

Singer, Michael, *50 Film Directors Talk about Their Craft*, Lone Eagle Publishing, 1998.

Talbot, Paul, *Bronson's Loose!: The Making of the Death Wish Films*, iUniverse, Inc., 2006.

Tarantino, Quentin, *Cinema Speculation*, Harper, 2022.

Tolchin, Martin, "Gangs Spread Terror in the South Bronx," *New York Times*, January 16, 1973.

Treaster, Joseph B., "Brooklyn Businessman Strangled in a Struggle with Police Officers," *New York Times*, June 17, 1978.

Variety's Film Reviews, Bowker, 1983.

Vognar, Chris, "A Bigot Walks into a Bar: The Politics of *Joe*, 50 Years Later," Rogerebert.com, December 4, 2020.

Walker, David, Rausch, Andrew J., and Watson, Chris, *Reflections on Blaxploitation: Actors and Directors Speak*, Scarecrow Press, 2009.

Westlake, Donald, and Stahl, Levi, *The Getaway Car*, University of Chicago Press, 2014.

Williams, Mason B., "How the Rockefeller Laws Hit the Streets: Drug Policing and the Politics of State Competence in New York City, 1973–1989," *Modern American History*, 2021.

Wilson, James Cameron, *The Cinema of Robert De Niro*, Zomba, 1981.

Winkler, Irwin, *A Life in Movies*, Abrams Press, 2019.

Wolcott, James, *Lucking Out: My Life Getting Down and Semi-Dirty in Seventies New York*, Doubleday, 2011.

Wykstra, Stephanie, "The Fight for Transparency in Police Misconduct, Explained," Vox, June 16, 2020.
Yule, Andrew, *Al Pacino: A Life on the Wire*, Macdonald, 1991.

Audio Commentaries

Bailey, Jason, and Hull, Michael, *Born to Win*, Fun City Editions, 2022.
Coppola, Francis Ford, *The Godfather Part II*, Paramount Pictures, 2022.
Gear, Matthew Asprey, *Across 110th Street*, Kino Lorber, 2022.
Kaufman, Philip, *The Wanderers*, Kino Lorber, 2017.
Kenny, Glenn, *The Anderson Tapes*, Kino Lorber, 2023.

Documentaries

Above and Below with Owen Roizman, Kino Lorber, 2018.
Bouzereau, Laurent, *Exorcising Cruising*, Warner Bros., 2007.
Bouzereau, Laurent, *The History of Cruising*, Warner Bros., 2007.
Bouzereau, Laurent, *The Making of Dressed to Kill*, MGM, 2001.
Bouzereau, Laurent, *Slashing Dressed to Kill*, MGM, 2001.
Buirski, Nancy, *By Sidney Lumet*, 2015.
Film Forum Q&A: *Wanderers*, 2016.
Garden, Allan, *The Magic of Hollywood . . . Is the Magic of People*, Paramount Pictures, 1976.
Geisinger, Elliott, *Klute in New York: A Background for Suspense*, 1971.
Going the Distance: Remembering Marathon Man, Paramount Pictures, 2001.
Haanen, Roel, "Look at the Hammer, man!" *The Flashback Files*, 2011.
Interview with Ron O'Neal, Warner Bros., 1972.
Jane Fonda and Illeana Douglas, Warner Bros., 2019.
Johnson, Derek Wayne, *John G. Avildsen: King of the Underdogs*, 2017.
Johnson, Keith, *Making the Connection: Untold Stories of The French Connection*, 2001.
Klute in New York, Warner Bros., 1971.
Leven, Russell, *The Poughkeepsie Shuffle: Tracing the French Connection*, 2000.
Samuelson, Edwin, *Back to the Bronx with Writer Richard Price*, 2017.
"Street Takes: Watching *Serpico* with Serpico," *New York Times* (video), January 25, 2010.

The Wanderers Filming Locations: Then and Now, year unknown.
Werner, Jeff, *The Godfather Family: A Look Inside*, Paramount Pictures, 1990.
Zippel, Francesco, *Friedkin Uncut*, Quiver Distribution, 2018.

Websites

Internet Movie Database (imdb.com)
On the Set of New York (onthesetofnewyork.com)
"Television Academy Foundation: The Interviews: Joseph Sargent" (www.emmytvlegends.org/interviews/people/joseph-sargent)
Wikipedia (wikipedia.com)

Author Interviews

Lawrence Appelbaum
Gabriel Bologna
Michael Campus
Anthony Caso
Rony Clanton
Larry Cohen
Max Allan Collins
Roger Corman
Andrew Garroni
Anne Gaybis
Jack Gill
James Grady
Gloria Hendry
Lloyd Kaufman
John A. Kuri
Novotny Lawrence
William Lustig
Mike Malloy
Mardik Martin
Charles Matthau
Allan Miller

David Selby
Frank Serpico
Ralph S. Singleton
Paul Talbot
Jonathan Taplin
David F. Walker
Kevin Wilmott

Index

Note: Photo insert images between pages 1 and 8 are indicated by *p1*, *p2*, *p3*, etc.

Abdullah, Salih Ali, 79
Across 110th Street, 4–5, 52, *p20*; assessment as blaxploitation film, 55; casting for, 53–54; literary source material, 53; music for, 55; "New York realism" and, 54; NYC locations for, 54
Across 110th Street (novel) (Ferris), 52
activism, political: Black Liberation Army, 18; in New York City, 8–9; Young Lords Organization and, 8–9
Adames, John, 222–23
Adams, Nate, 73, 75
Agnew, Spiro T., 14
Aiello, Danny, 180, 198
AIP. *See* American International Pictures
Allen, Karen, 195, 209
Allen, Nancy, 211
Allen, Penelope, 149
Allen, Woody, 20

All the President's Men, 156
Almussadig, Yusef Abdallah, 79
Alvarez Perez, Luiz, 9
American Dreaming (Carney), 225
American Film Institute, 165
American International Pictures (AIP), 85, 87, 99
Anatomy of a Murder, 118
Anderson, Lindsay, 126
The Anderson Tapes (film), 5; casting for, 21; critical response to, 22–23; literary source material for, 20; NYC locations for, 21–22
The Anderson Tapes (novel) (Sanders), 20
Anhalt, Edward, 174
Ansen, David, 225
Applebaum, Lawrence, 81–82
Argento, Dario, 226–27
Arkoff, Samuel Z., 211
Armstrong, Michael F., 135
Arnold, Gary, 84

240 / Index

Aubrey, James, 32–33, 44
Avakian, Aram, 89–90
Avery, Val, 223
Avildsen, John G., 13, 104–5

Badge 373, 19, 30, 108, 110; casting for, 83; critical response to, 82, 84; Egan and, 81–82; NYC locations for, 83–84
Bailey, Jason, 25, 42
Bain, Conrad, 21
Balaban, Bob, 154
Balm, Chas, 189–90
Balsam, Martin, 21, 136, 174
Bankston, Brian, 193
Baron, Mike, 111, 141
Barry, George, 179–81
Bart, Peter, 32
Baxter, John, 33
Beame, Abe, 79, 145
Beatty, Warren, 60
Beckerman, Sidney, 162–63
Begelman, David, 167, 221
Belafonte, Harry, 44, 53
Belasco, William, 132
Bell, Herman, 18
Belle de Jour, 28
Belli, Laura, 192
Benjamin, Paul, 21, 54, 124
Benson, Sheila, 212–13
Bercovici, Eric, 140
Berkowitz, David, 160, 172, 178–79, *p5*
Bernsen, Harry, 140
Birney, David, 107
Bitter Rice, 115
Black, Karen, 23, 60
Black Caesar, 84, 88, *p2*; American International Pictures, 85, 87; casting for, 85–86; cinematic influences on, 85; cinematic legacy of, 86; development of, 85; *Hell Up in Harlem* as sequel to, 91; music and score, 87; NYC locations for, 87; screenplay for, 86–87
"Black Film Revolution," blaxploitation genre as, 96
Black films, Black audiences and: *Cotton Comes to Harlem* influence on, 9–10, 73; *Sweet Sweetback's Baadassssss Song* influence on, 73. *See also* blaxploitation films; *specific films*
Blackkklansman, 10
Black Liberation Army, 18, 51
Black Panthers: Black Liberation Army and, 18, 51; NYPD conflicts with, 1–2, 19
Blakely, Susan, 152, 154
blaxploitation films, as sub-genre: *Across 110th Street*, 55; *Black Caesar*, 84–88; as "Black Film Revolution," 96; as cinematic sub-genre, 6; *Cotton Comes to Harlem* and, 10, 77; criticism of, 86; *Gordon's War*, 96–98; *Hell Up in Harlem*, 91–93; *Shaft* as, 4, 19–20, 46, 77, *p16*; *Slaughter's Big Rip-Off*, 87; *Super Fly*, 73–77, *p17*; *Sweet Sweetback's Baadassssss Song* as influence on, 73, 77; *Three the Hard Way*, 139–43. *See also specific films*
Bloom, Verna, 174
Blowen, Michael, 65
Bludhorn, Charles, 129
"Blue Flu" strike, by NYPD, 17–18

The Body Beneath, 24
Bologna, Joseph, 88, 90
Born to Win, 20, 53, 133; box office for, 25; casting for, 23–24; critical response to, 25; literary source for, 23
Bottoms, Joseph, 214
Bouzereau, Laurent, 211
Bowie, David, 219
Boxcar Bertha, 99
Boyle, Peter, 14–16, 115–16, *p4*. See also Crazy Joe
Brando, Marlon, 60–63, 97, 218
Brasco, Donnie, 177
Breakfast at Tiffany's, 2
Bregman, Martin, 104–5, 148
Breslin, Jimmy, 27, 31, 172
Brest, Martin, 192
Brickman, Jacob, 43
Bridges, Jeff, 166
Briguglio, Salvatore, 178
Brode, Douglas, 24
Bronson, Charles, 118–20, 191, *p7*
Brooks, Albert, 167
Brooks, Richard, 59
Brown, David, 41, 162
Brown, Drew Bundini, 71
Brown, James, 87, 93
Brown, Jim, 125–27, 140–42. See also The Gambler
Buckley, Michael, 220
Buffalino, Russell, 51
Buirski, Nancy, 149
Bujold, Genevieve, 60
Bullitt, 28–29, 64, 108–9
Buñuel, Luis, 28
Burger, Mark, 209
Burke, Jimmy, 177
Burnham, David, 7, 103–4
Buscetta, Tommaso, 9
Butterflies Are Free, 84

Caan, James, 60, 127, 128
Caine, Michael, 97, 211
Califano, John, 196–97
Cambridge, Godfrey, 11, 55–56
Cameron-Williams, James, 34
Campus, Michael, 122–23, 125
Canby, Vincent, 103, 111, 128, 142, 151, 182, 212
The Candidate, 39
Cannato, Vincent J., 2–3
Cannon, Dyan, 21
Capone, 115
Carey, Hugh, 146
Carlino, Lewis John, 115
Carmen, Julie, 225
Carney, Raymond, 225
Carradine, David, 60
Carson, Johnny, 219
Carson, Robert "Sonny," 121–22
Casey, Bernie, 45
Caso, Anthony, 61, 106
Cassavetes, John, 3, 98–99, 221–25. See also Gloria
Cassell, Seymour, 223
Castellano, Paul, 178
Cat Ballou, 148
Catch-22, 40
Cazale, John, 60, 148–49
Champlin, Charles, 15, 25, 38, 120–21, 128
Chapman, Michael, 180, 196
Chartoff, Robert, 31–32, 126
Chartrand, Harvey, 154
Chato's Land, 120
Chinatown, 62, 163
Chinich, Michael, 148–49
The Cinema of Robert De Niro (Cameron-Williams), 34
Cioffi, Charles, 37
Citizen Kane, 38
Clanton, Rony, 122–24

Clark, Arthur B., 43
Clayburgh, Jill, 60, 211
Clayton, Jack, 126
Cocks, Jay, 99–100
Cohen, Bert, 94
Cohen, Larry, 85–88, 91–93. *See also Black Caesar; Hell Up in Harlem*
Colombo, Joe, 18, 51, 178
Come Back Charleston Blue, 58, 120; *Cotton Comes to Harlem* and, 55–56; development of, 55; NYC locations for, 56–57
Comes a Horseman, 39
Comfort, Robert, 50
Connery, Sean, 21, 211
Connoisseur's Guide to the Contemporary Horror Film (Balm), 189–90
Contract on Cherry Street (novel) (Rosenberg), 173
Contract on Cherry Street (TV film), 53, 176, 219; casting for, 174; NYC locations for, 175; as television film, 173–74
Cool Hand Luke, 20, 148
cop films, as sub-genre: *Cops and Robbers*, 88–91; *Cotton Comes to Harlem* as "buddy cop" film, 10; in 1971, 17–20
The Cop in Blue Jeans, 107
Coppola, Francis Ford, 3; *The Godfather*, 4–5, 31, 58–63; *The Godfather Part II*, 4–5, 63, 128–32; *The Godfather Part III*, 63
Cops and Robbers: casting for, 88–89; NYC locations for, 90–91; production and development, 88–89; screenplay for, 89

Corliss, Richard, 221, 225
Corman, Roger, 99–100, 166
Cosby, Bill, 53
Cosell, Howard, 173
Costa-Gavras, 59
Costello, Frank, 4–5, 54, 80
Cottell, Louis C., 114
Cotten, Joseph, 191
Cotton Comes to Harlem, 9, 73; assessment as blaxploitation film, 10; box office for, 13; casting for, 11; *Come Back Charleston Blue* as sequel to, 55–56; literary source material for, 11; NYC locations for, 11; "otherness" themes in, 12; plot for, 12–13; screenplay dialogue in, 12; as seminal "buddy cop" movie, 10
Craven, Wes, 66–70. *See also The Last House on the Left*
Crazy Joe, p4; casting for, 115–16; critical response to, 117; NYC locations for, 116–17
crime films: as cinematic sub-genre, 6; methodological approach to, 6; 1970s as "Golden Age," 4. *See also specific films*
Cruising (film), 206; casting for, 207; critical response to, 209–10; Italian mafia role in, 207; protests against, 207–8; source material for, 146
Cruising (novel) (Walker, G.), 146, 206
Cunningham, Sean, 66

Dafoe, Willem, 29
Dane, Barbara, 35
Danner, Blythe, 60

D'Antoni, Phillip, 26–30, 107–10. *See also The French Connection* (film); *The Seven-Ups*
Davi, Robert, 175
Davis, Jerome, 18
Davis, Luther, 53
Davis, Ossie, 9–10, 12, 44, 55, 96–98
Davis, Sammy, Jr., 53, 85
Dawn of the Dead, 195, 227
Dead Man Walking, 15
Death Wish, 117, 213–14, *p7*; casting for, 118–19; as cult favorite, 121; NYC audiences' response to, 121; NYC locations for, 119–20; remakes of, 121; as wish fulfillment film, 114
Death Wish (novel) (Garfield), 117–18
Death Wish 3, 206
The Deer Hunter, 94
De Laurentiis, Dino: *Crazy Joe*, 115–17; *Dog Day Afternoon*, 151; early Italian films, 115, 155; *Serpico* (film), 104–5
Delon, Alain, 60
DeMeo, Roy, 80, 178
De Niro, Robert, 115, *p18*; in *Born to Win*, 24–25; *The Gambler* and, 126–27; in *The Gang that Couldn't Shoot Straight*, 33–35, 60; *The Godfather Part II*, 130–32; *Mean Streets* and, 100–101; *Taxi Driver*, 167–69
De Palma, Brian, 3, 166, 210, 211–13. *See also Dressed to Kill*
Devane, William, 164
Diamond, Neil, 166
Diamonds Are Forever, 21

DiCarlo, Michael, 178
Dickinson, Angie, 211
Didion, Joan, 39–40
DiGiamo, Louis, 207
Di Palma, Carlo, 4
Dirty Harry, 174
Does a Tiger Wear a Necktie (play), 40
Dog Day Afternoon, 4, 20; casting for, 148–49; critical response to, 151; inspiration for, 148; lack of score for, 150–51; NYC locations for, 150
Donnie Brasco, 178
Double Trouble, 31
Douglas, Illeana, 35
Douglas, Kirk, 53
Dressed to Kill, 210; casting for, 211; critical response to, 212–13; NYC locations for, 211–12
Driller Killer, 187; critical response to, 189–90; financing of, 188; NYC locations for, 189
Drumheller, Robert, 71
Dukakis, Olympia, 195
Dunaway, Faye, 36, 40, 158, 179, 220
Dunne, Dominick, 39–40, 42
Dunne, John Gregory, 39–40
Durk, David, 104
Duvall, Robert, 30, 61, 81, 83
Dylan, Bob, 1, 197
Dzunda, George, 94

Easy Rider, 182
Ebert, Roger, 22, 30, 56, 71, 72, 82, 128; on *Cruising*, 209–10; on *Dog Day Afternoon*, 151; on *Dressed to Kill*, 212; on *The Exterminator*, 217–18; on *The First Deadly Sin*, 220

Echevarria, Edgar, 104
Edelman, Rob, 225
Edelstein, David, 149
The Education of Sonny Carson: casting for, 123–24; critical response to, 124–25; cultural legacy of, 125; screenplay for, 121–22; source material for, 121–22
Egan, Eddie, 19, 25–26, 81–82, 108. *See also Badge 373*; *The French Connection* (book); *The French Connection* (film)
Eggar, Samantha, 214–15
Elfand, Martin, 148
Elizondo, Hector, 24, 136, 138, 154
Elliott, Peggy, 55
Endoso, Kenny, 215
Evans, Randolph, 160
Evans, Robert, 32–33; *The Godfather* (film) and, 59–62; *The Godfather Part II*, 129, 132; *Marathon Man*, 162–63
Evola, Natale, 80
Exterminator: casting for, 214; critical response to, 217–18; locations for, 215; as vigilante film, 213–14

Falco, Ed, 63
Falcone (TV series), 178
Family Business, 21
Farber, Stephen, 197
Fargas, Antonio, 54
Farrow, Mia, 41
Farrow, Tisa, 180
"Fear City," New York City as, 2, 146
Feinstein, Alan, 135
Fenty, Phillip, 73

Ferrara, Abel, 187–88, 190; *King of New York*, 189; *Ms. 45*, 189. *See also Driller Killer*
Ferraro, Geraldine, 185
Ferris, Wally, 53
Fertig (Yurick), 198–99
Fields, Verna, 158
The Films of Robert De Niro (Brode), 24
Fine, Marshall, 180
Fingers: casting for, 180; critical response to, 182–83; NYC locations for, 181–82; screenplay for, 179–80
Finian's Rainbow, 31
Finnegan, John, 223
The First Deadly Sin, 53; casting for, 219; critical response to, 220–21; development of, 218; NYC locations for, 219–20
The First Deadly Sin (novel) (Sanders), 218
Flatley, Guy, 166
Fleming, Mike, 29
Folsey, George, Jr., 93
Fonda, Henry, 118
Fonda, Jane, 35–39. *See also Klute*
Force, Ken, 195
Ford, Gerald, 145
Foster, Jodie, 167
Fox, Chester, 93–95
Foxx, Redd, 13
Franchina, Basilio, 223
Franciosa, Anthony, 54
Franco, James, 210
Franz, Dennis, 212
Frazier, Sheila, 74–75
The French Connection (book) (Moore, R.), 25, 81
The French Connection (film), 4–5, 19, 46, 108–9, *p11*; box office

Index / 245

for, 30; casting for, 27–28; critical response to, 30; NYC locations for, 26–30; screenplay for, 27; source material for, 25. *See also Badge 373; The Seven-Ups*
The French Connection II, 19, 30
French New Wave movement, in cinema, 3, 98
Friedkin, William, 26–30, 82, 108–9; *Cruising* (film), 146, 206–10. *See also The French Connection* (film)
Friedlander, Howard, 96
From Corleone to Brooklyn, 191; casting for, 192; critical response to, 193; NYC locations for, 193
Frumkes, Roy, 111
Fun City Cinema (Bailey), 25
Funke, Phyllis, 133
Furie, Sidney J., 59
Furrer, Urs, 71

Gage, Nicholas, 115
Gallagher, John, 217
Gallman, Brett, 95
Gallo, Joseph, 18, 34, 51, 115–16. *See also Crazy Joe*
Gambino, Carlo, 18–19
The Gambler, 179; critical response to, 128; De Niro and, 126–27; development of, 125–26; NYC locations for, 127
The Gang that Couldn't Shoot Straight, 20, 31; casting for, 32; critical response to, 34; De Niro in, 33–35; NYC locations for, 34; Pacino and, 32–33; screenplay, 32
Ganios, Tony, 194–95, 198

Garfield, Brian, 117–18, 121
Garroni, Andrew, 226, 228
Gasso, Michael V., 130
Gaybis, Anne, 95
Gazzo, Michael, 180
Gear, Matthew Asprey, 54
George, Christopher, 214–15
Gerard, Emanuel, 71
Gere, Richard, 152, 154
Giallo sub-genre, 191
Gill, Jack, 215–17
Ginsberg, Allen, 154–55
Ginty, Robert, 214, 217
Gleason, Jackie, 27
Glickenhaus, James, 213, 215
Gloria: casting for, 222–23; critical response to, 224–25; development of, 221–22; early titles for, 221–22; financing of, 221–22; NYC locations for, 223–24
The Go-Between, 43
Godey, John, 135
The Godfather (film), 4–5, 31; awards for, 62; backlash from Italian-American community, 61; box office for, 62, 84; casting for, 59–60; copycat films influenced by, 115; critical response to, 62; development of, 58–59; director search for, 59; legacy of, 58, 63; NYC locations for, 62; production process for, 61–62
The Godfather (novel) (Puzo), 58–59
The Godfather Part II, 4–5, 63; awards for, 132; casting for, 130; critical response to, 132; De Niro and, 130–32;

development of, 128–29; NYC locations for, 131; Scorsese and, 128–29; screenplay for, 129–30
The Godfather Part III, 63
Gold, Daniel M., 65
Goldman, William: *The Hot Rock* screenplay, 63–64; *Marathon Man*, 161–62, 165; Redford collaborations with, 64–65
Goldsmith, Jerry, 174
Goldwyn, Sam, Jr., 58, 194
Goodfellas, 177
Gordon, Lawrence, 199–200
Gordon's War: casting for, 96–97; critical response to, 97–98; NYC locations for, 97; screenplay for, 96
Gorman, Cliff, 88
Gotti, John, 80
The Graduate, 39
Grady, James, 154–55
Graham, William A., 175
Grant, Cary, 181
Greenberg, David, 132, 135
Greenberg, Jerry, 212
Greene, Joe. *See* Johnson, B. B.
Greenspun, Roger, 25, 38, 72
Gregory, David, 70
Gries, Tom, 44
Grimaldi, Alberto, 194
Grosso, Sonny, 19, 25–26, 81, 107–8, 174, 207. *See also The French Connection* (book); *The French Connection* (film); *The Seven-Ups*
Guardino, Harry, 174
Guess What We Learned in School Today?, 13
Guest, Christopher, 65
Guidice, Don, 158

Gunn, Moses, 65, 71
Guru, the Mad Monk, 24
Guzman, Pablo, 9

Haanen, Roel, 140
Hackman, Gene, 27–28
Haines, Larry, 108
Hamill, Pete, 83
Hamilton, Judd, 229
Hamilton, Margaret, 21
Hantz, Robert, 132, 135
Hard Hat Riot, 7–8
Harris, Burtt, 150, 196–97
Harris, Julius, 71, 74
Harris, Leonard, 168
Hauss, Michael, 95
Hayes, Isaac, 46–47, 71
Hell Up in Harlem, 88, 91; casting for, 92; critical response to, 93; music and score for, 93; NYC Locations for, 92
Hendry, Gloria, 54, 86
Henry, Buck, 223
Hepburn, Audrey, 2
Hernandez, Pedro, 186
Herzfeld, John, *p7*
Hess, David, 68–69
Hickman, Bill, 29, 108
Hill, Walter, 199–200
The Hill, 21
Himes, Chester, 11–12, 55
Hirschfeld, Gerald, 11
Hoffman, Dustin, 60, 91, 162–65
Holender, Adam, 42
Holland, Anthony, 21
Hopper, Dennis, 3
horror films, as sub-genre: *Driller Killer*, 187–90; *Giallo* sub-genre, 191; *Maniac*, 225–29; *Massage Parlor Murders*, 5–6,

80, 93–96; *Texas Chainsaw Massacre*, 187
The Hot Rock (film): casting for, 64–65; critical response to, 65; NYC locations for, 64–65; screenplay for, 63–64
The Hot Rock (novel) (Westlake), 63
Hudson, Frank, 121–22
Hurry Sundown, 13
Hutton, Brian, 218

Indian Wants the Bronx (play), 40
Inferno, 226–27
Italian mafia, in New York City, 10; *Across 110th Street* and, 4–5, 54; FBI investigation of, 177–78; intra-family violence within, 51, 186–87; popularity of *The Godfather* with, 59; Quinn and, 4–5, 54; Racketeer Influenced and Corrupt Organizations Act and, 9. *See also The Godfather* (film); *The Godfather* (novel); *The Godfather Part II*
Italian Neo-realism movement, in cinema, 3, 98
It's Alive, 91–92

Jackie Brown, 55
Jackson, Reggie, 171
Jacobs, Alex, 27
James, Steve, 214
Jarecki, Nicholas, 180–81, 188
Jaws, 147
Jeavons, Clyde, 72
Jenkins, Gordon, 219
Joe, 9, 13; box office for, 16; casting for, 14–15; critical response to, 15; inspiration for, 14; sociocultural context for, 10, 15; White audience responses to, 16
Joe II, 16
Johnson, B. B., 70
Johnson, Lamont, 166
Johnson, Van, 192
Jones, Grace, 97
Jones, James Earl, 76
Jones, Waverly, 18
Jurgensen, Randy, 26, 174, 207

Kael, Pauline, 102–3, 182–83, 202
Kalem, Toni, 195
Karate Kid, 68
Kastner, Elliott, 218
Katselas, Milton, 151, 153
Katzka, Gabriel, 136
Kauffmann, Stanley, 43, 151, 165
Kaufman, Lloyd, 14
Kaufman, Philip, 194–97. *See also The Wanderers*
Kaufman, Rose, 194
Keaton, Diane, 60
Keats, Steven, 135
Kehr, Dave, 39
Keitel, Harvey, 101, 167; *Fingers*, 180–82; *Taxi Driver*, 153
Keller, Marthe, 163
Kellow, Brian, 182
Kelly, Jim, 140
Kelsch, Ken, 188
Kemper, Victor J., 150
Kerkorian, Kirk, 32
Kersey, Paul, 114
Kershner, Irvin, 166
Kesten, Stephen, 224
The Killing of a Chinese Bookie, 221
King, Alan, 21–22
King, Tony, 152–54

King of New York, 189
Kinoy, Ernest, 55
Kluge, P. F., 148
Klute, 2, 20, 37, *p1*; awards for, 39; character research for Fonda, 35–36; critical response to, 38–39; NYC locations for, 36
Knapp Commission, 7, 50
Knight, Arthur, 43
Koch, Ed, 171–72, 186
Koch, Howard W., 83–84
Korshak, Sidney, 32
Kotto, Yaphet, 44–45, 53–54, 153–54
Kove, Martin, 67–68
Kratina, Richard, 133
Kuri, John A., 153–54

Laine and Abel, 188
Lancaster, Burt, 53, 59
Landers, Hal, 63, 118
Landon, Michael, 133
Larner, Jeremy, 39
The Last House on the Left, 52; banning of, 69; casting for, 67–68; critical response to, 69; development of, 66; documentary style approach, 68–69; early titles for, 67; influences on, 66; NYC locations for, 68–69; screenplay of, 66–67
Laszlo, Andrew, 201
Lawrence, Novotny, 76
Lawrence, Starling, 155
The Learning Tree, 10, 44
Lecot, Antero, 9
Lee, Carl, 74
Lemmon, Jack, 118
Lenzi, Umberto, 191–93
Leone, Sergio, 66
Levitt, Amy, 105

Lewis, Andy, 35, 39
Lewis, Dave, 35, 39
van Lidth, Erland, 196
Liebman, Ron, 65, 133–34
Lincoln, Fred, 67–68
Lindsay, John V., 5, 7, 18, 58, 79, *p12*
Little Murders, 24
Litto, George, 210–11
Lizzani, Carlo, 115, 117
Lo Bianco, Tony, 108
Lucas, George, 3
Ludwig, Jerrold L., 140
Lumet, Sidney, 118, 225; *The Anderson Tapes*, 5, 20–23; *Dog Day Afternoon*, 148–51; *Making Movies*, 4, 150; *Marathon Man*, 161–65; *The Pawnbroker*, 20; *Prince of the City*, 20; *Serpico* (film), 105–6; *12 Angry Men*, 20
Luparelli, Joseph, 51
Lustig, William, 225–29
Lynch, Richard, 108

Maas, Peter, 85, 104, 132
MacDermot, Galt, 12
MacDougall, Fiona, 42
The Magic of Hollywood...is the Magic of People, 164
Making Movies (Lumet), 4, 150
Malcolm X (film), 11
Malick, Terence, 3
Malina, Judith, 149
Malkin, Barry, 131
Malle, Louis, 224
Malloy, Mike, 191
Mancori, Guglielmo, 192
Maniac, 225–27; cinematic legacy of, 229; critical response to, 229; NYC locations for, 228–29
Mann, Abby, 154

Mantle, Mickey, 1
The Man with the Golden Arm, 24
Marathon Man: casting for, 162–63; critical response to, 165; development of, 161–62; NYC locations for, 164–65; screenplay for, 161–62
Marceau, Marcel, 93
Margolin, Stuart, 120
Maron, Marc, 165
Martin, Billy, 171
Martin, D'Urville, 92–93
Marvin, Lee, 118
Mascolo, Joseph, 71
Maslin, Janet, 106–7, 182
Massage Parlor Murders, 5–6, 80, 93, 96; casting for, 94–95; critical response to, 94–95; development of, 94; as grindhouse film, 94; release strategy for, 94–95
Mastroianni, Tony, 111
Matthau, Charles, 136
Matthau, Walter, 118, 136
Mayes, Wendell, 118
Mayfield, Curtis, 75–76
McBratney, James, 80
McElwaine, Guy, 221
McGilligan, Patrick, 64
McGregor, Charles, 74
McGregor, Paul, 35
McKiernan, Robert, 50
McMahon, Ed, 219
McQueen, Steve, 64
McSweeney, John, 224
Mean Streets, 4, 166–67; budget for, 100; casting for, 100–102; cinematic influences on, 98; Corman and, 99–100; critical response to, 102–3; De Niro and, 100–101; development of, 98–100; early titles for, 98–99; financing for, 99; NYC locations for, 101–2; screenplay for, 98–99
Medavoy, Mike, 126
Meeker, Ralph, 21
Merli, Maurizio, 191–93
Merola, Mario, 192
Metro, Douglas Anthony, 188
Michaux, Lewis H., 56
Mickey One, 13
Midnight Cowboy, 2, 32, 46, 101, 162
Midnight Run, 192
Milius, John, 166
Miller, Allan, 208
Miller, Arthur, 179
Miller, Jason, 226
Miller, Jeffrey Glenn, 8
Miller, Samuel, 179
Milligan, Andy, 24
Mills, James, 39, 154
Montgomery, Paul L., 123
Moore, Robin, 25, 81
Moore, Thomas, 148
Moriarty, Michael, 153–54
Morris, Garrett, 21
Morris, George, 142
Morrison, Jim, 40
Morrison, Susan, 197
Morrow, Vic, 215
Mostel, Zero, 65
Ms. 45, 189, 206
Mulligan, Robert, 166
Muntaqim, Jalil, 18
Murch, Walter, 131
Murder on the Orient Express (film), 21
Murphy, Patrick V., 7
My Life So Far (Fonda, J.), 35, 37

Nalo, Samuel, 50–51
Naturile, Salvatore, 148–49

Neufeld, Stanley, 58
Newman, Paul, 31–32
New realism movement, in American cinema, 3–4
New York City: Bronx locations, *p9*; as "Fear City," 2, 146; as film "character," 46; as film location for crime films, 4; financial crisis for, 145–46; Guardian Angels, 172–73; Hard Hat Riot in, 7–8; Italian mafia as criminal presence in, 5–6; mass exodus from, 2; movie coordination organization in, 5; New York Civil Rights Law, 160–61; in 1971, 17–20; in 1972, 49–52; in 1973, 79–80; in 1974, 113–14; in 1975, 145–47; in 1976, 159–61; in 1977, 171–73; in 1978, 177–79; in 1979, 185–87; political activism in, 8–9; public perception as crime-ridden, 2–3, 173; race riots in, 46; "Son of Sam" killings in, 160, 172, 178–79; subway crime in, 172, 186; subway images in, *p15*; Times Square in, *p6*, *p8*, *p10*. *See also* Italian mafia
New York Police Department (NYPD): Black Panthers' conflict with, 1–2; "Blue Flu" strike by, 17–18; corruption within, 7, 50, 80, 103–4; Knapp Commission and, 7, 50, 103–4; lack of accountability for, 160–61
"New York realism," 54
New York Times: NYPD corruption stories in, 7; political activism stories in, 8–9

Nichols, Mike, 40
Nights of Cabiria, 115
1969, films released in: sociocultural context for, 1, 9–10. *See also specific films*
1971, films released in: cop film sub-genre, 17–20; sociocultural context for, 17–20. *See also specific films*
Nixon, Richard, 8, 14, 79
Nolan, Chris, 94
Noonan, Tom, 223
Nussbaum, Albert, 89
NYPD. *See* New York Police Department

Obsession, 210
The Offence, 21
Olivier, Laurence, 59–60, 97, 162–65
Once Upon a Time in America, 206
O'Neal, Ron, 74, 76
O'Neal, Ryan, 60
O'Neill, Ed, 30
O'Neill, Jennifer, 60
Opening Night, 221
Orbach, Jerry, 32, 34
"otherness," as theme, in *Cotton Comes to Harlem*, 12
O'Toole, Peter, 97

Pacino, Al: *Cruising* and, 207–8; *Dog Day Afternoon*, 148–51; *The Gang that Couldn't Shoot Straight* and, 32–33; *The Godfather*, 60–61; *The Godfather Part II*, 132; *Panic in Needle Park*, 20, 39–43; *Serpico*, 105–7
Pakula, Alan J., 35–39. *See also Klute*

Palance, Jack, 191
Panic in Needle Park, 20, 42, *p14*; casting for, 40–41; critical response to, 43; NYC locations for, 24; screenplay for, 39–40; source material for, 39
Panic in Needle Park (novel), 39
Parks, Gordon, Jr.: *Super Fly*, 74–75; *Three the Hard Way*, 140–41
Parks, Gordon, Sr., 10, 74; *Shaft*, 44–46, 132–33; *Shaft's Big Score*, 71–73; *The Super Cops*, 132–35
Passer, Ivan, 23–24, 25
Patient Bill of Rights, 9
Patrick, Dennis, 15
Patz, Etan, 185–86
Paul, William, 11
The Pawnbroker, 20
Peabody, Sandra, 67–69, 94
Pearl, Sandy, 203
Peckinpah, Sam, 59
Pelligra, Biagio, 192
Penn, Arthur, 13, 59
Perl, Arnold, 11
Perl, David, 11
Perry, E. Lee, 100
Petkovich, Anthony, 120
Phillips, Julia, 166
Phillips, Michelle, 60
Piagentini, Joseph, 18
Pierson, Frank, 20, 148
Pistone, Joseph, 177–78
Point Blank, 27, 31
Poitier, Pamela, 202
Poitier, Sidney, 44, 53
Polanski, Roman, 3, 218
Poliziotteschi films, 192–93; as cinematic sub-genre, 6; Hollywood films as influence on, 190; Italian urban locations for, 191
Pollack, Sydney, 27
Popeye Doyle (TV series), 19, 30
Powell, Dilys, 217
Preminger, Otto, 13, 40, 59
Prentiss, Paula, 23
Presley, Elvis, 31, 175
Price, Richard, 193–98
Priestley, Jack, 53, 219
Prince of the City, 20, 206
Profaci, Joe, 116
Puzo, Mario, 58–59, 63
Puzzle of a Downfall Child, 40

Quinn, Anthony, 53–54. See also *Across 110th Street*

Racketeer Influenced and Corrupt Organizations Act (RICO), 9
Rafelson, Bob, 3
Raging Bull, 205
Raheem, Shulab Abdur, 79
Rahman, Dawd A., 79
Rain, Jeramie, 67, 69
Rain People, 31
Rapp, Paul, 100
Rayfiel, David, 156
Reagan, Ronald, 185–86
Redford, Robert, 60; Goldman collaborations with, 64–65; *The Hot Rock*, 64–65; *Three Days of the Condor*, 154–58
Reed, Oliver, 191
Reisz, Karel, 126–27, 179
Report to the Commissioner, 151; casting for, 152–54; documentary style for, 153; NYC locations for, 152–54
Reynolds, Burt, 136

Richardson, Tony, 126
RICO. *See* Racketeer Influenced and Corrupt Organizations Act
Riffi, 23
Rising Sun, 196, 198
Rivera, Geraldo, 141
Rizzo, Sol, 218
Robbery, 64
Roberts, Bobby, 63, 118, 121
Roberts, John, 221
Roberts, Sam, 160
Robertson, Cliff, 157
Robinson, Jay, 142
Rockefeller, Nelson, 79
Roizman, Owen, 29, 158
Rollover, 39
Romero, George, 227
Roos, Fred, 60, 131
Rosenbaum, David, 154
Rosenberg, Philip, 173
Rota, Nino, 131
Roth, Eli, 121
Rothenberg, Paul, 80
Roundtree, Richard, 45, 71, 73, 140, *p16*
Rowlands, Gena, 221–22, 224
Rubin, Mann, 220
Ruddy, Albert S., 4, 32, 59–60, 63, 129, 132. *See also The Godfather* (film)
Rudolf, Gene, 90, 126, 136–37, 164

Safdie, Ben, 25
Safdie, Josh, 25
Salt, Jennifer, 60
Salt, Waldo, 105
Sanders, Lawrence, 20, 218
Santos, Joe, 71
Sarandon, Susan, 15
Sargent, Alvin, 137

Sarris, Andrew, 22, 107, 117
Savalas, Telly, 191
Savini, Tom, 227–28
Sayre, Nora, 138–39, 154
Scarecrow, 149
Schafel, Robert, 96–97
Schatzberg, Jerry, 40–42
Scheider, Roy, 27–28, 108, 162
Scherick, Edgar J., 96, 136–37
Schickel, Richard, 102
Schlesinger, John, 2, 126, 162–63
Schrader, Paul, 165–70. *See also Taxi Driver*
Schrader on Schrader (Schrader), 165
Schuler, Fred, 223
Scorsese, Martin, 3, 20; *Boxcar Bertha*, 99; Corman and, 99–100, 166; early films for, 99; *The Godfather Part II* and, 128–29; *Goodfellas*, 177; *Mean Streets*, 98–103; *Raging Bull*, 205; *Taxi Driver*, 4–5, 46, 165–70; *Who's That Knocking on My Door?*, 99, 101
Scott, David Milton, 23
Scott, Walter, 80
Season of the Witch. See Mean Streets
Segal, George, 23, 65
Selby, David, 133–35
Semple, Lorenzo, Jr., 132–33, 155
Serpico (book) (Maas), 85, 103–4
Serpico (film), 4, 20; awards for, 107; box office for, 107; casting for, 105; cinematic legacy of, 107; critical response to, 103, 106–7; development of, 104–5; literary source material for, 85, 103–4; Lumet and, 105–6; NYC

locations for, 105–6; screenplay for, 105
Serpico, Frank, 7, 103–4, *p3*
The Seven-Ups, 19, 30; casting for, 108; critical response to, 110–11; development of, 107–8; NYC locations for, 109–10
Shaber, David, 199
Shaft (film), *p16*; awards for, 46–47; as blaxploitation film, 4, 19–20, 46; box office, 46; casting for, 44–45; cultural impact of, 47, 73; development history for, 43–45; film sequels, 47, 70–73; importance of NYC locations for, 45–46; musical score and album, 46–47; Parks, Gordon, Sr., and, 44–46, 132–33; screenplay for, 27, 45
Shaft (novel series) (Tidyman), 44, 47, 70
Shaft's Big Score: box office for, 73; casting for, 71; critical response to, 72; NYC locations for, 71–72; screenplay for, 70–71
Shaw, Robert, 136–37, *p13*
Shaw, Sam, 223
Shea, Thomas, 80
Shear, Barry, 53–54
Sheehy, Gail, 14
Sheen, Martin, 60
Sheeran, Frank, 51
Sheffler, Marc, 67
Shepherd, Cybill, 167
Shire, Talia, 132
The Sicilian (Puzo), 63
Silliphant, Stirling, 44
Silva, Henry, 174
Simon, John, 183
Simonetti, Claudio, 226–27

Sinatra, Frank, 60; *Contract on Cherry Street*, 173–76, 219; *The First Deadly Sin*, 218–21
Singleton, Ralph S., 29, 120; *Come Back Charleston Blue*, 56–58; *Contract on Cherry Street*, 174; *Crazy Joe*, 116; *Death Wish*, 118–19; *The Seven-Ups*, 109–10; *Taxi Driver*, 168–69; *Three Days of the Condor*, 157
Siskel, Gene, 15, 38, 72, 84, 209–10
Skinner, Margo, 43
Slaughter's Big Rip-Off, 87
Sliwa, Curtis, 172–73
Smight, Jack, 218
Smith, Bud S., 209
Smucker, Carl, 203
Sobel, Lee, 5
Sorel, Jean, 28
Soto, Erno, 51–52
Sounder, 97
Spacek, Sissy, 225
Spielberg, Steven, 3, 147
Spielman, Ed, 96
Spinell, Joe, 220, 225–27, 229
Spottiswoode, Roger, 127
Spradlin, G. D., 130–31
Spungen, Nancy, 178
Stander, Lionel, 32
Starr, Edwin, 93
Steiger, Rod, 60
Stern, Henry J., 145–46
Stevens, Alex, 94
St. Jacques, Raymond, 11, 45, 56
St. John, Nicholas, 189
Stockwell, Dean, 60
Stone, Peter, 136
Stonewall Rebellion, 1
La Strada, 115
Strasberg, Lee, 130, 132

Streisand, Barbra, 222
Strode, Woody, 191
Super Cops: casting for, 133; as comedy, 133; critical response to, 135; literary source for, 132; NYC locations for, 133–34
Super Cops (book) (Whittemore), 132
Super Fly, p17; casting for, 74; critical response to, 76; cultural legacy for, 76–77; early development for, 73–74; music and score, 75–76; NYC locations for, 74–75; screenplay for, 73–74
Sutherland, Donald, 36, 38, 194
Sweet Sweetback's Baadasssss Song, 73, 77

The Taking of Pelham One Two Three (film), 4, *p13*; casting for, 136–37; cinematic legacy of, 139; critical response to, 138–39; location issues for, 135–36, 138; screenplay for, 136
The Taking of Pelham One Two Three (novel) (Godey), 135
Taplin, Jonathan, 100–102
Tarantino, Quentin, 55
Tavoularis, Dean, 131
Taxi Driver, 4–5, 46, 165, *p18*; casting of, 166–67; critical response to, 169–70; development of, 166–67; film budget, 167; literary influences on, 166; NYC locations of, 168–69
Taylor, Rod, 27
Taylor-Young, Leigh, 32–33

Tell Me That You Love Me, Junie Moon, 40
Texas Chainsaw Massacre, 187
That Man Bolt, 91–92
They Shoot Horses, Don't They?, 27
Thomas, Danny, 60
Thompson, Howard, 97–98
Thompson, Robert E., 27
Three Days of the Condor (film), 154; casting for, 155–56; critical response to, 158; NYC locations for, 156–58; political context for, 156
Three Days of the Condor (novel) (Grady), 154–55
Three the Hard Way, 139; casting for, 140; cinematic legacy of, 143; critical response to, 141–42; film sequels for, 142
Tidyman, Ernest, 27, 45, 154; *Shaft* novel series, 44, 47, 70
Tierney, Lawrence, 14, 223
Toback, James, 125–27. *See also Fingers; The Gambler*
Together, 66
To Kill a Mockingbird (film), 35
To Live and Die in LA, 29
Torn, Rip, 116
Torsney, Robert, 160
Towne, Robert, 62, 163
The Toxic Avenger, 14
Troma Films, 14
Truffaut, Francois, 74
Turn on to Love, 13
12 Angry Men, 20, 105

Ullman, Liv, 211
Uncut Gems, 25
The Ungovernable City (Cannato), 2–3

Valachi, Joseph, 58
The Valachi Papers, 115, 117
Van Peebles, Melvin, 10–11
Van Valkenburgh, Deborah, 202
Variety, 98, 218
Venantini, Venantino, 192
Vicious, Sid, 178
Victory at Entebbe, 56
Vigilante, 206
vigilante films: *Death Wish*, 117–21; *Exterminator*, 213–14; as public wish fulfillment, 114
The Village Voice, 11, 142
Villechaize, Hervé, 32
Vineberg, Steve, 117
Voight, Jon, 101
von Sydow, Max, 157

Wadler, Joyce, 173
Wag the Dog, 91
Wahl, Ken, 194
Wahlberg, Mark, 128
Waites, Thomas, 202
Walken, Christopher, 21
Walker, David F., 45–47, 72, 86
Walker, Gerald, 146, 206
The Wanderers, 4, 193; audience screenings for, 197; casting for, 194–95; critical response for, 197; cult following for, 198; NYC locations for, 196; soundtrack for, 195
Ward, Richard, 54
Warren, Mark, 55
The Warriors, 2, 4, *p19*; casting for, 200; critical response to, 202–3; cult following for, 203; development of, 199; gang involvement in, 200–201; literary sources for, 198–99; NYC locations for, 200–201

Washington, Albert, 18
Washington, Denzel, 137
Wasserman, Lew, 92
Watermelon Man, 11
Wayne, John, 53, 63
Weathermen, 1
Weiner, Bob, 27–28
Weintraub, Jerry, 206–7
Weintraub, Sandy, 99
Weisberg, Arthur, 188
Weiss, Joel, 201
Weitman, Robert, 20
Weld, Tuesday, 60
Werner, Louis, 177
Westlake, Donald, 63–64, 88–89
West Side Story, 2
Wexler, Norman, 10–14, 105. *See also Cotton Comes to Harlem; Joe*
White audiences, *Joe* and, 16
Whittemore, L. H., 132
Who's That Knocking on My Door?, 99, 101
Williams, Billy Dee, 45
Williams, Tennessee, 169
Williamson, Fred, 191; *Black Caesar*, 85–86; *Hell Up in Harlem*, 91–92; *Three the Hard Way*, 139–40
Willis, Bruce, 121
Willis, Gordon, 39, 131
Wilmott, Kevin, 10
Wilson, Gerald, 119
Wilson, Malcolm, 114
Winegardner, Mark, 63
Winfield, Paul, 96–97
Winkler, Irwin, 31–32, 126
Winn, Kitty, 41–43
Winner, Michael, 118–20
Winning, 31–32
Winston, Stan, 215

Wojtowicz, John, 148–49
Womack, Bobby, 55
Wood, Elijah, 229
Woodhull, Victoria, 179
Woodruff, Maurice, 53
Woodstock music festival, 1
Woodward, Joan, 31–32
Wyatt, Rupert, 128

Yablans, Frank, 122
Yablans, Irwin, 121–24
Yanni, Nick, 25
Yates, Peter, 59, 64–65, 108

Yew, Peter, 147
YLO. *See* Young Lords Organization
Young, Burt, 24, 32
Young Lords Organization (YLO), 8–9
Yurick, Sol, 198–99

Zanuck, Richard, 27, 41
Ziegler, Evarts, 162
Zinner, Peter, 131
Zippel, Francesco, 29

About the Author

Andrew J. Rausch is an award-winning film journalist who has written or co-written many books on cinema, including *My Best Friend's Birthday: The Making of a Quentin Tarantino Film*, *The Films of Martin Scorsese and Robert De Niro*, and *Turning Points in Film History*. He is a former editor at *Diabolique* magazine, is a regular contributor to *Shock Cinema*, and writes a regular column for *Screem* magazine.

Jami Bernard is an award-winning film critic who has worked for both the *New York Daily News* and the *New York Post*. She has written a number of books, including *Quentin Tarantino: The Man and His Movies*, *Chick Flicks*, *First Films*, and *The Incredible Shrinking Critic*.